NO PLACE SAFE

"A gracefully written, vivid, heartfelt and deeply intimate work. Against the backdrop of Atlanta's infamous and still controversial child-murder spree, thirteen-year-old Kim Reid demonstrates uncanny wisdom, grit and confidence as she overcomes the fear and panic gripping Atlanta's children, to narrate her compelling personal story; all the while bringing to heartbreaking life each of the murdered boys."

—**Robert Hooks**, actor/ producer/ cultural activist

"Though a child herself, Kim Reid sat on the edge of a front row seat to one of the twentieth century's most bizarre and baffling murder cases. With *No Place Safe* she delivers her experience as a compelling story told from a sensitive gut and a formidable intellect. A narrative woven with strands of threatened innocence and Southern gothic gives *No Place Safe* the texture of a modern, urban *To Kill a Mockingbird*."

—**Elyse Singleton**, author of *This Side of the Sky*

"Like every great memoir writer, Kim Reid bares her heart and soul in this powerful account of growing up in a world of danger. Her honesty and storytelling skills make every page come alive."

—**Kien Nguyen**, author of *The Unwanted*

"*No Safe Place,* a dazzling memoir, is so compelling you won't stop reading until you finish. This outstanding offering is sure to safely place Kim Reid in the company of best-selling authors. So don't blink or you will miss this author's meteoric rise to the top."

—**Carolyn Quick Tillery**, author of *Southern Homecoming Traditions*

NO PLACE SAFE

a family memoir

KIM REID

KENSINGTON PUBLISHING CORP.
http://www.kensingtonbooks.com

DAFINA BOOKS are published by

Kensington Publishing Corp.
850 Third Avenue
New York, NY 10022

All Kensington titles, imprints and distributed lines are available at special quantity discounts for bulk purchases for sales promotion, premiums, fund-raising, educational or institutional use.

Special book excerpts or customized printings can also be created to fit specific needs. For details, write or phone the office of the Kensington Special Sales Manager: Kensington Publishing Corp., 850 Third Avenue, New York, NY 10022. Attn. Special Sales Department. Phone: 1-800-221-2647.

Dafina Books and the Dafina logo Reg. U.S. Pat. & TM Off.

ISBN-13: 978-0-7582-2052-3
ISBN-10: 0-7582-2052-9

First Kensington Trade Paperback Printing: October 2007
10 9 8 7 6 5 4 3 2 1

Printed in the United States of America

For my mother and Bridgette, and for James

Acknowledgments

A sincere thank-you to everyone on the Kensington team who turned my story into a book, including Kristine Mills-Noble, Selena James, and Laurie Parkin. A special thanks to my editors Stacey Barney, for believing in this story, and Michaela Hamilton, for being the best champion a new writer can luck into—I appreciate your guidance.

For her generosity and spirit, I thank my agent Kristin Nelson, who put her faith in this book before I'd written it, and wanted to see it in print as much as I did.

Atlanta and its people were with me as I wrote, and they have my respect and appreciation, especially those who lost their most precious ones. For those who lived it, we may have moved on, maybe even healed, but we can't forget.

I have friends who gave unending moral support as I wrote this book. My two percent team never thought I was crazy for leaving my corporate gig to write—thanks to Ann, Dottie, Erin, Karla, and Sandy. Also thanks to Gwen for her motivating phone calls, Jenny for our candid conversations about writing one's own life, and Kelly for dreaming and planning over beignets and coffee. Nik convinced me I could do whatever I damned well pleased, including becoming a writer.

My family made it safe for me to take a risk, and I'm grateful to all of you, even if there isn't room here to list every name. Thanks to Derek, Quentin, and Meghan for always cheering me on. When I wrote my earliest stories as a kid, my cousin Chet encouraged me; his words carried weight. Thanks to my grandparents, Mattie Lucille Fuller for her amazing memory and Jesse Fuller for being my guardian angel.

I have forever love for my mother and my sister Bridgette, because they are my roots, and there would be no story without them. They gave me hours of discussion and a box full of notes to fill in what I didn't know or remember. Thank you both for giving me room to write this the way I wanted to write it.

Finally, I am blessed with a husband who is happy to read my pages and talk me down from my drama moments. Thank you James for believing when I was unsure and for giving me the chance to find out for myself.

Chapter 1

The summer before I started high school, two boys went missing and a few days later, turned up dead. They were found by a mother and son looking for aluminum cans alongside a quiet wooded road. It was already ninety degrees at noon, even with an overcast sky, because it was the end of July in Atlanta, Georgia, which I imagine is similar to the heat in hell, except with humidity. The mother thought she saw an animal at the bottom of a steep embankment that started its descent just a couple of feet from the road. The combination of heat and damp created a smell that frightened her. Something about the odor must have told her it wasn't an animal at all, must have made her call her young child to her lest he discover the source. They left off the search for discarded cans and walked to a gas station where the mother called her husband, and he called the police.

The boys were friends; one was about to celebrate his fifteenth birthday, the other had just turned thirteen, the same age as I at the time. One went missing four days after the first, but they were both found on the same day, not two hundred feet apart in a ravine just off Niskey Lake Road. The two detectives first on the scene, responding to a signal forty-eight (person dead), noted in their report that either side of the road was bordered by trees, like most streets were in Atlanta at the time. Loblolly pine, white oaks, and the occasional stray dogwood that played unwitting hosts for the creeping kudzu vines that threatened to take them over completely. The officers also noted that the woods and ravines lining both sides of the road were "used as a dumping ground for trash." This was where they found the first body. A vine growing from a nearby tree had already wrapped itself around the boy's neck, unaware that his last breath had been stolen from him days ago.

While making notes of how the child's body lay among other thrown-away items littering the road's shoulder, the detectives caught an odor on a small, hot breeze coming from the north. Being detectives, they knew the smell immediately, and it led them to the second boy's body. At the time, no one knew the boys were friends because the police didn't know who they were. By the time school started, only one boy had been positively identified. More than a year would pass before a name could be given to his friend.

It wasn't much more than a blip in the news—two black boys being killed in Atlanta in 1979 didn't get much news coverage. The only reason I knew what I did was because my mother, an investigator with the Fulton County District Attorney's Office at the time, told me to be a little more careful. She said it was probably just a coincidence, but just as likely not, that the boys were close in age, black, and found in the same wooded area.

Warning me to be a little more careful because those boys were killed was a waste of words. By my thirteenth summer, I'd learned to be nothing but careful, whether I wanted to or not. I couldn't help but think like a cop. Even though they were my favorite, I rarely drank frozen Cokes because I avoided going into the convenience stores where they were sold (an off-duty cop still in uniform is a sitting duck if she walks in during a robbery). At restaurants, I never sat with my back to the door (you need to be aware of everyone who comes in and out, and know your entry and exit points). I always tried to carry myself like I wasn't scared of shit (even if you are, don't let them know or they have you). My friends called me *Narc.*

Ma told me about the boys while we got ready for work, sharing her bathroom mirror. I combed my hair while I studied her use of blush—the sucking in of cheeks to find the bones, the blowing of the brush to prevent overapplication. This girly part of her never seemed to go with the other part, the other woman—the one who, as a uniformed officer, carried a .38-caliber service revolver in her thick leather holster, along with other things difficult to associate with a woman, especially a mother: handcuffs, a nightstick, and the now illegal blackjack, solid metal covered in leather for handling an uncooperative perpetrator, or *bad guy* as I called them. Perpetrator filled my mouth in an uncomfortable way.

My use of cosmetics was limited to tinted lip gloss and a brush to tame my thick and unruly eyebrows. But I watched her anyway, filing away the technique for the time she'd let me use real makeup to turn my face into something that resembled hers.

"I'll call a friend at the department to see what other information I can get on those two boys," Ma said, while she softened the tip of her eyeliner pencil over a match's flame.

"Why?" I asked. "People are all the time turning up dead in Atlanta."

"Something's not right about it—them dying a few days apart, both being teenage boys and black, turning up in the same location. I'll look into it, and in the meantime, you be watchful and look out for your sister."

Ma didn't need to add the last part. When wasn't I watchful? And I didn't know any other way than to look out for my sister. Bridgette was only nine. I was the oldest, which meant looking out for her was my job.

I just told Ma, okay, I'd be careful. She was thinking there might be a pattern. She was always looking for a pattern in *everything.* The fact that the two boys were found so close together but in different stages of decomposition, a clue that they hadn't been left there on the same day, made Ma think their killer was the same person and was using the wooded spot just off the road as a dumping area. I imagined a car slowing just long enough to open a door and toss out some mother's child, like an emptied beer bottle or a treadbare tire.

Beyond that bit of theory, Ma couldn't come up with more. Even if she was right about a connection between the victims, I didn't see what I had in common with the dead boys other than being black and our ages being close. For one thing, they were boys, and everybody knew boys liked risk. Boys looked for trouble, and if none could be found, they'd make some up.

Ma said herself that most homicide victims were left not too far from where they lived or where they were killed. Niskey Lake Road was in southwest Atlanta, a good fourteen or fifteen miles from our house. Though they didn't know it for sure, the cops were already speculating the boys were poor and messing around with drugs. There was nothing new in this theory—according to the police and the media, all black boys in inner-city Atlanta were poor and dealing. I didn't know much about drugs other than the joint I'd sampled when I was twelve, during a summer vacation in Cleveland with my grandparents that freed me from Ma's surveillance.

We did okay financially, considering we lived on a cop's salary and there were no child support payments waiting in the mailbox, no sugar daddy to take up the slack. Neither of those income sources was my mother's style. Maybe those boys were from the projects or nearby, and I lived in a house with a pool in the backyard. True, I lived within a couple of miles of two housing projects myself, but that was on the other side of Jonesboro Road—the side that led down to Cleveland Avenue and its pawnshops, check-cashing stores, and fast-food joints that filled our passing car with the smell of old grease. To me, it seemed a world away.

In between filling the dog's water bowl and making sure Bridgette didn't add more sugar to her Frosted Flakes, I began the morning countdown, telling Ma the time every three minutes to keep her on track because she was never on time for anything. You'd have thought she was an actress instead of a cop, as much time as she took in the morning. It probably would have made her cop life easier, but she didn't pretend to be a man. She wore her hair long, although as a street cop, she'd had to wear it up. Long hair could get you into trouble when you're trying to take down a bad guy. This is probably what made her popular with some of the more open-minded male cops, those who didn't see anything wrong with a female cop as long as she was something to look at.

We rode together in the mornings because we both worked downtown, and I pestered her about the clock until the moment we were in the car. I hated being late for anything, much less a place where I was responsible for things. The source of my obsession with being on time is a mystery because Ma didn't give me much of an example. Or maybe it's because she didn't. There were too many times when I was the last kid picked up from daycare, or school, or basketball games that she couldn't get to early enough to watch me play. Put-out babysitters, teachers, and coaches would give me the evil eye in between checking the window for any sign of her, though when she finally arrived, they'd say, "Not a problem at all, I understand."

Normally, I'd catch MARTA, the city bus system, to avoid having to depend on her. She let me start taking public transportation when I was eleven. After that, my tardiness could only be blamed on the bus driver, and even that rarely happened because I always tried to take a bus earlier than I needed to just to make sure I wasn't late. But it was summertime and I was already getting up earlier than should be legal during summer break. Riding with Ma gave me an extra thirty minutes of sleep. When I'd finally get her out the door, I always thought we'd make it on time as long as we didn't get stuck at the train tracks. More often than not, we did.

I left Ma in the parking lot in front of her building, the Fulton County Courthouse on Pryor Street, and walked the last half mile to work. Past the old entrance to Underground Atlanta, once a tiny city beneath the city (and now is again). Down Martin Luther King to Courtland and into the Georgia State University campus. And finally, over to Butler Street, where all kinds of things could be seen and heard: fights between spouses, patrol cars coming and going, people grieving, the homeless, people going about their every day, and ambulances screaming to be heard over all the rest.

My job wasn't a paying one, but it should have been. I was a candy striper at Grady Hospital, which was like being a candy striper in hell. It seemed like a good idea when Ma said I needed something to keep me busy during the summer. I figured I'd get to wear a cute nurse's outfit, and Ma said I'd wanted to be a doctor since I was six when she bought me a microscope for Christmas, complete with specimens pressed between small rectangles of glass. The job would give me a chance to find out whether this life of medicine was Ma's dream or mine. True, I lied to the volunteer agency about my age, saying I was fourteen, but the job shouldn't have been given to anyone under twenty-one, and even then, I'd have warned them to think twice.

The uniform was the first disappointment because there was nothing cute about it. Instead of being white and form-fitting as I'd imagined, it was a smock of blue-and-white-striped seersucker worn over a white blouse. The top half of the smock was apron-like, square-necked, sleeveless, and a size too small, pressing down on my breasts like binding. The bottom half flared out, giving the impression my hips were far wider than they were. The candy striper uniform did nothing to help me broadcast my recently acquired curves. And the job wasn't like what I remembered from the movies—handing out magazines, filling cups with ice chips.

Back then, Grady was the largest hospital in the Southeast. It was where people were sent when no other hospital wanted them—because they were on Medicaid, because they were shot while trying to kill the person who shot them, because they had no place else to go. It was where the ambulance took Ma after a car chase that ended badly. She said when you're on the wrong side of the white light, Grady was the place to go if you weren't ready to check out just yet. Once they saved you, though, it was another story. You had better get moved to another hospital quick.

Grady served its purpose, but that didn't keep it from being a scary place. Everything about it was functional and institutional—brightly lit rooms, echoing hallways, and no thought given to softening the waiting areas with silk plants and paintings to distract visitors from whatever bad thing had brought them there. When I started the job, they gave us a tour and told us how many miles of corridors there were. I don't remember the number, but after spending my first few days there, I do recall thinking that it meant a lot of corridors filled with sick people, forgotten people, hopeless and hopeful people, overburdened nurses, and pushed-to-the-edge doctors.

It didn't help ease my initial fear of the place when they put me on the gynecology ward during the middle of a nurse shortage, requiring me to do a lot more than fluffing up pillows. Within the first week, I'd learned a couple of things: The whole idea of being a doctor was shot to hell regardless of whose idea it had been, and I planned to avoid those stirrups for as long as possible. According to the nurses I worked with, I didn't have to have the exam until I was eighteen or having sex, whichever came first. I thought that if the girls at school could see what I did, heard the screams I heard outside the examination rooms, they'd keep their legs closed for life.

Part of my job was to put together admissions packets for

the patients. I put the appropriate blank forms into the folders and stamped each form with the patient's insurance cards using one of those machines they used for credit cards at the department stores. It was always the same card—Medicaid, cornflower blue with patient information embossed in white. When I stamped one card in particular, I was certain the date of birth information was wrong, because it would have made the patient ten years old. When I showed it to the nurse at the desk, she said, "No, it's correct." She had checked the girl in herself.

The girl was back in the ward, the room where we'd put lots of people, the people who were either too poor—or not sick enough—to have a semiprivate room. We had no private rooms in our department that I can recall, which was too bad for the patients, because nearly everyone was there for something they probably didn't want too many people to know about.

I knew that, in the suburbs, the candy stripers weren't allowed in certain places, weren't allowed to see certain things. At Grady during a nurse shortage, I saw things and went places I'm sure I should've been nowhere near. I was a responsible thirteen-supposed-to-be-fourteen-year-old. People forgot I was a kid after spending a little time with me. And they were so short-staffed I had to help wherever I could, as long as it didn't require actual medical work. I wheeled patients on gurneys and in wheelchairs to x-ray, and shuttled blood and plasma *stat* between floors (I liked saying *stat*). On my trips to Pathology, always colder than the rest of the hospital, I tried hard not to think of the cadavers and body parts in jars that I imagined were stored inside the huge metal refrigerators, especially if I had to run this errand right before my lunch break. This kind of work was why I thought I should have been paid. Instead, my reward was supposed to have been satisfaction in helping others. At thirteen, it was difficult to see the reward in that.

When I went back to the ward, the girl I saw in the bed

didn't look ten years old. I was certain she was at least fifteen when I looked at her face, but when I made out the shape of her under the sheet, I could tell she was still a little girl.

"They sent me in here to take off your makeup," I said, trying to talk as I would to a small child even though she looked older than I did.

"Who the hell are you? Whoever you are, I don't want you touching me." She looked fifteen, but her mouth sounded thirty. "How old are you? You don't look like a real nurse."

"I'm not a nurse. All I want to do is take off your makeup. The nurse will be in soon to get you ready for your exam."

"All right, but don't touch the lashes. They fake, and it's hard as hell to get them on just right."

"They have to come off too."

"You try and I'll slap you."

I saw at this point that I was no match for the woman-child, and decided I'd remove everything but the lashes. The nurse could handle that. I tried to make conversation, and besides, I was dying to know what a ten-year-old was doing in the gynecology ward.

"What procedure are you in here for?"

"None of your damn business." She folded her arms over her chest and stared at me while I wiped cotton over her clown-red cheeks.

"You know I can just look at your chart."

"Then why you asking me?"

I realized that was the end of our conversation and removed the rest of the makeup in silence, a little embarrassed that the woman-child scared me. I didn't scare easily—I'd been in more fights than a girl ever should, had a knife pulled on me once by some high-school girls, and hid in a closet while a man who had been stalking Ma broke into our house. But this ten-year-old made me nervous.

When I finished removing her makeup, the girl touched her lashes to make sure I hadn't tricked her. She watched as I walked to the end of the bed and picked up the chart hanging there. I avoided her stare but felt it just the same. The doctors in Emergency had her admitted because she had gonorrhea. I wondered if she'd have to get the D&C procedure that made grown women cry out. I'd seen the makeup, knew of the diagnoses with women who had the disease so advanced that it had spread throughout their bodies, but would never have connected those women to this girl. I bet none of the candy stripers in the shiny, new suburban hospitals ever removed the makeup of a ten-year-old prostitute.

I'd thought about the doll-sized prostitute throughout the rest of my day, wondering if she was afraid of being in the streets since those two boys had died. Did it make it any more dangerous for her, or was her world scary enough that two dead boys she'd never met were the least of her problems?

Ma was reading the paper that night after dinner while Bridgette and I watched TV. Normally, talking to Ma while she had the paper in hand was not a wise thing. She'd shush anyone who disturbed her while she watched the TV news or read the newspaper—my grandparents, houseguests, it didn't matter. But thoughts of the girl in the hospital wouldn't let go of me.

"Ma, guess what happened today." Right away, I knew I should have just told her, and the look she gave me over the newspaper confirmed it. It said, *I know you don't want me to play guessing games while I'm reading the paper.* I pretended not to notice. "I had to take makeup off a prostitute's face."

"Mmm."

"She was wearing fake eyelashes and said she'd slap me if I touched them. She just about jumped out of the bed when I tried to take them off." I thought I should liven up the story a bit to get a better response.

"You should've let the nurses take care of it," she said from behind the paper.

"The craziest part of it is that she had gonorrhea *and* is only ten years old."

Ma said nothing, just kept reading the paper like meeting a ten-year-old prostitute with the clap happened every day. I was getting mad, and I wished I had the nerve to tear the paper from her hands. My story was every bit as interesting as whatever she was reading.

"Don't you think that's something?" It was more a demand than a question.

Ma just said, "You wouldn't believe the things I see." She didn't look up from the paper when she said it.

Chapter 2

Sometimes, no matter where you live, how nice the neighborhood is, or how friendly the people are, you're bound to hear your neighbors fight. Parents yelling at kids, lovers threatening to kill each other for the hundredth time, so you figure if they really were going to do it, it would have been done by now. Some people get up enough nerve to call the police and hope their neighbors never find out who called. Most folks just try to ignore it rather than get involved. That's how it probably goes in most homes, just pretend the bad thing isn't happening and hope it'll end soon.

Not at my house. On an August night when it wasn't hot enough to justify turning on the air-conditioning and running up the electric bill (which in Ma's mind meant no one had fallen over from heatstroke yet), we had the windows open and could hear an argument building next door. Our neighbor was single, mostly kept to himself, and rarely had visitors. Being these were often the traits of single men who ended up on the evening news for committing some shocking crime that surprised their neighbors, I'd already decided he was slightly suspect.

But recently he'd gotten himself a girlfriend, and their relationship must have been based on the kind of passion created by antagonism, because they often made us an unintentional audience for their bickering. The houses on our street sat on half an acre each, some more than that, so it wasn't as if we were right on top of each other, but still we could hear them clearly. It started out like a loud discussion, quickly turned into an argument, and soon enough, it sounded like our neighbor might be beating the hell out of his girlfriend.

There was something about a man beating a woman that agitated Ma more than other crimes. It was the thing that made her talk angrily to the TV set when she heard mention of a husband killing his wife during the nightly rundown of all the bad things that happened in Atlanta that day. The other murders, the robberies and corruption, she'd let go by with only a disgusted sigh, but wife beaters made my mother cuss without apology. Even though she'd told me a million times how a domestic dispute was the worst call for a cop to go on because tempers are high, passions are fired up, and people do things that don't make a damn bit of sense, Ma headed over there anyway. When I asked her if I should call the police, she said, "I *am* the police." She put her gun into her hip holster and clipped it on before she left the house, for which I didn't know whether to be grateful or afraid.

These were the times when it was hard for me not to blur the line between my mother and the other woman. When I tried to make the distinction, I could see only my mother going into a situation that might get her killed. It was difficult to see a cop with six years' experience, one who could kick some ass when she wanted to, according to her police friends. Still, I didn't see why she couldn't just call some uniforms to come over and deal with it.

Bridgette and I ran to her room to watch what would happen from the window. Both our bedrooms were on the side of the house that faced our neighbor's, but our house sat farther back from the road, so his front door was out of sight. We had to listen to it instead, which wasn't difficult because the neighbor was loud and Ma was loud right back at him. The conversation went something like this:

Ma: Stop beating on your girlfriend.

Man: This is none of your business. (I remember him being very proper talking, and I think he said something like "this is none of your affair," but probably not.)

Ma: Everyone on the street can hear you, so you're making it everybody's business.

Man: So call the police.

Ma: I am the motherfucking *po-lice.* (Ma liked saying this, and she could curse like nobody's business when provoked, probably something she had to learn to sound tough on the streets.)

I don't remember much else of the conversation, but the police never came and the couple stopped fighting, at least for that day. I don't recall ever hearing them fight again, but I'm certain they didn't stop. They just made sure to do it more quietly from then on. After Ma went *Kojak* on them, I went out of my way to avoid the man and his girlfriend, not certain why I was the one embarrassed when it should have been them.

On Friday, Ma was working while I took care of Bridgette. I didn't have to work at the hospital on Fridays, which meant Bridgette didn't have to go to the babysitter. When I was her age, I didn't much have a babysitter, but Ma said me being the oldest made me more responsible. Bridgette wasn't at all responsible; she didn't have to be because doctors had diagnosed her when she was six as being *hyperactive,* a condition that made her a scary combination of aggressive and reckless, and required her to take little pills that Ma or I had to cut in half or else they turned her into a zombie. She was also the baby, so Ma had fewer expectations of her.

We were watching reruns of *Gilligan's Island.*

"You're sitting too close to the TV," I told Bridgette. I liked to act as if I were her boss, mostly because Ma said I was completely in charge when she was at work. Sometimes I pushed it too far, like the time I tried to spank Bridgette with a wooden spoon like Ma used to do to me before parents started getting into trouble for that. Bridgette nearly kicked my ass and would have if I didn't outweigh her, so I never tried that again.

"Move back from the TV." I had to repeat myself because she was ignoring me. "You don't move back and I won't put any cheese on your Spaghettios."

She moved back, but only by an inch or two. I didn't ask for any more. I wasn't even worried about her eyes; I just wanted to make sure she knew who was running things. I kept all kinds of threats and bribes ready for those times she wanted to give me trouble, like when I had to comb her hair after lunch. To make sure she held still, I'd tell her she couldn't go down the street with me to play basketball later. Of course, I'd never leave her alone in the house—Ma would've killed me—but Bridgette hadn't figured that out yet.

"Remember when Ma would be home most of the time, and not always be at work?"

She turned down the volume on the TV, maybe so I could focus on the question, but I didn't remember such a time because Ma was always at some job. I figured Bridgette was old enough to have only four years of fully reliable memory, and Ma had been a cop for longer than that, so whatever days she was recalling she'd made them up. But she must have taken my silence as agreement.

"We used to watch *The Carol Burnett Show* in her room and crack pecans with that raggedy pair of pliers because you lost the nutcracker, and the next day she'd fuss about the shells in her bed."

The pliers and pecans were familiar. "I remember us watching that show. Is it still on?"

"No, and I don't know the last time we went to the farmer's market for pecans. Nothing is like when I was little."

That was funny to me because she was still little in my

book, but I didn't laugh because she looked so serious about it. In that moment I wanted to call her Little Bit, which was my nickname for her until she was five and told me she hated that name. I'd always assumed it was better than Monkey, which everyone else called her because she could climb anything and went a long stretch where the only food she'd eat willingly was bananas. She told me she hated that name too.

"Next week I'll buy some pecans from the market downtown."

Bridgette looked just about done with me. "Pecans aren't in season until fall."

After I warmed the Spaghettios, I told her to go wash her hands before she came to the table.

"You're not Ma, stop trying to act like it," she said, but she did it anyway.

When Ma would get home from work, she'd make us tell her what we did all day, but only after she went around the house inspecting furniture and opening closets, making sure we did our chores, which included vacuuming, dusting, and laundry. She liked a neat house, but getting chores done was also Ma's way of making sure we weren't getting into any trouble while she was gone. If everything was done on the list—and it was always a long list—she figured we didn't have time to do much else. She was usually right, but always suspected us anyway.

"You played basketball down the street?" she asked me.

"Yes."

"Did you have any company over here?"

Ma always asked this, trying to find out if my boyfriend had come over. Kevin had been my boyfriend since the summer before, when he kissed me on a warm night while a bunch of us kids played a game of hide-and-go-seek, the night lit only by lightning bugs and the glow from some parent's porch light. He'd caught me hiding between a house and a thick forsythia bush growing against it. He was fourteen and experienced, given his reputation around the neighborhood. I was twelve and it was my first real open-mouth kiss. It had come earlier than I'd expected, which meant I hadn't prepared for it, and my teeth were more involved than they should've been, but it was still exciting.

Kevin was handsome, even as a boy, with the strength of a man's face barely masked behind the softness of a boy's. His eyes were brown like just about every black person I knew, but hinted at the possibility of something gold warming the brown. Or perhaps that was just my imagination. He opened up a world of conversation for me at school, allowing me to add descriptions of my first kiss to those of the popular girls in eighth grade, who allowed me close enough to listen, but never expected me to contribute. And when they doubted my veracity, the wallet-sized school picture Kevin had given me was produced as proof. An unattractive boy would have gotten an immediate laugh, then dismissal. When they gathered around to silently scrutinize his picture, I knew they were impressed. When they questioned where I'd gotten the picture, suggesting maybe it was a cousin instead of a boyfriend, I knew they were jealous. I wouldn't respond, only returned the picture to my wallet and let my silent smugness tell them exactly what I thought about their skepticism.

Once I got my period, Ma was always saying, "I'm not raising any babies that I didn't bring into this world. Don't have any babies while you're in my house." When I was six years old, she made sure I understood how that might happen. She'd lectured me on the availability of birth control many times since buying my first box of Kotex, and had warned me that it was best to keep my legs shut until I no longer lived in her house. I understood that these warnings were well intended and had much to do with the fact that she got pregnant with me when she was eighteen and unmarried.

Ma couldn't stand the idea that I was only thirteen and had the same boyfriend for a year. Kevin lived one block over, and his father was a cop too. Ma knew him from the Department. I think that's why she never made me break up with him—she figured between her and his father, they'd catch us if we were doing anything. She preferred having that kind of surveillance over me, something she wouldn't have if I was going with a boy whose father wasn't a cop. She didn't realize that Kevin and I were scared shitless of both of them and wouldn't get into any trouble—at least not with one another (it wasn't until later that I learned my first love's reputation had been honestly earned).

"Kim didn't have any friends in the house, did she?" Ma treated Bridgette and me like her suspects, waiting for one to turn over on the other, but we rarely did, even if there was something to hide. She'd catch us at the front door, immediately send one into another room, and question us separately on where we'd been, what we'd done, and whom with. She caught us lying only a couple of times before we learned to get our stories straight before we reached the front door.

I prayed Bridgette wouldn't bust me, because on that very day my boyfriend *had* come by, though I didn't let him in the house, which was Ma's specific question. Instead, I led him around to the windowless side of the house, safe from Bridgette's watch. There, we kissed until the prospect of being caught by the neighbors and the thrill of the kiss itself made it difficult for me to keep his hands from wandering.

Bridgette said, "No boys came in," and I knew I'd owe her something later.

When Ma was satisfied that no boys had been in her house, she relaxed and stopped being a cop. I helped her make dinner, chopping vegetables for the salad and mixing up the corn bread, which were my regular dinner tasks any time Ma was home early enough to cook. When she wasn't, I cooked the whole dinner.

"They've identified one of the Niskey Lake boys, the older one," Ma said after sending Bridgette off to watch TV. When she sent Bridgette away so we could talk about her work, it always made me feel like I was a grown-up. And it was a chance to have Ma to myself. When she was home, it seemed to me most of her time went to Bridgette, because that's how it works when you're the youngest. Or maybe I was just jealous.

"How do you know he was older if you don't know who the other boy is yet?"

"The medical examiner can approximate their ages." Ma sounded too business-like about something so dark, until I considered figuring out the ages of the unidentified dead was part of her business. "His name was Edward Hope Smith, and he was just a month shy of his fifteenth birthday. Last time anyone saw him was at that skating rink you go to. *Used* to go to."

"What's that supposed to mean?" I knew what it meant, but asked anyway.

"Until they catch whoever did it, I want you to stay away from there."

Greenbriar skating rink on Campbellton Road had been a favorite hangout since I was eight or nine when we still lived in Southwest. My girlfriends and I would loop yarn around two cardboard doughnuts, snip the yarn along the edges, and tie string between the doughnuts to create pom-poms, which we tied onto our skates. I had pom-poms to match every outfit. Ma or a friend's mother would drop us off and leave for wherever they went to get a few hours' relief from being mothers. I'd skate until I grew sweaty and tired, timing my strides to the beat of Chic's "Good Times," made dizzy by the squares of light reflected from the disco ball as they moved round and round across the floor, walls, and skaters. I wouldn't leave the floor for an hour straight, except during Slow Skate, when the DJ would play something meant for couples, and fake smoke would blow from the ceiling, which made me cough despite it being fake.

And here Ma was trying to keep me from one of the few places a thirteen-year-old could go to have some fun. Since I didn't have any skating plans in the near future, I let it go and

decided to cross that bridge when I got to
have caught the killer.

"What's taking so long to identify the ot

"They're working on it."

"But it's been two weeks. No one's calle

"There's a missing report on a boy na
who hasn't been seen since he got on a bus heading downtown to watch a movie at the Coronet, but the police want to be as sure as they can before asking the family to identify the boy's body. As it is, there wasn't much left of him to identify when he was found."

That was a sad thing to me because it meant there was no one to cry over him, and somewhere in Atlanta there was a family wondering where their child was, hoping he wasn't the boy lying in the morgue.

"They still aren't tying the two boys together yet," Ma said, absentmindedly poking a spatula at ground beef that was long since cooked through. "But they're wrong on that."

Sometimes, I was sure she missed the Department. She wouldn't get involved in the investigation until the case was brought to the district attorney. By the time she got her hands on it, much of the early discovery was already done. Ma never wanted to see anyone hurt, especially not kids, but she did like to solve cases. I could tell she wished she could work on this one.

"Do they have any suspects yet?" I asked. I always asked Ma about this stuff, although most folks would probably say this wasn't the kind of thing to discuss with a thirteen-year-old. But who else was going to ask her? She had to let go of her work at the end of the day just like a professor did with her husband, or a businessman with his wife, except Ma didn't have a husband to tell it to. Besides, I'd never been thirteen a day in my life.

"Nothing so far. I guess they won't be bringing it to us any time soon. You know these things take a while." She handed me the plates to put on the table.

What about the boy from the skating rink? What else do ou know about him?"

Ma didn't answer, and I knew she was in her own head, thinking about patterns.

"Maybe you can help out with the investigation," I said, trying to bring her back to me.

"That's the city's business for now. I think those boys are tied together, and so do some of the detectives working the case. The city doesn't want to raise that question, though. People will freak out if they think somebody's out there killing kids."

I thought about the boys, wondered what the one from the skating rink did that night, the one named Hope. Maybe he skated with his girlfriend during the Slow Skate, maybe he had a quarter get stuck in the pinball machine that was always taking kids' money. He probably left there wondering what lie he was going to tell his mother for getting home late, and it turned out it didn't matter.

"I hope he at least had fun," I said. Then Ma looked at me as if to say, *Who?*

Chapter 3

My friend Cleo from middle school worked in the Municipal Market where her parents owned a stall. The market was in the middle of Sweet Auburn, the cradle of civil rights in Atlanta—home to Dr. King's Ebenezer Baptist Church and the *Atlanta Daily World*, the city's first black-owned daily newspaper. Before desegregation, black people couldn't shop inside where the best selection could be found, and had to make purchases from curbside vendors. By 1979, it seemed only black folks ever shopped there, and only on the inside.

It was like a farmer's market but better, because it had all the flavor of Atlanta wrapped inside of it in the form of food prepared from the soul, or soon to be, at home in someone's kitchen. While the vendors sold you tender collards, fat garlicky pickles, or let you sample just a little taste of pulled pork, they'd talk to you as if they'd known you forever, even if you'd never been inside the place. And the regulars they *had* known forever, they'd remember to ask how a child was doing in school, or whether an elderly father was recovering all right from his stroke. People who didn't go there that often complained about the smell, but that's because they couldn't sniff past the fish on ice to get to the good stuff—fresh melons and berries, home-style fried chicken, or fresh baked sweet potato pie.

Since it was only two blocks from the hospital, I'd walk down there after my shift and try to pull Cleo away from her job running the cash register so we could hang out somewhere downtown. Sometimes we'd window-shop the latest styles, visit Walter's Clothing on Decatur Street for a new pair of Converse high-tops, or maybe check out the record store for new 45s. Almost always her father would let her go, but not before handing us whatever fruit was at peak season—a handful of strawberries when summer was just getting started, or blueberries about the time it seemed the days couldn't get any hotter. (Bridgette was right—it was much too early for pecans.) Since it was on the waning side of August, he handed us a peach, sweeter than any you'd ever find in a grocery store. We walked toward Central City Park, talking about the things important only to thirteen-year-old girlfriends, trying to keep peach juice from running down our arms and staining our shirts.

"I can't stay away too long," Cleo said. "It's our busy day and Daddy'll need me back soon. You killing time until your mother gets off work?"

"Nah, I catch the bus back home. Never sure what time she'll get off work. I just figured we won't see each other much after summer vacation ends."

"Why do you want to go to that school way out in the middle of nowhere, anyway? Not like it's the only Catholic high school in town. It isn't even in town, for that matter."

"It's a good school," I said, wishing immediately that I hadn't.

"The school I'm going to is a good school too."

"I know. That's not what I meant." I pointed out a bench in the park, saying that the large shade tree it sat beneath would give us some relief from the sun, in hopes of changing the subject. She sat beside me but didn't change the subject.

"You're going to that white school like you think they want you there. They just want to make their quota."

"There isn't any quota." I knew she wasn't saying it to be

hurtful, that she was still angry that I'd reneged on our deal to attend the same high school. Neither of us had been part of the popular crowd at school, though they tolerated us, like a football team puts up with the mascot and the band, part of the team but not really. So Cleo and I mostly stuck together. After three years of being each other's confidantes, having each other's back in an after-school fight, sharing the angst of our secret and unrequited crushes, it was painful to imagine not seeing each other every day. But I told myself there would be weekends and summers.

Cleo folded her arms under her breasts, as though she was cradling them, an absentminded habit she'd developed to hide the psoriasis that had plagued her elbows and forearms for as long as I'd known her. A hundred or so pigeons gathered around our feet in anticipation of being fed, but moved away quickly when they discovered our hands were empty. I watched white and black people walk through the park—businesspeople, fast-food workers, homeless men, government employees—and wondered if there was any truth to what Cleo said.

"You'll change, going to school way out there. Next thing I know, you'll be talking white."

"No, I won't."

"And acting white too."

"No, I won't." I knew how weak and childish it sounded. But what else could I have said? I hadn't prepared for an argument defending who I was to the person who knew me better than anyone.

"I won't hardly recognize you anymore."

I wasn't sure which feeling took me more by surprise—the anger, or the hurt caused by her words. More confusing was how far apart we already were, even before school had begun. I hadn't set a foot on the new school's property, and already I was being called a sellout. There was little worse than being told by my own that I'd forgetten who I was, as though any neighborhood, any dialect, any race of people surrounding me could pull the brown skin from my flesh, my soul right from my heart.

"I'd better start walking toward Five Points if I want to make the next bus," I said, hoping the heat growing behind my eyelids wouldn't show how she'd wounded me before I could walk away. I don't recall how many times we talked after that, but I know it wasn't many more.

It was my fading friendship with Cleo that made me start one with Cassandra, the girl next door. She had lived there a couple of years by then, but we were never tight because I had Cleo, and the sometimes friendship of the popular girls at school. Also there was something about Cassandra I always thought strange and put me off from her—the way she was like an old lady and a little kid at the same time. She had the forgiving and innocent ways of a four-year-old, but none of the adventure of one. Cassandra never wanted to do anything, content to sit on her porch and watch everyone else even though she was only thirteen. She even had the physical presence of an old person, standing back on her legs so they bowed backward, hands on her hips, looking tired but willing to call up enough energy to give a sermon on the dangers of whatever the rest of us kids were doing.

On that day, Cassandra and I, along with two girls from the neighborhood we sometimes hung out with, all decided it was too hot for doing anything but sitting around, so we went down to the girl's house with the card table on her patio, protected by the shade of a big magnolia tree. Cassandra was reluctant to leave her porch, where she sat fanning herself with a folded newspaper and remarking on how fast people were driving down our street, but she followed us anyway.

Like most Atlanta streets outside of downtown, there were no sidewalks, so we had to walk in the street. This caused Cassandra no small amount of stress when cars flew around the curves going forty-five miles an hour instead of the thirty posted on the sign the city had planted in my yard. The speeders didn't live on our end of the street, where people had what Ma called *pride of ownership*. They lived on the other end, in apartments and Section 8 housing that either a landlord or the government owned. Today when I pass through (because my mother still owns that house and we have family living there), I see drug deals made openly at the stop sign where I once caught my bus, and I make only a rolling stop, fearful of being caught in the middle of a deal gone bad.

Twenty years earlier, my street had been part of a solidly middle-class neighborhood. In the summer of 1979, it was slipping toward the lower end, but I didn't know that. I saw mostly well-kept houses, large yards full of white oaks and peach trees, and at least one car in each driveway, even if they were older models with neglected dents aged with rust or patched with Bondo. I was just glad I didn't live in an apartment building as we had the four years before Ma bought the house. No more listening to the man above us pee in the morning, or the rhythmic banging of a headboard against the wall of the bedroom my sister and I shared, accompanied by sounds that made Bridgette ask whether the couple next door was fighting. My street was full of trees, houses were far enough apart that no one knew your business unless you wanted them to, and we had a pool in the backyard that made other kids on the street envious.

"Sitting under all those trees, we'll be eaten alive by mosquitoes," Cassandra said in a low voice so the others couldn't hear while we walked to the girl's house. I ignored her. "Plus, they have that small creek running behind the house. Mosquitoes love hanging around water."

"Then go back home."

"That's okay. I put on some Skin-So-Soft this morning. That should keep some of them away."

Our game was Spades, playing in pairs. There were five girls, and Cassandra was more than willing to be the odd girl out. She sat in a chair on the periphery of the card table, barely moving except to swat away mosquitoes, so that we almost forgot she was there.

After we bid our books, me certain that my partner was overconfident in the number of books she could win, we started into another game. From three houses down, I could hear the woodpecker going at one of the apple trees in my backyard. Every summer he returned, as if circling the branches and trunk with shallow holes was a pilgrimage. Our world was quiet except for the bird, and the occasional tiny thud of shiny red magnolia seeds falling from grenade-looking pods. It was at least a month too early in the season for the seeds to be falling, and I briefly wondered what omen my grandmother might read into it. We focused on our card game and didn't talk about how the humidity pressed down on us like a shroud, because that would have only made it feel more miserable.

One girl cleared her throat. Silence can make teenage girls uncomfortable if it goes on for more than a minute or two, so the rest of us were grateful.

"I can't wait until school starts," the girl said, causing us to look up at her with worry she'd taken ill with the heat stroke. "High school, I mean. It'll be fun to be in high school."

"There's nothing special about it," Marie said. She was the oldest, on her way to tenth grade, and she belonged to the Beautiful Family, as I called them. There were four kids—two boys and two girls—all of them pretty. They came in all shades, from redbone to cocoa, but all had flawless skin that seemed gilded, the same full lips, the same round eyes and lush eyelashes that made me think of babies. The girls I wanted to look like, the boys I wanted to go with, but neither thing ever happened.

The rest of us listened to Marie because not only was she the oldest and beautiful, she was also worldly. Her mother was a teacher, and she, like her sister and brothers, spoke in the most beautiful way—every syllable enunciated, no lingual shortcuts taken, and sometimes with words I'd have to pretend to know and then look up in my *World Book* dictionary later.

"It's just more of the same. College is what I'm looking forward to."

"What about the football games and pep rallies?" I asked.

"Oh, and the pep squad," my Spades partner said. "I'm going out for the pep squad."

"And all the cute boys," from Marie's partner.

"All what cute boys? The boys are the same ones you knew in eighth grade. Everyone's the same, just in a new building. Status quo." Marie laid down a card with a slapping sound, as if to say, *and that's that*, and won the book.

"Not for Kim," Cassandra said from behind me, startling everyone because we'd come to believe there were only four of us. "The boys will be different 'cause she went to private school, and now she'll be going to George High with us."

"I'm not going to George. I'm staying in Catholic school." I was waiting for the fallout, the questions about whether I thought I was too good for public school.

"Now that's a strange religion," Marie said, repositioning the cards in her hand. "Not strange, but with so many rituals and symbolism. So dark. I guess you have to be Catholic to understand it."

I was happy Marie was there. With a few sentences, she made it seem like my decision was too bizarre to question, too complex for the other kids to understand, and made me seem slightly exotic all at the same time. I was certain she'd become my best friend, fill in the opening left by Cleo, but that never happened either.

The dead boys weren't enough to take my mind off starting high school. I'd been in Catholic school since kindergarten, and was headed to a Catholic high school. People were sometimes surprised to learn black Catholics exist, even other black folks. We had all the traditional doings at our church, like the holy water, stained glass windows with the

Stations of the Cross, and the smoky pot the priest waved around to fill the church with the spicy scent of incense. There was the constant kneeling I had to do, so that by the time I was five or six, I'd learned to hate the kneelers that never had enough foam covering them to keep my knees from hurting. As a younger child, I'd always thought of the kneelers as one of the many burdens Catholics were supposed to bear for Jesus having saved us from our sins.

But everything else about our church was Southern Baptist or AME—the gospel music, the unintentional fashion parade put on every Sunday by the women parishioners, and the fund-raising fish dinners held in the church basement. True, no self-respecting Catholic would ever fall out in church—we were too low-key for that—and it was rare to hear an "amen" in response to the priest above more than a murmur, but we did have more flavor than your usual Catholic church.

Now I was going to an all-white Catholic high school in an all-white neighborhood across town in Northeast. At the beginning of eighth grade, Ma and I had our minds on what it would take to get me into a good college, and when the Knights of Columbus offered me a scholarship to attend the school that we normally couldn't afford, we had to accept. I had no idea what it would be like, but if it was anything like what I experienced when I took the entrance exam for the school, I expected to be uncomfortable.

On the day of the exam, I woke up nervous, my stomach pulling at my insides from every angle. It didn't help matters that Ma got me there late. I had to depend on her to take me because there was no bus to the test site. When I arrived, the other kids were already seated and the proctor was just about to hand out the tests.

In a room of about two hundred kids, it seemed mine was the only dark face, and everyone looked at me as if I'd walked through the wrong door. It was the first moment that the term *CP time*—colored people's time—held any meaning for me, even though I'd heard the term before. The experience only deepened my addiction to punctuality. I just held on to my Number Two pencils like I dared anyone to take them from me, and walked in like I'd been coming there all my life. When I got the acceptance letter, I wished I could show it to every kid and teacher who looked at me funny. It wasn't until later that I realized I'd be sitting next to a lot of them come late August.

Now it was two weeks before class started, and I was stepping off the bus in front of the school with plans to buy my books for the first semester. My school was way out in Ashford-Dunwoody, a place I'd never heard of, much less visited. All I knew about that part of Atlanta was that it was rich and white. The whole experience was like walking into the Twilight Zone.

The campus, as they called it, looked nothing like I expected. It was huge, and the soccer field alone was bigger than the space that my old school stood on, including the blacktop where we had recess and the new building they had to add on when the old building got too crowded. Everything at the new school was green grass except for the parking lot and driveways, and the school itself sat about an eighth of a mile off a road that looked like something from a fairy tale, with its huge magnolias, houses set far off the road and buffered by rolling green yards, and nothing remotely commercial for at least two miles. There was even a babbling brook running alongside the school's property, as if it were a scene pulled from the pages of a children's book.

My old school sat forty feet off busy Gordon Street in the West End, across from a mom-and-pop grocer, and shared a block with Krispy Kreme Doughnuts and a New York deli. The deli had the best ham Po'Boys, and even though I gave the place up after noticing a couple of roaches crawling up a wall behind the man working on my sandwich, I ended up coming back a few months later because the food was good, cheap, and I'd worked hard to block out my memory of the roaches. Across the street was the Shrine of the Black Madonna bookstore, and two blocks down was the Wren's Nest, home of Joel Chandler Harris, the author who gave the world Uncle Remus, Brer Rabbit, and Tar-Baby. Even as a child, I saw the irony in how such different literary messages were housed just a few doors apart.

I had talked Ma into a new outfit just for the occasion, but it didn't look anything like what the other kids were wearing. They looked like younger versions of their parents. The girls wore denim skirts, vests covering plaid shirts with matching satin ribbons tied at their necks. It seemed every boy in the place was wearing a white cotton shirt with dull beige pants. It was an understatement to say I stood out from the crowd: I didn't have at least one parent in tow, and I was wearing my skintight jeans, gauzy peasant shirt, and lace-up wedge-heeled sandals. And *everyone* was white. Lucky for me I had Ma's blood and could always fake like I just didn't give a damn, even when I did, because everyone was staring at me.

Chapter 4

Fortunately, I didn't have much time to think about the new school and how foreign a place it was, how it was clear I wouldn't be a candidate for a picture in next year's catalogue. The current issue, creased and worn by a daily search for answers that might relieve my fear that I'd chosen the wrong school, sat on my nightstand brimming with the earnest and happy faces of dull beige boys and white cotton girls. Next thing I knew, the summer was over and I was on the bus heading across town to my new school. It was still dark outside because I had to catch a 5:30 bus to get downtown in time to take a connecting bus at 6:10. I tried not to think about the two dead boys as I walked through Central City Park.

During the day, it was my favorite part of downtown Atlanta. But in the shadows of dawn, when trash cans looked like crouching men and park benches might be hiding child killers, I began to regret cutting through the park as a shortcut. My pace quickened into a near run until I reached the other side of the park, still telling myself I wasn't worried about dead children or how the person who killed them hadn't been caught yet. Once I made it to the bus that would take me into the suburbs, I thanked God for getting me there and promised to walk around the park from then on.

I felt more confident about my first day, thinking the school uniform would make it a level playing ground. But when I arrived at school, I saw that I couldn't even get the uniform right. We had been given instructions to buy our uniforms from a specific store, but I figured I'd save some money on the blazer and buy only the skirt. The skirt was in a plaid cloth specific to the school, but the only requirement of the blazer was that it be navy blue. I made the twenty-mile bus trip to the nearest Buckhead Men's Shop, on the north side in a part of town I'd never visited. There were kids in the shop buying uniforms for my school and other private schools. Their mothers picked out the full ensemble of plaid skirt (gray pants and striped tie for the boys), blazer, shirt, and socks. At the cash register, a mother rang up a full set for each day of the week, except for the jacket, because she told her son he could get by with three. Ma had given me enough money for two skirts and one jacket. The shirts I was to buy someplace less expensive.

I was the only kid in the store without a mother, and it struck me as odd—Why did teenagers need their mothers to shop with them? But I must have struck them as odd, too, because they looked at me as if I was the one who had it wrong. I bought my blue-and-gray plaid skirt and school crest, and crossed Peachtree Street for the bus south. I decided I'd buy the blazer and shirts at a department store, not tell Ma, and pocket the difference. That was the advantage of shopping alone.

I saw the error in my plan when I realized that standing next to all the other blue blazers, mine wasn't navy at all, but closer to cobalt. The topstitching around the lapel called attention to its cheapness, and the fancy-looking school crest I'd sewn on the left pocket as instructed did nothing to enhance the quality. Instead, it highlighted the fact that I'd paid only sixteen dollars for the blazer, which until now I thought had been a bit of shrewd bargain hunting. My bra was visible underneath my thin, cheap white blouse, which kept me from taking off the jacket once outside in the late August heat. When the other girls took off their blazers, I noticed their collars were pinned down neatly by tiny buttons on the tip of each collar, not flying every which way like mine. And my blouse had no polo player on a tiny horse running across the front.

We were required to wear black-and-white saddle oxfords, which I'd never worn before. Every girl in the school had the same shoes on—leather, thin-soled, slightly tapered at the toe. Not me. I bought my shoes at Butler's downtown because they were the only saddle oxfords I could find that were stylish, as far as saddle oxfords went. My leather shoes had a round toe, thick black soles, and a flap of notched, black pleather covering the laces. Originally, I'd planned to switch the black flap with homemade yarn pom-poms in the school colors, which I'd thought would give the otherwise ugly shoes a little style. I was grateful Ma had talked me out of that. As it was, everywhere I went, girls stared at my feet.

I'd been in school only a week and the dead boys had already been pushed off my list of worries, replaced by schoolgirl concerns like wearing the right clothes, making new friends, and wondering what the next four years would be like with little to no black boys being part of my new school's population.

As if a reminder to heed Ma's warning to be more careful, another boy went missing the day after Labor Day. His name was Milton Harvey, and he was fourteen. I tried to keep in mind that he was only missing, that he might be found. I speculated that he got tired of his parents and ran away from home. Instead of some really terrible thing happening to him, maybe he'd only been knocked in the head, had amnesia, and couldn't remember where he lived.

But living with a cop, you knew even as you made up such scenarios that you were being childish, that if the boy wasn't found within the first twenty-fours that he went missing, he likely wouldn't be found alive. This was what Ma said every time a TV news story talked about an abducted child, chastising the police spokesperson being interviewed for giving false hope to the terrified parents who always appeared in the story to plead for their child's safe return.

"What else can they say?" I'd ask her.

"Nothing, really. It's just sad knowing how things will probably turn out."

Just the same, I tried to imagine the boy hanging out with a friend somewhere, trying to make his parents feel bad for some wrong they'd done him.

A week later, Milton Harvey still hadn't turned up. An article ran in the newspaper, "Police Ask Help in Finding Teens." It showed pictures of the two boys still missing, the fourteen-year-old who'd been missing a week now, and one of the boys who disappeared at the end of July. Ma said the police felt certain that the boy missing since July was the one still lying in the morgue unidentified, but that his parents were just as certain the body wasn't their child's. All I could think was how regular they looked, how much like the boys at my old school they were. One had a smile that reminded me of a boy I liked in seventh grade, a smile full of bravado created by anticipation and fear of a fast-approaching manhood. I don't know what I expected to be different, but I hoped for something that would set them apart from me and my world.

Milton Harvey had just started ninth grade. So had I. He'd asked his mother if he could miss the first day of school because he didn't have the latest style of sneakers and was worried about being teased, reminding me of my own shoe embarrassment. The last time he was seen he'd gone to pay a bill for his mother at a bank two miles from home. I'd completed similar grown-folk's tasks for Ma, usually dropping off a payment at a branch downtown before I changed buses between school and home. The bike he'd borrowed from a friend to run the errand had been found behind a tree in some woods along the route between his home and the bank. The bank said he'd completed the transaction, so someone got him on his way back home. The police didn't think he'd run away. I rode my Huffy Strider ten-speed everywhere. If I ever ran away, it would be the first thing I'd take, but I didn't believe the boy had run away either.

There was also a description of what the boy who might be the second boy from Niskey Lake Road was wearing when he disappeared—black knit pants and a black T-shirt. Ma told me later that it was a Kiss T-shirt like the one she brought home for me after working an extra job as security for the band. Just like mine, which was probably wadded up in the back of a dresser drawer or torn into dust rags in the broom closet. Maybe just being black kids living in the same city, having to be in the same streets every day, taking the same routes and unknowingly crossing paths meant that what we shared outnumbered the things we didn't.

I wanted to ask Ma more about the boys from the newspaper article, and saw my chance when she sent Bridgette out of the kitchen before she began cleaning her gun. I knew my sister was somewhere pouting, jealous of my time alone with Ma. Our dog Copper left the room, too, either to follow Bridgette or maybe because his dog sense told him that a gun was something he wanted no part of. Ma wanted me to watch her clean the gun so I'd learn. I was the oldest, and she'd already given me my first shooting lesson with her personal revolver, which consisted of shooting cans off tree stumps on some family land out in the country. First, I had to get used to the gun's weight, how to steady it when holding it out in front of me. Then, Ma taught me how to use the site on top of the .38's barrel to line up my target. She stood behind me and braced me the first time I experienced the gun's kick from a fired round, and I remember smelling Chanel N° 5 and gunpowder, a nauseating mix of sweet and acrid, like burned brown sugar.

There was no getting around the fact that guns were a part of how she paid the mortgage, and they were kept in the house. They were out of sight but not under lock and key every minute of the day. So she wanted to make sure that I understood how they worked, but mostly that I respected what they could do. She didn't think Bridgette was old enough to learn how to use guns, but she'd also been schooled in what they could do, how they worked, and had been allowed to hold an unloaded gun.

We sat at the kitchen table, and I tried to think of questions to ask about the missing kids that wouldn't give away my worry. Once I did that, she'd have more justification for keeping me from places like the skating rink. While Ma spread out the old towel kept around for this job, her red nails a fiery contrast against cold steel, she emptied the chamber of its bullets and went right on talking about whatever trivial thing we'd been discussing when she sent Bridgette from the room, plans for next summer's family reunion, I think. As I watched her, I forgot about the missing boys, and instead remembered the man she shot when she was a street cop, a clean *through and through* in the shoulder that left the man wounded but alive. It left Ma alive, too, despite the man's attempt to make me an orphan that day.

She lined the bullets up on the towel, the pointy ends all going the same direction. In most things, Ma was haphazard, disorderly, and usually made things up as she went. But in her police work, she always had a plan, a pattern that was not to be disrupted. She went on and on about whether we should reserve space at a public park or hold the reunion in someone's backyard, but I couldn't help staring at the gun. I only wondered how quickly she could pull the gun from its holster if she surprised some bad guy during a robbery in progress.

Some professions can't be gone into half-assed. Some require being called to them, like giving your life to the church or the throne or the mob. To be successful at those jobs, it should be something you feel in your bones is the thing you have to do, or someone has to catch you at a young age and groom you into it. Being a cop should be the same way, but that's not exactly how it was for my mother.

It was the man who'd stalked Ma that convinced her to become a cop in the first place. She'd been working a combination of part-time jobs that barely paid the rent, kept the lights on and our stomachs full—usually as a bookkeeper or an apartment-leasing agent. The leasing agent job got us free rent, but it came with a price. I remember her boss being the nastiest sort of man, mostly because he was always asking for some "chocolate pie" from her, right in front of me. I guess he figured calling it that would fool a seven-year-old, but I knew exactly what he was talking about. Ma was able to keep him off of her, but he always threatened her with eviction. She was sick of the man holding her and her children's fate in his nasty hands, and started looking for a job that would pay a twenty-six-year-old single mother with no college degree a decent wage.

She was friends with an off-duty cop who worked security for our apartment complex. He teased her that since she liked to think she was so big and bad, why not take the police exam? When she received yet another threat of eviction from her lecherous boss and landlord, she asked her friend how she should go about applying for a police job. He laughed and told her he was just messing with her. She couldn't be a cop—she probably couldn't even pass the physical agility test. Ma told me later that he was probably right about the physical exam, but she wanted to try anyway. Besides, she was going to need rent money. She figured being a cop was as good a job as any.

Ma still wasn't fully sold on the police officer business until something happened that changed her outlook on a few things, including making a living, keeping her kids safe, and not ever letting a man hold her fate.

While Ma was working in the leasing office at the front end of the apartment complex, Bridgette and I were playing in the grassy area between buildings, just outside our patio and the wooden fence that enclosed it. A man came from nowhere and stood about twenty feet from us. He asked me something about Ma that I can't remember anymore, maybe he asked us her name. I didn't say anything to him, just grabbed Bridgette's hand and ran onto the patio and into the apartment, locking the sliding door and putting the broomstick into the track for extra measure.

Our apartment was like a townhouse, with an upstairs. I watched the man from behind curtains in a downstairs window. He stood in the grass separating the back of our building from the back of the next building over, watching our upstairs window, the one for Ma's bedroom. I kept the phone with me, ready to ask Ma to come home from the leasing office if I got too scared being by myself. After about ten minutes of staring at the window, he walked away.

I'd never been as happy as when Ma finally got home. I told her about the man and gave her the best description I could. She wrote it all down, and told me next time something like that happened to call her right away. Before we went to bed, she must have checked the locks on the doors fifty times. It worried me because I'd never seen my mother frightened of anything. Even before she became a cop, she was not a woman you wanted to mess with. Nothing happened that night, but the next morning when Ma opened her curtains, he was there, staring up at her bedroom window again. By the time she went to the phone to call the police, he was gone. She figured, or hoped, that was the end of it.

That night, Ma checked the windows and the doors, but she turned down a friend's offer to spend the night. She took a bat upstairs to bed with her, just in case, and made Bridgette and me sleep in her bed. I figured that was as much for her nerves as our protection. Only Bridgette could sleep, being three and not old enough to be afraid. Ma kept looking out the window, expecting to see him, but relieved when she didn't. Eventually, I went to sleep but woke up when I felt her get out of the bed to check the window again. This time he was there, and he saw her. In the time it took her to run around the bed to get to the phone, we could hear the crash of glass downstairs. Ma told me to take Bridgette into the closet and hide behind the suitcases she had stored in there. While Bridgette and I hid in the closet, Ma closed the bedroom door and pushed some furniture against it.

Using the two suitcases and a corner of the closet, I made a tiny, four-walled room. We sat in the tiny room cross-legged, facing each other and knees touching, making a ceiling of Ma's skirts and dresses. Bridgette was still half asleep, but she was awake enough to be afraid, even if she wasn't sure of what.

"What happen?"

"Shh, whisper, okay? It's like a game of hide-and-go-seek," I told her, hoping it was enough to keep her quiet, trying hard to sound calm and grown-up when I really just wanted to cry.

"We hide from Mommy?"

"Yeah, so hush, or she'll find us."

"She's not counting. I don't hear counting."

I put a finger to my lips, even though Bridgette couldn't see it in the dark of the closet, and listened for what was happening outside the door.

I could hear her on the phone, calling her off-duty cop friend who worked in the little gatehouse at the entrance of the complex. Ma was trying to sound like everything was okay while she told her friend to come, to hurry, but I could hear the panic in her voice. That scared me even more.

"Now I hear Mommy, but she still not counting. Who she talking to?"

"I don't know, but if you stay quiet you can have my turn for the prize in the cereal box."

That shut her up finally. I could hear more furniture being pulled across the carpet. Ma was pushing something against the bedroom door, probably the tallboy. I wondered how she was able to move it alone.

Then it was quiet in the room, and I imagined the man coming up the staircase at that very moment, Ma waiting beside the closed and locked bedroom door with the bat in her hands, ready to swing, like on TV. Except this wasn't TV, it was real, even if it didn't seem like it. The closet smelled of Chanel and mothballs and worn-in shoe leather. Bridgette smelled like baby, good baby. She was three years old, but Ma still gave her a bath and washed her hair with Johnson's in the pink bottle. I breathed in all the scents, and the mix made me feel a little better, even the mothballs.

It seemed like we were in the closet forever from the time Ma had called the guardhouse, but it was only another minute later when I heard someone banging on the door downstairs. I was grateful that Ma had made good friends with that cop. A few minutes later, I could hear his voice yelling upstairs for Ma, and not long after that, she was opening the door of the closet. When I walked into the room, I could see that I'd been right about the tallboy. It had only been pushed away from the door enough to let in her police friend.

Ma hugged Bridgette and me, and called me a smart girl for taking care of my sister.

"You didn't count. No fair."

Ma looked at Bridgette, confused, then at me. Then she gave us another hug, which was when I could feel the tears coming, but I wiped them away before she could see them. I was no baby like Bridgette, and Bridgette wasn't crying. Ma's friend turned the man over to some uniform cops who took him away, but it was a few days before I could get to sleep without being in her bed.

We never learned why the man was stalking her, but soon

after that happened we moved into another complex, and just two years after the Atlanta Police Department had hired its first black female officer, Ma enrolled in the police academy. She said the first thing she wanted to do was learn how to shoot a gun.

Chapter 5

School wasn't so bad after the first few days. Ma gave me money to get some new saddle oxfords, even though she fussed at me about having to spend more money when she told me the first pair were wrong the day we bought them. She kept telling me what they looked like in her day, so I was certain those were not the shoes I wanted to wear. It turned out she was right.

Black kids made up a whopping one percent of the school's population. I figured it would be an easy thing to make friends with those kids since we naturally had something in common. It's the thing you can always count on—black folks finding each other wherever we are few. As with every other thing I was learning about the school, it turned out this wasn't the case. The kids had been attending since seventh grade and had already established their groups, and most surprising, not all together. They were friendly enough, but I knew they'd likely never be my friends. Not like those in my neighborhood, or the kids I went to middle school with in the West End. Those kids talked like me, listened to the same music, could see the style in a pair of straight-leg jeans cuffed over a new pair of white Converse high-tops.

Not the black kids at my new school. They were about as unlike me as the rich white kids, and they seemed bland and assimilated. They'd heard of the bands that were unknown to me—bands with names like Lynyrd Skynyrd and AC/DC. They could use the word *crap* without it sounding foreign on their tongues (in my neighborhood, we called it what it was—shit). Somehow they could actually dance to the song "My Sharona." I decided that trying to make friends with them would be no less difficult than making friends with the white kids. At least with the kids whose differences showed readily in their skin, in the intonation of their words, in their shiny Trans Ams and Corvettes that blasted "Sweet Home Alabama" from the radio, there would be no guessing where I stood, wondering where our similarities ended. So I did something I never would have expected I'd do a month earlier—I began making friends with some of the rich white kids.

They asked me stupid questions, and our initial conversations often involved discussions I'd never imagined I'd be part of.

"Does your hair get wet?" What, did you expect water would slide off as if my hair were a duck's feathers?

"Can I touch your hair?" This I allowed only once. That one instance made me feel too much like a rabbit in a petting zoo, or a misunderstood circus freak, to allow it again. Each time someone asked to touch my hair after that I had to fight an urge to hurt them. I wondered how they'd react if black people were all the time asking to touch their hair. But I didn't really care to know, and besides, I already knew. In books, hair was always described as flaxen or being like corn silk, and I'd shucked enough ears of corn to know what that felt like. Smooth, shiny hair came on all the Barbie dolls, even the black ones. White people were hardly a mystery to me by the time I'd reached high school, because even though I didn't know many personally—my teachers at the old school, a girlfriend of one of my aunts—their presence in my world was felt everywhere.

"Oh, you just have to come to the first school dance. You can show us all the new moves." The most I could muster in response was a serious roll of the eyes. This being my first real experience with "overcoming stereotypes," I wasn't adept at doing so. No one asked me about a love of fried chicken or watermelon, but they wondered whether I'd be going out for the basketball team. I found it difficult to say, "Yes, I play basketball. I *love* playing basketball."

I hated some of the things that I felt I had to do to make them comfortable with me, like talking differently when I was around them. It took nearly a year to let go of using "to be" as a present tense verb, as in "I be tripping when he tells a joke," or "She be wearing a cute outfit to school every day." It wasn't as if I didn't know how to conjugate verbs, not as though the nuns at my old school didn't try to pound this particular verb usage out of our heads. It was just the way we talked around friends who wouldn't suspect our intelligence because we talked that way. I realized early that people at the new school expected me to be less from the start, in a Catholic missionary "save the savages" kind of way, so I learned to speak the "right way" around kids when it used to be a requirement only around teachers.

It was like another chore outside of just attending school—learning to live this second life. I pretended to like The Eagles (until one day I realized I really did). When my classmates discussed ski vacations, I nodded as though I knew where Breadloaf was and tried to see the logic in wearing a down jacket with no sleeves during the winter. I wanted to ask, *Aren't your arms cold too?* Going five class periods without seeing a face like mine is not that big a deal, I told myself. I tried to call someone a "spaz" without it sounding ridiculous, but it always did. At first, it wore me out, made me grateful when I got off the bus downtown in a world that didn't expect anything of me than what I was. Eventually, it got easier. Sometimes it was the fact that it *did* get easier that bothered me most.

* * *

New differences between the kids and me showed up daily. In the spirit of getting us more involved in PE instead of seeing it as a drudgery that caused our curling-ironed flips to fall before midday, the teacher suggested everyone bring an album or two that could be played during the PE hour. It was still early in the school year, before I'd really figured out just how foreign a place it was. I knew I'd never pass around the latest frosted blue eye shadows and pale-pink lipsticks in the locker room the way my classmates did (I'd look like a clown in those colors). On the one Friday a month when we didn't have to wear our uniforms, I knew I'd never be able to ask if anyone had a spare package of L'eggs pantyhose because I'd put a run in mine (Nude didn't apply to bare brown skin, and Suntan didn't refer to the shade of mocha I turned after a day in the sun). But my music was something I could share with them. I was excited about getting home and going through my album collection, which was impressive because one of my aunts was dating a DJ who spun records in a nightclub and he gave her his duplicates, which she always gave to me.

After much consideration, and recognizing that a PE class demanded something upbeat, I chose two songs that were hot in 1979, at least in my world: Gloria Gaynor's "I Will Survive," and Anita Ward's "Ring My Bell." True, all I'd heard around school so far was a sound I didn't know much about, Southern Rock from groups like .38 Special and Molly Hatchet, but I was sure my music would inspire the girls in class to move through whatever lame activity the teacher would inflict on us. This certainty made me get changed quickly and out to the gym floor first, where I handed my albums to the teacher so they'd get the first play. She took the albums from me without asking anything about them, and was lowering the arm on the school-issued record player just as all of the girls arrived in the gym.

The first few notes of "Ring My Bell" came out of the player's speakers, sounding small and tinny compared to my stereo at home, and something like the special-effects sound that always accompanied the firing of laser guns in seventies sci-fi movies. I looked around the gym floor at the girls to see if the music would have the effect I'd hoped for. Instead, there were small snickers, which grew into giggles, until finally all of them were laughing out loud.

"What *is* this?"

"Disco. Someone brought *disco.*" It was as if I'd introduced the plague into the gym. "God, I can't believe it. Who brought disco?"

It didn't take more than a quick glance around for them to conclude it must have been me, the one who least fit in and who looked most likely to spread the dreaded disco among them. The teacher tried to ignore the girls, I suppose out of kindness toward me, and let the record play, trying to tap her foot to the beat until a funny look passed over her face and she lifted the arm of the record player abruptly.

That's when it dawned on me that I hadn't considered the lyrics when I made my selection, so involved was I in making sure the music would get the class fired up. About the same time I thought of this, the teacher must have figured out that "Ring My Bell" didn't have a thing to do with alerting Anita to her man's presence at the front door. She put the record back in the sleeve and handed both albums to me, not even willing to give old Gloria Gaynor a try. On top of that, every girl in the place now knew for sure who had brought the records.

"I'll take these back to my locker," I told her. It was a good ten minutes before I showed up on the gym floor again, and hoped that by then I'd pushed my anger and embarrassment down enough to get through the class without cussing out the next girl to say disco. The teacher must have said something while I was gone, because the laughs and comments had been reduced to knowing glances, the kind that only high-school girls can give, the kind that can decide and relay to the rest of the pack a girl's social standing in an instant. I just acted like it didn't faze me, but I decided that would be the last time I'd try to bring some of my world into theirs.

* * *

On a Saturday in October that still had the makings of a summer day—warm and sticky, the air feeling almost too heavy to breathe—we kids were taking a break from playing basketball on the driveway of the boys with the hoop. Our hosts were three brothers—one a year younger than I, one a year older than Bridgette, and a third who was too young to hang with any of us. His parents made his brothers look out for him anyway, which meant he tagged along after the older kids like an afterthought and always seemed to have skinned knees from falling while trying to keep up. All the kids from the Beautiful Family were there, a good thing because the boys were the best players on the street, and the best-looking.

Marie and I were the only girls the boys would take when choosing teams. We were the only girls willing to go hard to the basket and scrap for the ball without fussing about getting scratched, or worrying about our hair coming loose from our ponytails. Plus, we could shoot from the outside, a skill learned to avoid some of those under-the-basket skirmishes. Cassandra and her younger sister Latrice were there. Bridgette and Latrice were friends, and we gave them the job of chasing down a runaway ball or holding on to valuables that might get damaged in a game—eyeglasses (mine); a bracelet; loose change; a pack of Bubble Yum that would be returned to the owner soft from sitting in the sun or a pocket, and usually missing a piece. In return, they got to hang out with us older kids. Cassandra would never join a game, even if she knew how to play, because it required bumping up against sweaty boys, one of the reasons I enjoyed the game.

Playing basketball was one of the few occasions I wasn't nervous around boys. I loved their awe when I hit two points from the outside while being defended by a boy six inches taller. The moment my feet left the ground in the jump shot, when I felt the ball leave the fingertips of my shooting hand, watched it arc through the air and fall into the basket, heard the whisper of leather moving through net without touching rim or backboard, I was all confidence. By the time a boy from the other team had grabbed the ball and run up the driveway to take it out again, my shot was forgotten. But in the seconds between the shot and the next play, hearing a player from my team say "nothing but net," or taunting the boy who'd been playing me with "in your face" or "you let a girl play you like that?" was the sweetest thing. Cassandra would never know that feeling (and probably wouldn't care anyway) because she always sat on the porch steps watching the game, along with the second daughter from the Beautiful Family, who was another prissy girl.

We had just finished a game of Twenty-One, my side victorious, and were resting up so we could start another. I sat on the porch steps and could smell the pine needles someone had raked from the lawn and spread under the holly bushes that grew in front of the porch. It was barely a smell, the pine oil long since faded, just enough to remind me of something warm and pleasant.

"We play Fulton High tonight. Who's going to the game?" asked one Beautiful boy, who was the oldest of us and in the eleventh grade. Along with his brother and Marie, he went to George High like everyone else in our neighborhood. He tried to spin the ball on his middle finger like Meadowlark Lemon, but managed no more than a few rotations before the ball fell and he had to try again.

No one outside the Beautiful Family had planned to go to the game.

"Why not, Cassandra? You go to George, show some school spirit." Marie said.

"I don't like sports."

"No one goes for the sports. People go for the cheering and socializing, and to hear the band and watch the steppers at halftime."

I didn't say anything, only thought how different it was at my school, where the football game was everything, where the team ran the show because they had a tradition of going to the state finals every year since dirt was created. The band had no soul, and I was certain no one at the school had ever seen a step show, much less knew what one was. In my head, I kept hearing, *Who brought disco?*

Everyone was quiet for a while, and then Cassandra asked, "What about these kids turning up missing?" It was an attempt to keep the conversation from returning to her not going to the game. Or she may have asked because she was like an old person that way, bringing up the news or talking about the weather the way old people do when there's nothing else to say.

"Not just missing. Dead. Two dead and one missing," Marie said. "You think it's just a coincidence?" She said it in a way to make the *you* addressed to anyone, but we all knew she was directing it to me. I was the one most likely to know.

"We don't think so, but it's too soon to tell." I was good at giving just enough information to titillate, but not enough to get into any trouble. It was a politician's skill I'd learned listening to Ma answer similar questions. I liked the way I could let *we* slide off my tongue as though I had anything to do with it, and the way none of the kids ever questioned my knowledge. "Just too soon to tell."

One of the boys who lived in the house went inside for a few minutes and returned with a stack of Dixie cups and a plastic pitcher of Kool-Aid full of ice. The drink was so sweet we knew he'd made it, not his mother, and were glad. The cups were tiny, with riddles and cartoons on them, made for preschoolers instead of sun-weary, half-grown kids, so we drank the first cup greedily, then settled into a resting spot to savor the second cup. We all had red mustaches as Kool-Aid dried on our upper lips in a breeze that briefly hinted at fall.

Someone had brought a boom box, and now Sugarhill Gang's new song was playing, "Rapper's Delight."

"That's my song," I said.

"That's *my* song," said a Beautiful brother, and the challenge was on.

After the music intro, I started singing along with Wonder

Mike, hitting every word on beat, as if I'd written the lyrics. When Wonder Mike passed it over to Hank, the Beautiful brother picked up the lyrics, and everyone waited to see if he'd stumble on a word, making me winner of the battle. We sat on porch steps, lawn chairs, and grass, and took turns singing the parts we knew, laughing when somebody didn't know the rhyme and tried to make up words. We weren't thinking of dead kids anymore. I wasn't thinking of mean white girls who couldn't see the beauty in a dance beat so tight you couldn't resist moving to it.

After I finished my homework, Bridgette and I were watching the news and heard that another boy was missing. They still hadn't found Milton Harvey, the boy who was last seen at the bank, but it had been over six weeks and I'd already stopped making up reasons why he went missing. I didn't bother to imagine what this fourth boy was doing, where he might be. I knew he was dead, just like lots of people in Atlanta knew, just like his mother must have known while she cried in the film that the newspeople were running, praying publicly for his return. I turned to Channel 17, which had no news hour or crying mothers, and played a constant loop of sixties sitcoms and Braves games during baseball season.

Ma walked into the den and told me to turn the TV back to the news. She wanted to hear it. This I didn't understand because whatever information she had must have been better than the story they told on the news. But Ma was a news junkie. No matter what was on, boring human-interest stories or the most terrible murder, she had to see it. Even after the crazy stuff she saw all day, she could come home and watch more.

This time the boy, Yusef Bell, was only nine years old.

"That's the same age I am," Bridgette said.

I asked Ma to tell me what she knew about him, because even to a thirteen-year-old, nine seemed too young.

"Why do you want to know?"

"So I can be safer," I lied. I guess that could be true, but now I just wanted to know. Was this boy more like me than not? Did our paths ever cross?

"Don't go sharing this with your friends."

"Do I ever?"

I never did, even when I was younger and first understood that Ma being a cop gave me the kind of attention I'd never attract under other circumstances. She helped me earn my grade-school friends' respect when she'd turn on the blue lights of her patrol car, and my high-school friends' envy when I hinted that I could have a traffic ticket fixed if I ever got one, but I never betrayed her trust.

"He was last seen in Southwest, but closer to us, only six miles away."

"Anyone see anything?"

"Nothing. His mother had sent him to the corner store to pick up something for her neighbor friend, and he just didn't come back."

Like the boy from the skating rink, I wondered what this boy was thinking, what he was doing, before he was taken. He'd probably run the same errand so many other times before. Was he hoping he'd have enough change left over to buy some Pop Rocks? Did he plan to stop off at a friend's house before returning home to pick up the football he'd loaned him? I wondered what his last thoughts were, what his last happy act was, and hoped it gave him something sweet to hold on to.

Chapter 6

Ma threatened to keep me from going downtown on the weekend with Cassandra and some other kids to watch a kung-fu movie at the Rialto. The Rialto was one of those old-time theaters that had been around forever and couldn't compete with the wider screens and armrest drink holders of the newer shopping mall theaters. Downtown Atlanta didn't make it the most attractive location either, since people with the most discretionary income only spent time downtown Monday through Friday, nine to five. After their weekday, they beat it out of there, packing cars onto I-75 or I-20, heading for the suburbs in every direction.

The Rialto understood its weekend audience—young black folks who needed a theater on an easily accessible bus route—and ran the movies we wanted to see, sometimes a picture with black actors in it, but usually an old Bruce Lee movie or some kung-fu flick that tried but never matched the style of the old Bruce Lee movies. It was where all my friends went, and I always took the bus down there with no flack from Ma, but when children started dying and disappearing, she was all of a sudden worried.

I was sitting at the kitchen table, Ma standing behind me while she applied permanent relaxer to my hair and canceled my weekend plans. I wondered how far I should push the matter. Ma didn't much like being questioned, and at that moment, she was applying lye to my head. Putting up a fight just then would be foolish, not because Ma would do anything to hurt me, but once I set her off on a lecture, she might have forgotten how long the chemicals had been burning into my scalp. But I did it anyway.

"Those boys were found in Southwest—I won't be anywhere around there. I'll be downtown."

"One of the missing boys, the one that might be the unidentified body laying in the morgue right now, was on his way downtown to the movies the last time anyone saw him alive."

"There's more than one theater downtown. He was going to the Coronet, not the Rialto."

Ma didn't hear me, and only said, "The other boy was last seen leaving the same skating rink you go to sometimes."

"What's that got to do with the Rialto downtown? I don't want to go to the skating rink."

"Watch your tone, girl. You can't go because it's too close, and because I said so." As usual, the reasonable logic she applied to her cases, the weighing of facts, had no place in our house. In our house, everything came down to *because I said so*.

I tried again because her tone hadn't yet changed from *I'm mildly peeved* to *you've gone too far*. "The skating rink and the Rialto are miles apart."

"I don't mean too close in proximity. I mean too close to *you*. The same skating rink? You might've skated right past that boy once. You could have been there that night and they picked you instead."

I knew then it was useless to fight. When something happened to a child, that child became any child, all children, to Ma. In her mind, she could easily substitute me or my sister with the kid who had been kidnapped, or raped, or beaten up in whatever case she was working. No more logic in the discussion. I shut up about it and hoped that by Saturday either the case would be solved and have nothing to do with my world, or the dead boys would have been pushed out of her mind by some other terrible thing. In a city considered the murder capital of America, this last option was not at all impossible.

They say bad things come in threes, but in this case, there was one extra. In November, Milton and Yusef were found, bringing the number dead to four. The mother who'd sent her boy on an errand for her neighbor was angry and made herself heard; we saw her on the news, read about her in the paper. People began paying attention to what she was saying, instead of comforting themselves with the idea that it was all just a coincidence. She said in the news report what Ma had been thinking, what other cops had been thinking, but what the city denied—that the boys' murders were related. People started to talk about it wherever you went. There were even rumors that the Klan was behind it, and how we might see race riots like they did up North and in Los Angeles in '66 and '67. When I asked Ma what she thought about the Klan theory, at first she waved her hand to dismiss it, but then she said, "You never know."

At the time, the only thing I knew of the Klan was what I'd seen on TV, or the stories told to me by my grandparents and my great-grandfather. They grew up in a time when black folks knew more about the Klan than they'd ever wanted to, mostly about how to stay out of the Klan's way. I'd yet to have rocks thrown at me by men in hooded robes, or hear my white friends called nigger-lovers by the same men (and women and children)—something I experienced seven years later during a march in Forsyth County, Georgia, where black people were outlawed from owning property simply because they were black.

But in 1979, Klan involvement wasn't impossible. The Klan was still burning crosses with regularity on Stone Mountain, in a suburb of Atlanta and official home of the Ku Klux Klan's national organization. Stone Mountain is Georgia's answer to Mount Rushmore, with its carving of Confederate leaders. The fact that the carving was officially completed only seven years earlier, and that the Klan used it as its base of operations well into the 1980s, should disabuse anyone of the thought that the Old South and its slave heritage was hundred-year-old history. Its roots wound deeply through Georgia clay. The weekend before the last two boys were found, the Klan had killed five Klan protesters in North Carolina. It wasn't at all unlikely that they could have something to do with the boys.

As a child uninitiated in the ways of the Klan, I tried to imagine a Klansman in his white hood, driving down Campbellton Road in Southwest, past Wingo's Restaurant with its loud rainbow-colored sign and the best chicken in the world, looking for a fourteen-year-old black boy to steal away. He would sit behind the wheel, moving slowly down the street populated by black folks going about their day while he tried to figure out which life was most valuable, would be held more dear, once people on the street got word that it had been taken away. Taking which life would cause the most fear, the most panic?

It could never happen if he was wearing a hood. So I imagined him without the hood, looking like any other white man in Atlanta, and I still couldn't see it happening. Most black folks, at least in the 1970s South, came out of the womb mistrusting white folks, and one as racist as a Klansman? Any black person could probably tell you—no hood is needed to see the truth in people who hate a race for simply being. The danger just rises from them like steam from just-rained-on asphalt in summer. I just couldn't see those boys getting into the car of one. But maybe they were too young, especially the nine-year-old, to know any better. At nine, you still trust everyone.

Four boys turning up dead only gave Ma more ammunition to keep me from hanging out like I used to, not that she needed any because I was scared enough of her to do what I was told in most cases. After the two boys were found, Ma said, "See, good thing I told you to stay away from the Rialto. From now on, no hanging around downtown between buses. There's no reason for you to mess around in Five Points, going into McCrory's and Woolworth's. Whatever you need, I'll take you to the mall to get."

First off, it was never as easy as just saying I *needed* something. Ma had to first know why, understand why something we already had wouldn't do just as fine, and *just because your friends have it doesn't mean you need it too.* And second, I didn't see what the Rialto, or Woolworth's and McCrory's, had a thing to do with the boys being found miles away. Of course, I kept these opinions to myself.

"How far is six miles?" Bridgette asked me. We were raking leaves in the front yard, a job that took a month of weekends to complete and made me dream of having enough money to rent one of those riding lawn mowers that sucked up leaves in no time flat. When I suggested this to Ma, she said that if I ever had enough money to rent a lawn mower, we'd use it for something worthwhile like replacing the cracked pane in the kitchen window or fixing the rip in the screen door. We didn't need to rent a lawn mower when Bridgette and I had two good arms and legs.

"Six miles from where?"

"That's what I mean. Is it like from here to your school, or from here to my school?"

"Hold the bag open wider or I can't get all the leaves in. My school is twenty miles away. More like here to your school, maybe closer."

"How much closer?" Bridgette was nearly useless as a bag holder, and I dropped more leaves back onto the ground than into the Hefty bag.

"Why are you so worried about how far six miles is? You're starting to get on my nerves. When Ma gives us the money for raking, you better believe I'm getting more than half."

"That's how far away from us that last boy went missing. Now he's dead."

"Who told you that?"

"Ma. When y'all were talking about him going missing, she said it was just six miles from our house."

"Don't worry about that." It seemed a patronizing thing to say even to a nine-year-old, but I had nothing else to offer. I decided I'd still give Bridgette half even though she'd been no help to me at all.

"I think the saddest thing about dying would be not seeing your mother. I can't imagine not being able to see Ma every day. Maybe you could see her from heaven, but it wouldn't be the same."

I reached the wet, heavy leaves at the bottom, my nose startled by the rank smell of decay, and stopped to stretch my back. Maybe Ma and I shouldn't talk about missing kids when Bridgette was around.

"Six miles is farther away than your school, I had it mixed up. It's a good ways from here," I said. But I don't think she believed me.

My boyfriend Kevin was two years older than I, and this made him exotic to me. Before that first kiss during a game of hide-and-go-seek, I thought him exciting and out of reach because he'd ride his bike up and down the street, sometimes stop at the top of the driveway of the boys' house where we'd all play basketball, but never come down to join us. I'd go up to him because even at twelve I loved men, or men-in-the-making. We'd make small talk about what school I went to, or I'd ask him about his bike, but I could never convince him to join me and my friends. I'd tell him he didn't have to play ball, that we also had fun just hanging out and watching whoever was playing. When he turned down my offers, that made him all the more interesting.

That's why I was surprised when he finally decided to hang with me and my friends that night. I was glad I'd been wearing my favorite peach-colored shorts and the black T-shirt that was a little snug. Anytime he came near me, which he did often for no reason I could see, I hoped I wasn't too funky after a day of basketball in the summer heat—broken up only by bathroom and Kool-Aid breaks and no attention to personal hygiene. When lightning bugs came out from wherever they go during the day, I wondered why he suggested hide-and-go-seek when the rest of us complained that it was a child's game, and being twelve, thirteen, and fourteen, we had no use for children's games. But he insisted, and later, crushed between yellow flowers and red brick, I found out why.

Every meeting with him after that first kiss was ripe with the tension of children wanting to play adult games, wanting to no longer be children. There was the date at Six Flags when we went through the It's a Small World ride a dozen times so I could let him feel me up in the dark. When the boat ride began with pastel colors and smiling mechanical bunnies, I played nice girl. During the middle part of the ride, the tunnel darkened, ogre-like characters made sinister sounds, and sprayers misted us to give the effect of a swamp, and I'd pretend to be scared and huddle against him. And when he kissed me, I let him. Each time we went through and we'd reach the swamp segment, his hands would get bolder and I'd let them.

That was early summer, before two boys were found at Niskey Lake and Kevin fit a killer's profile. Now our meetings were full of that same tension, but worry too. I worried about him being the kind of boy the killer might want. He didn't worry at all. That night, he was giving a house party and I was there to be his girlfriend, not to worry about killers.

The basement was mostly dark, illuminated by a mix of bare bulbs in blue, green, and red. We fast-danced to Donna

Summer's "Hot Stuff" and Foxy's "Get Off," the boys hoping the lyrics might give the girls ideas. Like every other girl at the party, I wore double-cuffed Levi's and Candies, except that my Candies had only a two-inch heel because Ma said any more than that was hookerish. And mine weren't really Candies but knockoffs from Butlers. On my walk over to Kevin's house, I applied lipstick stolen from my mother's cache and opened another button on the shirt she made me wear over my glittered tube top. (*No child of mine is going out the house looking like a Stewart Avenue ho.)* Within an hour, the shirt was gone completely, and the tube top left little mystery. Kevin told me I was a fox, and I ate it up.

He was a thoughtful host, leaving me every now and then to check on his guests or run upstairs for more soda and chips. It seemed to me he checked on the girls more often than the boys, but I didn't mind because he'd be coming back to dance with me. Kevin would stop his mother on the steps when she tried to come and check on things, not by pleading like most kids would, but with smooth talk. She never made it past the third step, which allowed the kids to continue whatever it was they were doing—kissing in a dark corner, dancing a little too close. *It works on her, too,* I thought. *She's probably where he learned the skill.* I wondered if Kevin was ever a boy, whether he came out a man and was just waiting for his body to catch up. It occurred to me then that the killer didn't know him the way I did, that the killer would see only a boy.

Kevin went around the room turning off some of the lamps, as if they'd been giving off much light in the first place. Things slowed down a bit when he put Rick James's "Mary Jane" on the turntable, a nice bridge from fast music to the slow ballads that were sure to come as the evening progressed. When someone put on Peaches & Herb's "Reunited," our song after several brief breakups that year (mostly over my unwillingness to move beyond the feeling-up stage), I tried to push the killer out of my head.

"You worry too much," Kevin said into the air above my black-girl version of a Farrah Fawcett flip, not a flip at all but a stiff curl still holding the shape of the sponge rollers I'd slept in the night before.

We were slow-dragging, my arms around his neck, his around my waist. One of my legs between his, one of his between mine. Hips dipping low and slow to match the beat. Me feeling the reason between two layers of jeans for why he'd be pressing me with his most persuasive lines later in the evening when all the other kids went home, before he'd walk me home, while his parents were upstairs wondering why it was so quiet in the basement.

"I know. But I can't help it. You're too much like the other boys."

"I'm nothing like them." I wondered if that was true. I wondered if the boy from the skating rink had a girlfriend, if they'd slow-dragged one night and felt certain they'd be slow-dragging forever. "Forget all that tonight. It's my birthday party. We're supposed to feel good."

I listened to Peaches & Herb croon about how good it was to be together while I swayed slow and low against Kevin, certain I understood what they meant, thinking I was grown. I breathed in his scent, some cologne he'd probably borrowed from his father mixed with a little sweat that comes from the warmth of a basement full of teenagers dancing slow. I was in heaven. I forgot.

Later, when the last of the kids had gone home and I both anticipated and feared our inevitable moment on the sofa in his basement, we heard his father's feet on the steps. I didn't have to worry whether Ma's warnings about getting pregnant would be enough to hold him at bay. I was both grateful and disappointed.

"It's time to walk Kim home," his father said. His voice made it clear there would be no sofa time.

"You mind driving us, Mr. Scott?" I hadn't planned to ask, had looked forward to making the five-minute walk stretch into fifteen, but the words came out of my mouth before I could stop them. Kevin looked at me like I was crazy.

"Not feeling okay?" his father asked me.

"It's just that it's late, and I'd be worried about Kevin walking back alone."

His father went to get his shoes and keys, and Kevin flopped down onto the sofa looking defeated. It wasn't until then that I realized my worry for him was the same as asking whether he was a man. I tried to make it better. "I was worried about both of us being out so late." I made it worse.

"I can look out for us." He looked down when he said this, rubbing his hands on his Levi's as if he could rub away my lack of confidence. But he looked straight at me when he said, "I can look out for *me*."

When Mr. Scott drove me home, there were only the two of us in the car.

Chapter 7

One November night, Ma got home a little later than usual from her night class. She was working to finish her degree and took a class whenever she could scrape together enough money and time. Even though Ma was always late for everything, it was still hard for me not to get that sick feeling in my stomach. The one that always came after fifteen minutes of checking the window, trying to remember what she said she'd be doing before coming home, and wondering if this would be the day a uniform showed up at the door with news that might kill me.

By the time Ma walked in, I'd gotten Bridgette into bed and had already run through my mental list of all the bad things that could have happened to her. I was relieved and angry at the same time. She could have called.

"Sorry I'm late. I was pulled over for speeding."

Ma was always speeding, and this wasn't the first time she'd been pulled over. Cops always let each other go, so I knew she didn't get a ticket.

"Where'd he stop you?" I asked.

"Just up the street, if you can believe it. Right at the corner where you catch your bus. I was almost home."

"Did you know him?"

"No, he must be new on the beat. I showed him my badge

and driver's license, and for a second I thought he might actually give me a ticket."

"Cops don't give each other tickets."

"Most don't, but we're supposed to. Every now and then you get an Officer Do-Right. We didn't know each other. He was young and looked like he was afraid not to ticket me."

"Why didn't he?" I figured Ma was able to smooth-talk him the way she could just about any man if she was of a mind to, even a Do-Right rookie.

"I told him I was rushing home to my two girls, that I'd just gotten out of class. He asked what I was studying, and I told him I was finishing my degree with plans to go to law school. Turns out he wants to be a lawyer, too, and he asked how he could get into the DA's office as an investigator. I gave him the short version of how I did it, and he let me go. That was that."

But it turned out that wasn't the end of it, after all. The next night, the doorbell woke me. I thought it might be our neighbor, the one that liked to beat his girlfriend. The girlfriend had finally had enough and moved out the week before, when Ma's urging to press charges didn't work, but the suggestion to get out before he killed her did. The neighbor had already come over twice since then, drunk and blaming Ma for his woman leaving him. Ma had told Bridgette and me to watch out for him, he was strange anyway, but now he was angry too. She'd told the man to stay off her property, unless he was looking to give her a reason to shoot him.

But even our crazy neighbor knew better than to come knocking in the middle of the night, drunk or not, after Ma's warning. When I looked at my clock and saw that it was two in the morning, the sick feeling grabbed my stomach until I was coherent enough to realize that when I went to sleep, Ma was in her room watching the eleven-o'clock news. The two-in-the-morning visit wasn't the one I always dreaded. By the time I went into Ma's bedroom, she was already out of the bed. My stomach flipped again when I looked out her window and saw a patrol car parked in our driveway. Maybe she had slipped out after I went to sleep. I'm the lightest sleeper in the world, but she was trained to go undetected. My heart tried to slow itself when I heard her voice at the front door.

Her bedroom was right off the front entrance of the house, separated only by a pass-through bathroom. I stood behind the bathroom door, listening to find out why there was a uniform at our door at two in the morning. I could hear Copper on the other side, growling low but convincingly. The only thing I could guess was that one of her friends had been hurt, or some perpetrator was loose in the area and a beat cop who knew where she lived wanted to make sure she watched herself. As soon as the cop spoke, I knew it wasn't any of her friends, because the voice belonged to a white man. There was still a lot of racial animosity on the force. Until the early sixties, black officers could arrest only black citizens. In 1979, white and black patrolmen had been allowed to partner only in the last ten years, and black cops were still a minority, which meant they stuck together outside of work. The only tie that bound black and white cops then was the fact that on the job, they were cops regardless of what they looked liked. Fortunately, that was usually enough.

"Hi, I was just on patrol and saw your car in the driveway and thought I'd stop by."

"At two in the morning?" Ma said. Cop or no cop, she sounded like she was ready to bless the man out. There weren't many things that pleased Ma as much as a good night's sleep, which I always believed was her escape from having to work extra jobs, being a cop, a single mother, and just being a black woman in general.

"Well, you were so helpful giving me that information about the DA's office. And I let you off on that speeding ticket. I thought we were getting to be friends . . ." He was quiet then, as if giving Ma room to finish his thought. When she did not, he continued, "It's such a chilly night. I thought maybe you wouldn't mind letting me visit a while, maybe give me a little hot chocolate to keep me warm."

"No the hell you did not just say that," Ma said, kind of

laughing, but I knew she didn't think the situation was funny because it was her *I don't believe this shit* laugh. I prepared myself to hear every four-letter word in her arsenal, but all she said was, "Get the fuck off my porch."

When Ma slammed the door, I wasn't fast enough to make it through her bathroom and back to my room. I had to admit I was eavesdropping when she asked, and all it took was the evil eye from her to know I'd better not ask her one word about the man at the door. From her bedroom across the hall from mine, I heard her talking to herself, saying she couldn't believe the man disrespected her and her children that way.

I closed my door and tried to go back to sleep, but wondering what gave him the nerve to treat Ma that way kept me awake for a while. Would he have done the same to a white lady cop? Would he have requested some "warm milk" from her? If he thought saving Ma from a traffic ticket that she could easily get fixed the next day held the same value as her body, I figured he must have been a straight-from-the-academy-yesterday rookie.

At dinner the next night, Bridgette was complaining about her babysitter. Mrs. Ingram lived near Bridgette's school and would pick her up after class and keep her until Ma could pick her up when she got off work, which could be a couple of hours or well into the evening, depending on Ma's caseload. According to Bridgette, Mrs. Ingram was a mean woman who gave her own children most of the Hydrox cookies and Hawaiian Punch that Ma bought every Monday for Bridgette's afternoon snack, intended to last the week. By Friday afternoon, there was never any left and she had to go hungry until Ma picked her up, so she claimed. My sister could work drama, so I never knew when to believe her.

"Yesterday I had to kick that boy's butt," Bridgette said, referring to Mrs. Ingram's oldest son, an outsized boy who was destined for some football team's offensive line.

"You did not. He's two years older than you."

"Did too. You think I'm afraid of some boy two years older? You slap me, I don't care how old you are. He won't hit me again, I bet you."

I was certain he wouldn't. Bridgette wouldn't back down to anyone, a fact I knew well because I often had to bail her out, like the time she took on three brothers, and a neighbor friend had to come running to tell me what was happening. I found Bridgette tussling in the dirt with one of the boys at the playground of our apartment complex, a second brother about to join in, and a third cheering them on from his perch atop the monkey bars. The sight of my six-year-old sister being ganged up on by three boys, all older than she, sent me into a rage more fierce than my ten years should have allowed. At the end of it, we had busted lips and torn clothes, but those boys never messed with either of us again.

Bridgette started telling me all the horrible things Mrs. Ingram's children had done that day, calling them juvenile delinquents even though she was only nine years old herself. Usually Ma would say, *Stop exaggerating, it's not that bad.* Instead, she interrupted Bridgette to say, "Oh, Kim, you remember what happened last night?"

As though I could've forgotten.

"What happened last night?" Bridgette asked.

"None of your business," I said before Ma could say it.

"You're not grown, don't tell me . . ."

"Hush, the two of you. Anyway, we won't be seeing that cop on our beat anymore."

"How come?" I asked.

"I made a call to his captain, a good friend of mine," Ma said, forking her salad with a little too much violence. "He'll be working Hartsfield from now on."

I shook my head and thought how that young uniform had no idea whom he'd messed with. Ma had two sides like the Gemini that she is. There was the crazy side that let you know when she was thoroughly pissed off, because she either cussed you out or decided you were too low ranking for her wrath and looked for someone else to cuss out. If a salesperson watched us like thieves as we walked through a store, or a clerk at the DMV got a nasty attitude, Ma was quick to say, "I don't have time for this. Where's your manager?" Then there was the side that let the anger simmer, and the attack came just when you thought everything was forgotten. This was the side unleashed on that patrol cop. His request for "hot chocolate" got him assigned to the Atlanta airport, an invisible detail that did nothing for the career of an ambitious, promotion-seeking rookie.

Chapter 8

It was Christmas break and we'd gone more than two months without any children turning up missing. Already people were starting to drop the dead kids from their conversations, although the boy's mother who'd sent him on an errand was still letting folks know what she thought about the police and their silence on whether the deaths were related. Even Ma didn't mention the cases anymore. She had plenty of other murdered people's cases to investigate.

On my fourteenth birthday, it appeared nothing exciting would happen, as usual. It was a tough time to have a birthday—a few days before Christmas. It got mixed in with everything else, lost in all the fuss over the main event. It was the same with Bridgette since her birthday fell a few days after. Maybe it was worse for her. At least for me, people were still filled with anticipation and plans. By the time Bridgette's birthday came, everyone was fat, tired, and whining about how broke they'd be for the next six months.

When we were younger, Ma did a good job of keeping everything separate. Everyone else just handed us one present, and said, "Here's your birthday *and* Christmas present," like it was some great trick, instead of the cheap and easy way out that it really was. And always wrapped in Christmas paper. It didn't bother me so much as a teenager, but it did when I was younger and saw how my friends and cousins with birthdays in the summer got gifts that had nothing to do with the presents they'd receive at Christmas. Later, even Ma became slack. She still gave us birthday and Christmas gifts, but the birthdays themselves just blended right into the red and green of Christmas day.

My birthday fell on a Sunday, and Ma surprised us by saying we would have lunch and see a show downtown. The idea of it excited me more than the act, since Ma was never spontaneous about having fun, and it had been a long time since she'd taken us to a movie. We picked *The Fish That Saved Pittsburgh* because it was showing at the Omni and I loved hanging out there. Besides the theater, it was where the Atlanta Hawks played and wrestling matches were held, though I never went to the games or matches. There was an ice rink (where I watched Peggy Fleming skate the following year and decided I wanted to be a skater, but only briefly), a video arcade, a food court, and plenty of people-watching. Mostly it was a place for me and my friends to meet, easily accessible by bus. It wasn't until we got there that I got worried about running into friends on my birthday with my mother and kid sister. But even that worry left quickly, I was so excited just to be doing something fun with Ma.

Usually her weekends were spent making extra money doing security and traffic detail for Braves baseball games in spring and summer, or concerts and ice-skating shows at the Omni during the winter. For a while, she worked security at a high-end clothing store, mostly for the discount because it was hard to be fashionable on a cop's salary, and my mother liked to look good. The owners were grateful because Ma figured out it was the store manager who was stealing from them, pretending she was taking out garbage in those big plastic bags. Sometimes I'd benefit from the discount if she thought an outfit didn't look too grown for me. She worked a lot so we could have nice things, so I tried to understand her lack of spontaneity and good timing. I never felt short-changed. Her presence was so big to me that even a small bit of it filled me up.

We arrived at the theater early enough to get the best seats since there were hardly any people in line.

She handed me two ticket stubs. "Take your sister in and get a seat on the aisle so I can find you. And not too close, or I'll get a headache. I'll get the popcorn."

"And Goobers?"

"And Goobers."

I tried to take Bridgette's hand, but she shook me off saying, "Always thinking you're somebody's mother." Inside the nearly empty theater, we found four seats on the aisle. Bridgette sat in the inside seat and I sat next to her, leaving the two outside seats empty, one for Ma and one for buffer. We watched the coming attractions for a few minutes when a man sat down in the end seat.

"That seat's saved," I said, immediately wary. A man sitting down one seat over when most of the theater was free set off alarms. The man didn't say anything, just smiled at me funny. I pretended to stare at the screen, all the while trying to keep one eye on him. The man hadn't done anything yet, and maybe I'd just look crazy making a scene over nothing. I hoped Ma would come soon.

Next thing I knew, the man had unzipped his fly and had his hand in his pants, still smiling at Bridgette and I, his hand working away. In the time it took me to figure out whether to take Bridgette and climb over the seat to the next row, or just scream, or try to cuss the man out like Ma would have done, there she was, her arm around the man's neck as she leaned over him from the row behind us.

"I oughta kill you right here, but it's my child's birthday."

She pulled the man from the seat and yanked both his arms back, and with no more words, she led him out of the theater. I was surprised he didn't fight back, but I wouldn't have fought her either. By the time she came back to us, *The Fish That Saved Pittsburgh* was nearly over. To this day, I couldn't tell you much of what the movie was about, and I never asked what happened to the man. Some things I knew not to question, though I always figured she called a uniform and filed a report.

There was another occasion, just a couple of weeks after the movie, that's as vivid for me now as it was then.

Ma, Bridgette, and I were at the Greenbriar Mall exchanging birthday/Christmas gifts. Whenever we got clothes, mine were always too small. Maybe people were trying to be nice by not getting me the size they knew I really was. In seventh grade, I was jealous of the girls around me who already had their periods and were buying bras because they needed them, not because they wanted them. Careful what you wish for is right, because I hit a serious growth spurt in eighth grade, and halfway through ninth, I was wearing a C-cup.

We were walking through the parking lot back to our car when we heard a woman cry out. At first, we didn't see anyone else in the parking lot but us, but after another scream, we saw a man hitting a woman inside a car parked in the row across from us, two or three spaces down.

"Take Bridgette and get in the car," Ma said, handing me the keys and the packages she was holding.

I did what she said but I also rolled down my window and watched her walk toward the car the screams were coming from. By now, the man and woman were out of the car, and the woman was using her jacket sleeve to wipe tears from her face.

"What's going on here? You all right?" Ma asked the woman.

"Ain't none of your damn business how she doing," the man said, taking a step toward Ma.

Ma put her hand into her purse. I was scared then, and realized I should be distracting Bridgette from what was going on, but I couldn't help watching myself.

"I'm making it my business. Lady, do you know him?"

"It's okay, he's my man. We all right." I could tell from her shaky voice and her swollen face that nothing about her was all right.

"Look, I want you to come with me," Ma said to the woman. "He can go and do whatever he needs to, but you don't need to get into that car with him."

"She ain't going nowhere," the man said. "And I'm about to give you some of what she got if you don't get the hell out of here."

Before he could take two steps, Ma raised her purse in front of her, her hand still inside of it.

"You move another inch and I'll blow it off."

I wasn't sure if Ma was really carrying, she didn't always when she was off-duty, but her voice must have sounded like she was. When he finally moved, it was back toward his car. When he tried to get in, it must have scared Ma because she told him to stop. Again, her voice convinced him he'd better do what she said.

"Come with me," Ma said to the woman, but she refused.

Now Ma was in a risky situation—me and Bridgette in the car, the woman she was trying to rescue not cooperating, and a man in front of her who was still excited by the adrenaline that had flooded him while he was beating his girlfriend. I wondered if she would try to arrest him, but that would've been dangerous without backup. All she could do was back down or be ready to shoot him if he did something crazy. *If* she was really carrying. And even then, she couldn't turn her back on him to get into our car, and she couldn't let him get into his car. He could have had a gun in there. I was so afraid I was ready to wet myself.

"Who the hell you think you is telling me what . . ."

Ma made a movement with the hand that was still inside her purse, which I hoped was cradling her .38.

"Ah shit, you a damn cop," the man said, finally realizing that no average woman would be going through all of this unless she was either crazy or a cop—in Ma's case, both. The man stared at her for a second, then said, "I know you. You the bitch cop that put me in jail for five years."

"If you know I'm a cop, then you know what I got in this bag."

"Hey, I ain't trying to start no shit with you."

"Unless you want me to call this in, ya'll need to go your separate ways. Give her the keys, and you walk back toward the mall."

The man handed the keys over to the woman and started walking toward the mall like Ma said, but not without calling her a bitch again.

Once the man was far enough from our car and the woman had backed out of her parking space, Ma got into our car. I watched the woman as we left the parking lot. She pulled alongside the man and he got into the car; then they drove away.

"Stupid woman. He'll probably kill her tonight." Ma said this out loud, but not to Bridgette and me. "Stupid, stupid." I got the feeling this last thing was meant for herself and not the woman with the swollen face.

"You girls forget about that, okay?"

Bridgette and I nodded our agreement, but she was crazy if she really thought I'd forget. I couldn't have if I wanted to, and I didn't want to. When we got home from the mall, I peeked into Ma's purse and saw her gun, and wondered how things might have gone—how differently and badly.

Chapter 9

On the first day back to school after Christmas break, I didn't look forward to getting used to a new round of teachers. With the exception of homeroom and French, I had new teachers in all my classes. In math class, the teacher went down each row of students, assigning the names in her roll book to the unfamiliar faces in the class. I didn't pay much attention because I was watching the girl in the row ahead and to the right of me constantly flipping her hair. It was clear she'd spent a long time with her curling iron to get the flip just right, uniformly shaped all the way around her head, and now she was letting the flip fall into her eyes just so she could use her hand to swing it away.

Constant hair flipping was an activity I'd never seen before coming to this school, so I didn't get it. Then the girl reminded me of when I was younger, how my friends and I used to put bath towels on our heads and pretend we had long flowing hair like white girls, flipping it behind our backs like Cher did during the opening act of her show with husband Sonny. I'd outgrown the desire for silky, swingy hair, knowing even my hair relaxer chemicals wouldn't make it so. Apparently, when you came by it naturally, the need to toss it about was something you never outgrew.

I broke away from staring at the hair-flipping girl when I

heard the boy in front of me give his name to the teacher, ready to give mine next. The teacher looked at her roll sheet and made a mark with her pen.

"And you must be Kim," she said smiling, like I should be flattered that there was some kind of mark on her list indicating that I was the *black one*.

"I must be," was all I said.

The hair-flipping girl swung her hair for the millionth time, and I imagined taking a big pair of scissors to it.

Even without the disco episode, I hated PE, unless we were playing basketball. At my old school, the options were basketball on the blacktop or kickball in the city park next to the school. Since the park didn't have much in the way of grass, kickball meant dirtied socks and dusty legs from running across dry red clay. Besides that, it was a kid's game that no one higher than fifth grade would be caught dead playing. Between the high tuition and gifts from affluent parents—some of whom were celebrities, including the coach of one of Atlanta's professional sports teams and a Hollywood actor—the rich school had plenty of money. There were two gyms, one with a basketball court layered with shock-absorbing foam that protected young knees but still allowed the ball to bounce. No dusty socks or hot blacktop here. All that money allowed them to come up with all kinds of crazy sports for us to play. This week, we were playing badminton. If we were going to knock things over a net, I didn't see why we couldn't play tennis—a real game, one I'd at least heard of even if I'd never played.

We were playing doubles, and my partner was the kind of girl who was always the last one named when kids were choosing teams. Combine that with my first-time-playing-badminton skills, and things didn't look good for our side. It didn't help that the girls on the other side were cheating.

"That was out," I yelled across the net, using my racket to

point to the spot the birdie fell just over the line, knowing that proof would be required.

"It was fair." My opponent looked at me, then my racket, then the birdie. There was a toss of red hair before she approximated a model's pivot, turning her back to me. I'd been dismissed, along with my play call. My face warmed and I knew the anger was beginning to rise, but I responded as calmly as I could.

"You keep calling shots fair when everyone can see it's outside."

"What did you say?" She looked around for support from her partner and girls on the other courts, so I knew something was about to happen. She wasn't one of the truly popular girls, those with influence, but a hanger-on. That type tended to be the meanest, the in-between girls who are angry because they didn't make the first cut and so take it out on those at the bottom of the social ladder, the very people who kept them from being last. I was today's target, though it was clear she was a little concerned about backup.

There was no way she didn't hear me, because I'd gone around the net to her side of the court. But I said it again anyway, "You aren't calling your shots fairly. Anyone can see it."

"Who can see it? You're the only one claiming it's out."

I looked over at my partner, who was studying the strings of her racket like it was an oracle, and I knew there'd be no support from her.

"Take a look. I left the birdie where it fell."

"I'm not walking *all* the way over there when I already know it's fair."

"Because you know I'm right." My tone had nothing but threat and dare in it. She didn't back down, but she also didn't look at me when she spoke her next words.

"She's saying I'm cheating," the girl said to her partner. "Stupid nigger."

She directed this comment to her friend instead of me, and

I stood there for about half a second before I swung my racket at her. It took all my restraint not to drop the racket and just go at her, but I thought of Ma saying, *They always expect the worse; don't ever give them justification.* The girl looked at me like I was crazy, like she never expected me to do anything about her calling me a nigger. I dropped the racquet and readied myself for her to come back at me, but she never did. Instead, she called out for the teacher.

A few minutes later, I was in the principal's office trying to explain my side of it—what the girl had called me, and the fact that being hit by a badminton racket was hardly as dangerous as everyone was making it sound. The thing didn't weigh but a few ounces. It was only a gesture, if anything. It didn't matter, Father was telling me that what I'd done deserved demerits, and reminded me that it took only thirty demerits to be kicked out of school. He explained this to me like I should budget mine. I guess he expected me to earn more before the year ended, even though this was the first time I'd been anywhere near his office.

Before I left, he told me that, of course, he'd be calling my parents. I wanted to correct him and say parent, singular, but it didn't matter. I knew Ma wouldn't have any problem with what I did when I told her what happened. She'd have probably given me her own version of a demerit if I'd let that girl get away with it.

I talked Cassandra into coming along with me to the beauty shop, one of my least favorite places because it was mostly about waiting, not styling. They always overbooked, so you'd have to wait an hour or two before you got a chair. And it wasn't even a real beauty shop. To save money, Ma sent me to get my relaxer at a school of cosmetology in a strip mall. When she dropped Cassandra and me off in front of the school, she assured me that they'd only let the students who were about to graduate do my hair. But it was either the beauty school or risk Ma applying the perm, which half the time meant her burning scabs onto my scalp that would take faithful application of Sea Breeze Astringent and a few weeks' time to heal and flake away.

Most of the patrons were old women, and most were having someone else's hair styled. Instead of fitting snugly against scalps, their tightly curled gray wigs perched on their heads as though they might take off at any minute. I hoped the cosmetology students would show them the proper way to wear a wig, but other than that fleeting concern, the grandmothers offered nothing in the way of entertainment. Cassandra and I settled into our long wait, sucking on the Lemon Heads and apple Jolly Ranchers that we bought at the convenience store next door. I was grateful she was with me to pass the time, and we made fun of the models in the ancient hairstyle magazines until that got boring. When I told Cassandra about the badminton game, she sympathized and sermonized at the same time.

"I would have done more than hit her with a badminton racket."

"Like what?" Kids always talked big about what they'd do when there was never any chance of them having to follow through.

"Some white girl calls me a nigger, I'm scratching her eyes out."

"Uh-huh."

"And snatching her bald-headed."

"Yeah, and you'd be kicked out of the school too."

"That's the problem right there. If you went to school with me, none of this would ever happen. There's only about ten white kids in the whole school, and all of them got enough sense not to ever call somebody a nigger."

One Sunday in January, Ma and I were in the kitchen making food for a playoff game while Bridgette worked as a runner between the kitchen and living room, refilling fast-emptying platters of food. It was something Ma started when she was still a street cop. Since she didn't work Sundays unless she was picking up a security job for extra money, she'd put together a big spread, usually sandwiches or chili or fried chicken livers and potato salad, and invite her cop friends over to watch football. Men would be all over the living room, relaxed on our brown-and-white plaid sofa or sprawled across the two wing chairs donated by some forgotten relative to my grandmother, and later to my mother, and reupholstered at least twice. When seating ran out, they sat on the rust-colored shag carpeting that Ma kept saying needed to be replaced to anyone who came over. The men didn't notice the condition of our carpet, only an empty plate, or for those off-duty, a drained beer bottle. The room was always full—one officer would jump up to go answer a call, and within a few minutes, someone else had shown up to take his place.

Ma used football the way I used basketball, to get closer to men, but for different reasons. She never had any interest in it until she became a cop, when she realized that mutual trust among cops could be the difference between living and dying. Men didn't trust female cops to get the job done, so she did what she could to make it clear to them she could handle herself, that she'd have their back on a call the same way any man would.

As a street cop, she was a trainer on the Department football team (there were some roles the female officers just had to accept to be included, despite the guns, badges, and blackjacks they wore), applying bandages to gashed knees and kind words to wounded egos. When she let me come along, I'd be shocked at the words that came from her mouth when she joked around with the male cops, words she never used at home. Occasionally, she'd apologize by saying, "excuse my French," but no one, including me, believed she wanted to be pardoned.

"Now, Yvonne, you know a man is better on the job than a woman—fuck *Ms. Magazine*, or what the chief says when he's in front of a TV camera," a cop said at one game.

"Fucking Neanderthal. Ask my partner who he'd rather have backing him up on a domestic, you or me?" Her partner said he'd pick Ma any day, and I beamed like he'd chosen me.

"Yeah, well, I think we know why that is, and it ain't got a damn thing to do with how you handle a weapon. Or maybe it does." Laughs all around, except I didn't get it.

"You can kiss my black ass."

"Is that an invitation?"

"You bad enough to try?"

They never were, at least not while I was around to witness it. Secretly, I wanted one to try, so I could see if Ma might put some karate moves on them. I imagined she knew martial arts, that she could stop a man with one blow to the right place on his throat. I never got to see her in action, so my speculation was never proved wrong, which was good because my Pam Grier-as-Coffy image of her kept me from being afraid every time she left the house for work. She kept the line drawn between friendship and anything else, so much so that the cops had a nickname for her—Blue Nun. *Blue* for the fact that she was a cop; *Nun* because she was religious about giving up *none*. It was also a name of the wine some of the cops liked to drink. When I was finally old enough to get the double meaning, I thought it kind of clever. I remember only one cop being romantically linked to Ma, though there may have been others and I just didn't know about them.

Even though she was now working for the DA and no longer on the force, most of her friends were, so she continued her Sunday football parties. Many of the cops who came by were still on duty, but they tried to arrange the visit when the game was at an exciting moment since they couldn't very well spend the whole three hours at our place when they should be out patrolling.

"Ma, there are a lot of cars in the driveway."

"Always worrying. You'll go gray before you're twenty. Hand me a mixing bowl."

"I'm not worried, I just don't want them to get into trouble."

"They're grown men. If they aren't worried about it, why are you? Besides, they have to eat lunch somewhere, why not here, in front of the game?"

"I'm just saying . . ."

"Don't worry about grown folks' business, you hear?"

That was the final warning, and I shut up, though I still wondered what our neighbors must have thought seeing patrol cars and unmarked cars that clearly belonged to cops to anyone used to dealing with cops, coming and going all Sunday long. I was sure that some do-good citizen would bust all of us. It never happened.

My mother had great fun hosting the football parties, laughing at the dirty jokes the cops told when she thought Bridgette and I were out of hearing range, but I noticed on that day she was still smiling when she returned to the kitchen. Still smiling while she scooped out the insides of cherry tomatoes and filled them with cream cheese. I found out why when she turned to me and said, "Guess what?"

Ma never started a conversation with guess what—*no time for games.*

"I met someone. Well, met someone again. I've known him a long time."

I thought of her old boyfriends, wondering who it might be.

Ma often had a date on those weekends she had free, though mostly we only heard about them, it was seldom we met them, because she didn't want to bring men around Bridgette and me unless she thought things might get serious. Some of her dates were fairly interesting. She'd been wined and dined once by Lionel Hampton. There was the psychiatrist who claimed to have Michael Jackson as a client, which impressed me because that was at a time when Michael was still normal and I still had a crush on him.

One boyfriend drove a Corvette convertible, and Bridgette and I loved going on long drives in it. He had a horse housed at a stable that we got to ride, and a boa constrictor as a pet. I'd never met a black person who had any of those things because of the money required, and because the black folks I knew didn't do life-threatening stuff like riding horses or living with killer snakes. Life in our world was difficult enough without adding more danger to it. (For the same reason today, I just don't see the allure of jumping from planes, skiing black diamond runs, or doing any kind of extreme anything.) If the black people I knew did life-threatening things, it involved a paycheck, like Ma being a cop. Like me working nights in downtown Atlanta at what would be my first paying job. Still, I hoped it was the dangerous-living Corvette man; it was cramped, but we'd look good riding around in it.

Even though neither of us had said anything funny, Ma let out a small laugh while she added butter to the hot bacon grease already in the cast-iron skillet.

"Don't tell the guys about it. They like to give me a hard time when they find out I'm dating someone new, like I'm their sister or something." She dropped battered chicken livers into hot grease, jumping back to avoid getting splattered.

"Who is it?"

"You don't know him. We dated a few years back when he was on the force, but he joined the navy and got shipped off somewhere, and that was the end of it."

"So now he's not in the navy?"

"No, he's still on active duty." Ma said it like it was a strange thing for me to ask, but I was thinking how the ocean was four hours away, making it tough to be a seaman in Atlanta.

"What's he look like?"

"Tall, good-looking, very deep voice. And let me tell you about . . ." She didn't finish the sentence, maybe remembering that I was a child, a fact both of us sometimes forgot.

* * *

"He's an officer now, assigned in Atlanta for a month or two to work on a special project with the army over at Fort McPherson."

She said it like her sailor was Batman and was working in his Bat Cave on a way to save Gotham. It bothered me that she was acting like that over some man I hadn't met, and at the same time I thought it cute that a woman who carried two guns and took down bad guys for a living could act as silly as I over the prospect of a brand-new crush.

Chapter 10

The killer had been silent over the winter months, and most of us let our guard down. Except for those in the neighborhoods where the four boys went missing, where the empty space left by the children still lay gaping, people didn't talk as much about the boys anymore. The city was still trying to figure out who killed them, but they were no longer at the front of people's minds. Too many other bad things had been in the news to take their place—American hostages were taken in Beirut, the Soviets had invaded Afghanistan. These places many of us had never heard of before, or at most could point them out on a map, we now knew of in detail—at least the details provided us by grainy film on the evening news. Atlanta got on with other things, like how expensive it was to fill a gas tank or how hard it was to find a job.

Just as we were ready to believe that whoever was committing the murders had moved on, something we could be thankful for even if he hadn't been caught, another child turned up missing in early March. This time it was a girl, twelve years old, with a name too pretty and hopeful to fit properly in a news article about missing kids: Angel. Now the bonds between the victims had fallen to two—young and black, but the killer was no longer partial to boys.

Maybe because she was a girl, maybe because it had finally sunk in how real this whole thing was, maybe it was her name, but she was the first one I really prayed for. Despite all the Catholic schooling and churchgoing, I wasn't much of a Catholic. The year before the killings began I'd told my priest that he'd heard my last confession. I just didn't see the point of bringing a middleman between myself and the Maker. Ma was called to the school to help the priests talk some sense into her heretical daughter, but it was useless. She'd done the same thing early in her own Catholic career. I haven't been in a confessional since.

But the missing girl made me go down on my knees, light a candle, and beg God to let her be okay. I tried to forget all the facts and statistics that living with Ma had taught me. Surely there were times when kids were found past the first twenty-four hours—hiding out in a basement to torment parents who didn't understand; the center of some communications mixup between family members who got the dropoff place and time wrong; found in a bus station with money stolen from piggy banks and fathers' wallets. When my friends spoke of her in past tense, I corrected them. She wasn't gone. She was only missing.

God didn't hear me, or chose to ignore me. I didn't have to wait for the TV news. I asked Ma daily what she knew about Angel. Almost a week after she went missing, Ma told me Angel had been found tied to a tree with the same electrical cord that was used to steal her last breath, panties that didn't belong to her wadded into her mouth. It was the first time I remember questioning God's omnipotence. I didn't think he controlled everything if he could let Angel die like that. The priests and nuns had been feeding me fairy tales.

At school the next day, I joined some friends in the cafeteria, which wasn't like most school cafeterias back then, but a kind of deli where we paid cash for sandwiches, soups, and salads. Most days I brought a bag lunch of bologna and yellow mustard on white bread from the day-old bakery, or leftover chicken with a piece of fruit. But sometimes I'd leave my sack on the kitchen counter and didn't have enough money to buy something from the deli. Luckily my friend Dana was generous and would loan me money. She also brought me gifts of Bonnie Bell Lip Smackers so I wouldn't have to use vitamin E capsules for lip gloss. (I'd lied and told her my doctor recommended it for chapped lips, but I guess she saw through my story.) She gave me a tin of peppermint when she noticed I was still trying to make a giant Christmas cane stretch into spring by breaking off bits at a time.

Dana never wanted the lunch money reimbursed, probably because she figured I needed it more than she did. She was right, but I always paid her back. I was nobody's charitable deed. The partial scholarship that allowed me to go to the school I earned through good grades. The rest of the tuition Ma earned working security jobs. I didn't want people thinking we couldn't come up with lunch money.

I'd say, "Dana, can you loan me fifty cent until tomorrow?"

She'd always give me the money, saying, "Fifty *cents*. It's plural. Why do you always make it singular?"

Because that's the way everyone I know says it, but if I told her that, she'd ask more questions about a world where people went around failing to pluralize properly and I didn't want the bother. By the end of the school year, she'd badgered me enough that I said it correctly. To this day, I think of Dana when I hear someone say fifty cent.

At one end of the lunch table we'd chosen someone was talking about a party. My lunch mates were not part of the conversation because I'd settled in with a group that had been marked as one that didn't get invited to parties. We were the kids with excellent grades but not much else going for us as far as school social standing went, so we had to take solace in the future, when we'd be the ones running corporations or emergency rooms or universities and throwing the fabulous, invitation-only parties. For fun at these parties of the future, I imagined we smart kids would speculate on which of the party kids from school were now pumping gas or living off trust funds, still being reminded by their parents of the thousands spent on their fine educations.

We've been called different names since the first school opened when time began, but I believe in 1980 at my school the term was *dweeb*. I'd never heard the word in my other life. I was grateful I had another life, where I got invitations to house parties that played music I wanted to hear, so I wasn't too broken up when I wasn't included on my school's social agenda. Even if I had been invited, I'd have no way to get there. None of the kids with cars was going to drive to Southeast to give me a ride. I listened to the conversation anyway.

"His parents won't be in town all weekend. Can you believe it?"

"I hear he's getting a keg."

"I heard two kegs."

It sounded like all the other parties I'd heard about around school. A few things still surprised me after nearly a full school year. Daily, I learned more words in a whole new vocabulary, words like *kegger* and *dweeb*. I also learned that kids of privilege seemed to have no fear of their parents. No one in my neighborhood would have even thought about throwing a party while their parents were away.

We didn't have much time to mourn Angel Lenair because a ten-year-old boy named Jefferey Mathis was reported missing the day after Angel was found. He was last seen not a mile from my old school in the West End, the same school Bridgette still attended, on his way to buy cigarettes for his mother. I thought of this boy's mother, wondered how she felt when she learned her last communication with her child would be about buying her some cigarettes. Anytime she lit a cigarette, or smelled the sulfur from someone's struck match, or sped by a cigarette ad on a highway billboard, I wondered if her heart would break each time.

I knew the service station where he was last seen, had bought candy and soda there more than once. I suppose that's something I was thankful for about my new school. Kids didn't show up missing from gas stations down the street, and I didn't have to worry about girls from Brown High teasing me and my friends about our plaid uniforms, using them as an excuse for an afterschool fight. At the rich school, I thought of myself as a tough kid. When a boy grabbed my ass once in the art supply room, he was shocked at the cuss words I let fly. And of course, people remembered the badminton incident for a while.

But Bridgette was still there, and sometimes I felt guilty for the green soccer fields of my new school while my sister's fourth grade class spent recess on a blacktop. She was too young for the Brown High kids to pick fights with, but she was the same age as the last boy to go missing. I told myself she was safe, probably safer than when I was still there, and we rode MARTA home together. Now she waited for a ride from Ma at Mrs. Ingram's house, or sometimes at the public library one door down from the school where we'd spent so many evenings waiting for Ma that the librarians considered us family. Bridgette was probably safer now with me out in the suburbs.

Remembering Angel, I noticed for the first time that no one at school really talked about the kids who were dying, so I asked a couple of classmates what they thought about it.

"What kids dying?" was one kid's reaction.

"Oh yeah, I think I heard something about it," said another. "Why? Did you know any of them?"

Yes, I know every black kid in Atlanta, I wanted to say it but never did because I liked them and realized they didn't know any better.

"No, I didn't know them. It's freaking me out a little; I just wondered what you thought about it."

"Well, it's not freaking me out. I mean, it's sad and everything, but weren't those kids poor or something?"

"Yeah, they live like a million miles from me."

I wanted to tell them that Angel had lived only eight miles away from me, but caught myself because I was still uncomfortable letting them know that I wasn't as well off as they were. They knew I lived far away, but having never been anywhere near Southeast, I thought they imagined I lived in a version of their world, only on the Southside, if they even thought about it at all. Not telling them that Angel and I shared far more similarities than I did with my classmates made me feel guilty later, made me feel small and weak and a traitor to Angel.

To my classmates, the dead kids and their world were more than just miles away. They were a whole life away. The private-school kids weren't black and just getting by, many didn't even have an Atlanta address. It was a story they'd heard on the news, and it touched them the same way the news about the Beirut hostages did—more bad news on TV that didn't really change how they got to and from school, didn't make them pick up the pace when a car drove too slowly past them on a city block.

On a spring day toward the end of the school year, I was walking the half mile from the bus stop to my house, noticing how the forsythia had all but gone from yellow flowers to green leaves. The pink and white of dogwood flowers in most of the yards hid the first signs of a middle-class neighborhood quietly sliding into lower class—a sagging shutter on one house that had been that way a couple of seasons now, a junk car sitting idle for months in more than one driveway, burglar bars on the windows of a few houses. Azalea blossoms had already peaked and were turning a faded version of their once magenta and coral selves, which meant summer vacation was less than two months away.

I was wondering whether I'd be able to get in some basketball after I finished my homework. This, and having safely reached my street after my two-hour bus trip from school, is what kept me from being as observant as I would have been downtown. I was walking on the wrong side of the street like I always did (that way, you can see what's coming and makes it tough for someone to pull alongside and snatch you into his car, Ma would say) when I paid only the slightest attention to a car driving slowly by, going in my direction.

The car disappeared over a hill and I'd already forgotten about it when I saw it crest the hill again, coming toward me. Like many streets in the south, ours had no sidewalk, so I stepped onto the curb and walked along the edge of someone's yard. As the car approached, I saw a man at the wheel—I didn't expect otherwise—and he was alone. He drove by me slowly, shouting something about how good I looked.

I started walking faster once he passed, worried that I was still a quarter mile from my house. I wondered what I'd do once I got home to the empty house. Ma had taught me never to go into the house if it was unlocked, and never get trapped someplace alone if you think someone's after you. Always go to a public place, preferably a police station or firehouse. I realized I didn't have these options, but I kept walking quickly toward home, hoping he'd had his say and moved on. I knew every neighbor within three houses of my home in any direction. I'd go to one of their houses.

He hadn't moved on. I heard his car coming from behind me again, and I started to run toward home. Before I could get any speed going, he turned left into the driveway ahead of me, cutting me off from home and neighbors I knew would help me. It's true what they say about how much the mind can process in a very short time when fear kicks in. In less than a second, but what felt like minutes, I recalled everything Ma had taught me to do if something like this ever happened. Don't get into the car even if he shows a gun. Once you get into the car, you'll never get back out. Run. Scream. Fight. (Remember a man's balls and eyes are weak points.)

I dropped my books and did all of those things—ran toward the house of the driveway he'd pulled into, screamed, readied myself to fight if he got out of his car and pulled me to the ground. The house was the most grand on the street, white and looking like something from a plantation. It must have been on an acre of land because it sat far back from the road, though I never knew how far until that moment. A stand of trees separated it from the house on either side, unlike all the other houses on the street. I knew nothing of its owners, other than they were an old couple and one of the last two or three white families on the street. I prayed they were home.

I never had to find out. As soon as I took off yelling and running, the man backed out of the drive and burned rubber getting away, going in the direction away from me and my house. I took off for my house, and once inside, checked the locks twice and watched out the window to see if he had doubled back, grateful that Copper was a chow and bred to do nothing but guard his people. I was still shaken up when Ma and Bridgette got home, and I didn't realize until then that I'd left my books in the yard where I'd dropped them. Ma walked down with me to pick them up.

"You think you could describe him?"

"I only heard him—I couldn't really see him. And I barely heard him over the car's engine."

"What about the car?"

"It was brown I think, American." Not a helpful description. I wasn't sure of the color, and everyone around here drove American models.

"Do you remember the plates? Maybe a couple of the numbers?" If Ma had her report book in her hand instead of my algebra text, I'd have felt exactly like one of her *alleged victims* and not at all like her daughter. "Without that, we can't do much about finding him."

"No, I didn't get any of the plate. I forgot to look." I felt guilty, like I'd been neglectful.

"Well, you did the right thing. You didn't end up in his car."

This made me feel better. I'd accomplished the main goal,

even if I hadn't gotten the plate or a description. I was safe, still here to talk about it. Maybe he was interested only in getting some time from a fourteen-year-old girl. Not to say I was so special to look at, but much of the downtown segment of my commute between school and home was saying no to the men who called to me on the street, taking care not to offend them in my rejection. No need in making one of them angry and forcing him to save face by saying something even nastier to me, hurling threats and put-downs—*You ain't all that, no way*. Maybe he was like those freaks on the transit train that got off on scaring young girls, staring at them while touching themselves underneath spread-open newspapers or folded trench coats. I had run into those too. Maybe he was the one snatching kids off streets.

Ma didn't throw her arms around me, kiss away my tears, and all that. I didn't cry, and that wasn't her style. Mine either. But she did make one of my favorite dinners that night, chicken smothered in cream of mushroom soup with fluffy biscuits from a can.

The next morning, Ma gave me a ride to the bus stop, but I still had to walk home alone. There was nothing we could do; I had to go to and from school, and she had to work. But from then on, I saved daydreaming for another time. My side of Jonesboro Road was no different than the other side, except for it being more green, a bit more quiet. Turned out that's what made it dangerous, what lulled me into thinking I was safe. After that day, I focused only on getting home, and walked a few feet away from the street, daring people to scold me about walking in their grass.

In mid-May, the seventh child was found dead just hours after his family reported him gone. He went missing and was found in Southeast, and this time I didn't tell myself all the ways his life was different than mine even if we lived only six miles apart. It seemed I had more similarities to Eric Middlebrooks than differences. He was fourteen, his bike found near his body. The last time anyone saw him alive he was riding his bike around ten or eleven at night. Like the others, he was doing something he did all the time—riding a bike, leaving a skating rink, running an errand—but this time he never made it back home. One thing different between us was that Eric had more courage than I did. He had provided evidence to police that led to the arrest of a school gang on robbery charges and was going to testify. Police had looked for a connection between the gang and his murder, but added him to the missing and murdered list after clearing the boys of suspicion.

We were shopping for a dress at Southlake Mall, I assumed for Ma's date with her new man, though she didn't tell me as much. I sat on the only chair in the dressing room area, making Bridgette sit on the floor because that's the way it works when you're the oldest and biggest. We waited for Ma to emerge in what seemed the hundredth dress so we could say it looked fine and she could disagree.

"I need a size larger." Ma always took a size too small into the fitting room, hoping she could still wear a size eight.

"Bridgette, go find this in a size ten," I instructed. She was happy to play grown-up and help out, and I was happy to let her.

Ma slid the curtain open and looked like she wanted to put the mojo on me. "You know better than to send that girl out there by herself, she's only ten." When the curtain was pulled closed again, she added, "You just never know." That was her newest one-size-fits-all explanation since the killings began. Before the killings, it had been, *Because I'm your mama and I said so.*

When I returned with the size Ma should have tried in the first place, Bridgette had stolen my chair and was pouting, arms crossed in defiance. "She acts like I'm a baby. What does she think—the killer is shopping in the dress department?" she asked, as though the curtain could muffle her words. I ran interference, distracting Ma by asking whether I should be worried about the similarities between the latest victim and me when she stepped out to model the size ten. She looked under the stalls before answering, because you never know.

"Worrying won't help a thing, but you should always be aware." I think as much to reassure herself as me, she added, "Whoever it is, he seems to want boys."

"What about Angel?" I'd forgotten the rule about not discussing the murders around Bridgette, but Ma must have too.

"I don't think it's the same person, whoever killed her."

"So now there are two killers looking for kids?"

"No, I think Angel shouldn't have been included with the boys. I think her murder was a one-time deal for whoever killed her, but it looks like the same killer or team of killers is going after the boys. They don't want a girl, for whatever reason."

Ma may have thought this gave me comfort, knowing that girls weren't wanted, but it didn't. Maybe Angel was only the first of the girls to be killed. Already six boys were dead. I didn't tell her that her words hadn't reassured me, knowing it made her feel better to think she'd put my mind at ease. Bridgette had been quiet while we talked, aware of a rare chance to hear about the case. When Ma requested a size ten in a different style, Bridgette didn't remind us of her age and ability to pick a dress and safely return to the dressing room, offering instead to put the tried-on dresses back on the hangers.

Chapter 11

I was grateful for the end of the school year, even though it didn't look like I was going to have much of a summer vacation.

"You may have to go to public school in the fall." Ma broke this news to me while she drove down I-75 as though it was an inconsequential matter and just a *by the way.*

"Why?"

"I can't afford it. That scholarship you got from the Knights of Columbus was for only one year. As it is, I'm working extra jobs to make ends meet."

I thought of the fur coat she got last winter though we live in a climate that made it impossible to wear fur ten months out of the year. When she'd brought it home, she said she got a big discount at the nice clothing store where she worked security, and besides, it was only fox. Our car was bought the year before, a brand-new Buick Regal. When Ma would pull up to my school in the West End wearing the fur coat and driving the new car, I felt good knowing my mother was the prettiest, best dressed of all the mothers, and sporting the nicest car. Now I wondered if the car note and the fur were all that separated me from the public school in our neighborhood.

"But I can't just leave the new school in the middle of everything."

"What everything? You're between school years. I didn't think this would be such a big deal. You're always complaining about how you can't stand those kids, how they're all stuck-up and rich and racist. So what's the problem?"

"I'm just thinking about getting into college." I was also thinking how the high school in my district served not only the kids from my neighborhood, but from the nearby projects too. How it had one of the highest teen pregnancy rates in the school system. I wasn't exactly sure what this meant to me, but it was a statistic cited whenever TV news and newspaper articles gave proof that an inner-city school was both dangerous and ineffective. I thought about how soft I'd gotten in the last year, and how the hard kids would read my softness from a mile away.

"Well, if you want to go, you'll have to make it happen." Ma drove through traffic like she always did, weaving and speeding as if she was on a call and there was a blue light affixed to the roof of the Buick. Normally I didn't much notice it, but that day it bothered me.

"Why me?"

"Don't get smart."

"I'm not getting smart, but I don't see what I can do about it."

"You can get a job."

I didn't say anything, but went silent so that Ma knew I was going into a funk. She stopped that right off.

"You like living in a house with a pool in the backyard, having your own bedroom, being seen by your friends in a nice car."

Silence from me.

"You don't have to answer, I *know* you. You got champagne tastes, and I got Kool-Aid money. If you want to keep going to the private school, you'll have to pay for half of it."

A year earlier, I'd have thought Ma was right, even if I didn't admit to it. But after a year spent with kids who drove new cars more expensive than ours, kids who came to school wearing ski jackets with the lift tickets still hanging from the zipper to broadcast where they'd spent Christmas break, I thought it was a bit much to say I had champagne tastes. All I wanted was a decent education. Besides, where did she think I got my champagne tastes? She had the same affliction.

A decent education wasn't the whole story. I'd convinced myself that the private school in a rich, white suburb of Atlanta was safer for me. No one was stealing kids away from that part of town. Whoever was doing the killing didn't want white kids, and they wouldn't come to Ashford-Dunwoody looking for black children. Around there, we were rare as snow in winter. True, I lived just a few miles from where the kids were being taken, and I had to ride the city bus through downtown in darkness for most of the school year, but I figured that going to the private school kept me safer for at least half of my waking hours. This line of thinking led me to my first paying gig.

Ma had a friend who owned several McDonald's restaurants and he offered me a job. Kids were supposed to be sixteen to work in a restaurant, or fifteen with a work permit. I was fourteen, which meant I had to lie to get mine. Ma was an accomplice in my birth certificate forgery. Even though she was a cop, she'd bend a few minor rules occasionally. My experience taught me that some cops did. They wouldn't do anything that would make for a TV movie, or get internal affairs into their business, but there was the occasional fudging of the lines. In the case of the forged birth certificate, I guess lying about my age in an effort to improve my collegiate prospects was allowable.

I worked in Five Points, literally the crossroads of downtown Atlanta, at the busiest McDonald's in the metro area. Across the street from the store was the main hub of the rapid rail system, which later grew new lines all over the city and beyond, like fissures spreading through sun-dried Georgia clay. I loved Five Points; for almost ten years it was the center of my world as I passed through it twice a day between home and school—through elementary grades, high school, and into college—a kind of border crossing as I traveled from one of my lives to the other.

There wasn't much fancy about that stretch of Peachtree—a pawnshop where I bought my stereo, turntable, and speakers on layaway; a Rexall Drugs; two shoe stores that always seemed to sell the same stock, Butlers and Bakers; Kesslers's Department Store; and McCrory's Five and Dime as the old folks called it, but I don't recall anything in the store being either five or dime. McCrory's is where I'd buy Squirrel Nut Zippers and apple Jolly Ranchers as a sixth grader, and my first set of sheets when I moved out of my mother's house and into my own apartment at twenty.

In the middle of that stretch was the only bit of elegance in that area—Rich's Department Store across the street from where I worked. It was where old ladies who peaked in the fifties still came to dine at a restaurant on the top floor called the Magnolia Room, and mothers remembering their own childhoods took their little kids to ride on the Pink Pig at Christmas. These women always looked out of place to me, mainly because they were white and dressed fancy, neither characteristic being a predominant one in Five Points in 1980.

A four-block radius of this point was the territory of a homeless drunk I called Not to Worry because for five years those were just about the only words I ever heard him say, which I thought was strange because if anyone had something to worry about, it was him. He'd say it over and over while he stood leaning against the concrete wall of Rich's, hoping for a handout from people who didn't have much more than he did. He'd watch me while I waited for my bus, and I'd pretend I didn't notice while I kept a quiet eye on him just in case. Sometimes I could smell Not to Worry before I actually saw him coming around the corner toward me, but I always heard him first: "Not to worry, people . . . not to worry." He used to frighten me, because even though he was ancient and far too broken down by his life to be much of a threat, he was still scary to an eleven-year-old, the age I was when I first met him. Now a child killer on the loose had made Not to Worry seem almost harmless. Still, a few years later when Bridgette was twelve and started to ride the bus with me again, I'd change positions with her so that I'd be closest to him as he stumbled past us.

The nature of Five Points meant we got all kinds in McDonald's, and witnessed all kinds of craziness. Cokeheads would come in asking for the coffee stirrers that looked like long, skinny plastic spoons. It turned out they were perfect for measuring the right amount of the white powder. In the cold months, we served homeless men who'd been fortunate to raise enough money for a burger and coffee while panhandling on the sidewalk outside. They'd make their purchase, find a seat in a corner downstairs (that's how big the restaurant was), and nurse one cup of coffee for seven or eight hours. I hated having cleanup detail downstairs because I never knew what or who I'd find down there. Luckily, they usually assigned us to that task in pairs.

It was nothing to see an argument between patrons, and those sometimes escalated to fights. In case this may seem exaggerated based on most people's fast-food experiences, our management employed off-duty Atlanta cops, armed and in full uniform, as security. You don't see that at your average neighborhood burger stand. I had a lot of fun there, too, or I wouldn't have stayed as long as I did. The kids there were more like me than those I went to school with. When school started in the fall, they offered a balance to my day after eight hours of playing chameleon. After a while, I looked forward to punching into the real world after a day at school.

Most of my paycheck went to paying for tuition, once in a while Ma needed some of it to help pay the light bill or the car insurance, and whatever was left over was mine—half into a savings account and the rest to spend, which didn't leave much. Usually I spent it on a new outfit for the one Friday a month we were allowed to wear something besides our uniforms to school. Sometimes I'd spend money on Bridgette, letting her pick out cheap toys from the Woolworth's in Five Points, or we'd cut out five-for-five-dollars coupons from the Sunday paper for Arby's sandwiches. We'd buy a sackful and take them home for dinner on nights Ma was working late at one of her second jobs. Bridgette and I ate a lot of roast beef sandwiches with Horsey Sauce back then.

On a Sunday evening after I had come home from a day of training on my new job and had showered the fast-food smell off of me, Kevin came by to visit. Ma and Bridgette were home so we went for a walk. By now I realized that there wasn't much to our relationship other than his asking for sex and me trying hard to turn him down. Most times I didn't mind this fact, because truth be told it was the only thing I really gave much thought to when I was around him. The way he'd make my whole body fill with the wonder of what might happen next, like the way my mouth would water with just the suggestion of chocolate. He was my first experience of man smell, the way a boy/man smells warm and so unlike me after he's played a short game of H-O-R-S-E in the sun, or after I've watched him mow the lawn without his shirt. Past the scent of soap from his morning shower, just before he crosses over into funky. Man smell. I could smell it on him as we walked the quarter mile to his house. It was a given that we'd mess around a little. The question was where.

"We can go to my house. My mother won't be home for another half hour."

The idea of going to his house when his parents weren't there scared me. It was getting increasingly difficult to stop Kevin from going further than groping, and he was becoming more insistent that he be allowed to go further. Being alone in his house, and him swimming in man smell, might finally wear me down, drown out Ma's warnings about no babies in her house.

"But what if she comes home a few minutes early?" I said,

hoping it was enough to scare him. For added effect, I said, "And you know she'd tell your father."

Kevin's father, from what I could tell, had the same effect on him that Ma had on me, and I wondered if it existed between other kids and their cop parents. It's a mix of emotions that goes beyond a typical child–parent relationship. There is awe in their courage to do what they do. Throw in a child's pride in being able to brag that his mother or father carries a gun—an exaggeration of the playground taunt "my dad can beat your dad," made even more exotic and intimidating when it's a mother. Underneath all that is fear; cops have a sometimes imperceptible aggression that, even though it's intended (and necessary) for dealing with bad guys, carries over into their emotional relationships and can sometimes be a bit scary even to their own children. You know your cop parent would never hurt you, but it doesn't escape you that they are paid to handle far greater threats than you could ever pose.

"Yeah, maybe we shouldn't go to my house," Kevin said. "Then there's only one place left."

"Where?" I asked, wondering why we were walking toward his house if that wasn't safe either.

"The path. No one will be on it now."

The George High path was a shortcut through the woods that separated our subdivision and the high school. Originally it was just a path worn into the dirt by the kids who preferred the short walk to taking the Bluebird school bus around the long way, but recently the city or the school had decided to pave it and make it official. Kevin lived just three houses away from the path, which made it a convenient place for our stolen kisses, his fumbling attempts to unfasten my bra while I slapped him away with one hand and ran the other up his becoming-muscular back. There was no comfort to it, no park bench or even a flat rock to sit on. The best I could do was lean against a tree while we kissed, reminding Kevin afterward to brush bits of white pine bark and dried moss from the back of my shirt. What it provided was cover and a measure of privacy, but we hadn't used the path in a few months for two reasons.

"You know I don't like going up there anymore, since that boy got jumped and beaten up so badly," I said.

"I told you they got the kids who did it. He shouldn't have been making a play for someone else's girlfriend."

"They put him in the hospital for it."

"Yeah, well, no one's waiting to jump us in there."

I wondered whether that was true, given the gossip I was beginning to hear about Kevin, that our arrangement wasn't exclusive, that he was quite the player. But jealous sixteen-year-old boys lying in wait weren't my only worry.

"I'm not going into any woods while the killer is on the loose."

"What? The killer is nowhere around here."

"But he's getting closer. I know more than you do."

"I know too. My father tells me."

"Yeah, but he's not working the case. My mother is unofficially assigned to it. I know more about it."

Kevin dropped the tactic of saying he knew what was what. That was the good thing about going with a boy whose father was a cop. He understood things none of my other friends did. But that didn't mean he was willing to give up a makeout session. He was smart, and a smooth talker who usually got his way, a combination that made him persistent.

"Ah, come on. If the killer's in there, I'll protect you."

I looked at him, beautiful and already more man than boy, his face becoming defined, the whisper of hair above his lips, the shoulders broader than I remembered them being that summer night behind the forsythia bush. But he was still part boy. I bet some of the dead boys, the older ones, thought the same thing.

"You're the one he wants. Who'll protect you?"

During my two-week training at the restaurant on Hightower Road, a twelve-year-old boy whose prize possessions included a Pete Rose baseball game and an Around the World notebook, disappeared. Christopher Richardson had last been seen in his nice, middle-class neighborhood on the way to the local recreation center. We didn't know until later in the summer that the killer was just gearing up, taking advantage of the warm months when kids could be found everywhere—playgrounds, recreation centers, public pools. It seemed memorials were made of places considered as much a part of being a kid in summer as eating tree-ripened peaches and riding bikes down hills to catch a cooling breeze. Those places were spoken of as *the last place so-and-so was seen.* When kids talked about them, they said, *No, Mama won't let me go there anymore.* The addresses of those places appeared in the *Special Bulletins on Missing Children* later printed and circulated by the police.

By the end of June 1980, seven-year-old Latonya Wilson had disappeared and ten-year-old Aaron Wyche was found dead the day after he disappeared, under a bridge that crossed railroad tracks in DeKalb County. The girl's disappearance didn't seem to fit; she was a girl for one thing, and her parents said she was taken from her bed while she and her family slept. Up to that point, all the victims had been taken off the street, and none from within a block of their homes. Aaron wasn't listed as a homicide at first because the coroner said he'd fallen from the bridge and smothered in the leaves and ground cover that he'd fallen into. It would be nearly a year before he would be added to the official list of missing and murdered children. Aaron's mother never believed the theory because she knew her child, and he was afraid of heights. He wouldn't have been playing around on a bridge in the first place.

Because he was last seen alive only two miles from my house, Ma became more strict about where Bridgette and I could go, how late we could be outside, even in our own neighborhood. One of my favorite things about summer was playing basketball late into the night around the neighborhood, at the house of whomever had the most lenient parents, those who didn't mind the sound of a basketball hitting their driveway long after dark. An hour past dark was the only time of day when the humidity didn't feel as real as a fourth player in a game of three-on-three, an extra man whose defense wore me down. The scent of honeysuckle nectar, made sickly sweet when it cooked in the midday sun, was pleasant on a night breeze. But Ma said no more late-night ball games, we had to be in by dusk. *And don't make me have to come looking for you.*

As summer got into full swing, the total of missing and murdered children had grown to ten. It was just the beginning.

Chapter 12

In mid-July, Ma told me that she was being assigned officially as an investigator on the newly created Special Task Force on Children. Along with the Task Force came the city authorities' long overdue admission that the murders were connected, though they were careful not to call them serial murders. Even before joining the investigation, at the District Attorney's request, Ma had begun looking for patterns. She first thought the child murders might be related to the John Wayne Gacy serial killings in Chicago. During the winter lull in the Atlanta murders, Gacy was on trial for killing more than thirty boys and young men, and Ma wondered if the Atlanta killings were the work of a copycat murderer or a Gacy accomplice who had escaped detection in Chicago and had moved south. But the fact that Gacy's victims were white was enough of a departure from the Atlanta killer's *modus operandi* for Ma to drop that theory.

She and her partner at the DA's office revisited a case they'd worked on when their boss brought it to trial the year before. In early April 1979, a nine-year-old white boy named Dewey went missing. His disappearance was widely publicized, and fliers and news reports stamped a slogan across the city: WHERE'S DEWEY? The boy's body was found a few days later near some railroad tracks. There was a lot of pressure from the white business community to find the killer—nine-year-old white boys just didn't turn up dead in Fulton County. The result of the investigation was the arrest of Donald Wayne Thomas, a black seventeen-year-old boy. Thomas was tried and convicted of the murder and received the death penalty, one of the first to receive a capital punishment sentence after the use of the death penalty resumed in Georgia in 1977. Months before the first black child went missing, that trial exposed the racial tension that had always lurked just below Atlanta's surface. A black man convicted of killing a white boy raised hard feelings that had roots going back to slavery, grown ripe through lynching in the twentieth century.

Ma and her partner thought they saw a connection between Dewey's murder and the current murders. Like Dewey, one of the boys discovered in June was found near railroad tracks. They got a tip that Dewey's father and some of his friends said they would "get some black boys" since it was a black boy who killed his son. That tip launched my mother into her official role as a Task Force investigator.

"I'll be working more hours, so you'll have to do more around here." She said this while standing outside the fence that surrounded our pool, watching me drag a net on a long metal pole across the water's surface. Ma had a serious fear of water, perhaps the only thing I remember her being truly afraid of, at least before the child murders began. She rarely came inside the fence, and when she did, she'd walk alongside it, holding on to the chainlink and being careful to stay away from the pool's edge. Now she was standing outside of it watching me, fingers of both hands wrapped around the metal, making me think of an anxious child.

"More of what?" Even now I was working as the pool man we couldn't afford to hire. What more did I have to do?

"Whatever I need you to do to help." She sounded tired and worn-out already and it was only her first day officially on the case, but I didn't care. I was already tired too.

"I'm working full-time now and all my money goes into the bank or to you. I cook dinners most nights; Bridgette and I do most of the housework. I have to watch Bridgette on my off days, or take her everywhere I go. When do I get to have some fun this summer?"

"Those dead kids won't ever have any fun." It was a silencing blow, and a cruel one. Her tactic was similar to the "kids are dying in Africa" ploy used to encourage the cleaning of dinner plates, but this one actually had teeth. I could already feel the guilt tightening around me.

"I shouldn't have said that. I'm just frustrated. You do so much already, I know that, and I appreciate it. I know it's hard sometimes, but it'll have to be a little harder for a while. Working this case means I can't take any side jobs, so money will be tight for a few months. Just a while until we can catch the son of a bitch."

Ma didn't cuss much around me unless she was mad or driving, so I knew she was angry, but at what I wasn't certain. Was it at the killer, or at the circumstances that forced her to ask her child to grow up sooner than later? I figured it was some of both.

We had just finished the five-hour drive from Atlanta to Hilton Head, South Carolina. The island was where well-off people from Atlanta and beyond escaped the city for long weekends of golf and tennis, or shopped at boutiques where you had to ask the price of things because they weren't always labeled, and dined in restaurants that took reservations. We didn't go into those boutiques more than once because they'd follow us around, and Ma said there was nothing we needed that got its allure just from being overpriced anyway.

It was a trip we would make for the next three summers, renting a condo at the Hilton Head Beach and Tennis Resort. I think it made Ma feel richer to say we vacationed in Hilton Head, the way her fox coat and new car made her feel, despite the fact that we were just two or three paychecks from poor. As my mother's daughter, I looked forward to conversations about summer vacations when I went back to school. I'd leave out the part about standing over hot grease and bagging fries and burgers for most of the summer. I'd make it sound like we owned the condo in Hilton Head instead of renting it by the night.

Bridgette and I left Ma making some lunch from the groceries we bought on the mainland where the prices were cheaper—enough food for the whole weekend—while we checked out the beach. We'd spent vacations on the Georgia and South Carolina coasts near Savannah before, so we were no longer surprised that the water wasn't blue like it was on travel brochures. But the first time we found out, it was a disappointment. Now I was willing only to let the murky brown water touch my feet and no more, but Bridgette was still young enough not to suspect anything, and she went in boldly, letting the waves knock her down onto the beach while I watched from the shore. I envied her fearlessness, the way she'd try anything once without considering the drawbacks or weighing the danger.

"I wish we remembered to bring a towel," she said when she walked to where I was sitting and dropped to the sand.

"We weren't expecting to get wet. Ma'll have a fit you going into the water wearing your new shorts and T-shirt."

"We'll stay out here until the wind dries me."

Some birds were flying low over the water, dipping in occasionally, searching for dinner. I thought it was a pretty scene, but I couldn't help thinking about acid rain and whether the fish swimming in the dirty water were at all connected to the fish in the grocery store. I hoped not.

"I bet soon as Ma starts on the Task Force, she'll find the killer in a couple of days," Bridgette said.

"She doesn't think so. She'll be busy working on the case and won't have much time for us. That's why she brought us out here, sort of like an 'I'm sorry' present to make up for something she hasn't done yet."

"That's not why."

"I'm just saying you shouldn't expect her to find the killer right away." I didn't admit that I also thought Ma would make all the difference on the case, but my rational self tried to believe otherwise. Low expectations meant less disappointment.

A warm breeze kicked up the odor of rotting fish. If Bridgette noticed it, she didn't say anything, just kept shoveling sand into a pile as if she'd lost something and was trying to find it. Not building a sand castle or searching for shells, just absentminded digging. She stopped when she reached packed wet sand.

"Well, I hope you're wrong. I'm tired of being worried about the killer."

"You worry about the killer?"

"Who doesn't? When that one boy disappeared from just down the street from the school, we all got scared, all my friends and me. It was near that gym where y'all practiced basketball after school, where we caught the number ten bus home sometimes, that gas station is where he went missing from."

"I remember."

"It could have been one of Mrs. Ingram's boys—they just live down the street. Even if they're all the time stealing my food and bothering me, I wouldn't want them to get snatched." She looked down at the hole she'd created in the sand and began refilling it. "It could've been me, for all I know."

I knew Ma couldn't afford to send Bridgette to private school anymore, but she hadn't told her yet. So I only suggested the possibility of change. "Maybe you won't have to go to school in the West End next year. Maybe Ma will take you out of the school because of the boy disappearing over there. Don't worry about it anymore."

Bridgette looked as though I'd just walked in from the moon. "Don't you know the killer can be anywhere?"

* * *

Later that night after Bridgette had fallen asleep watching *The Love Boat,* Ma told me things were going nicely with the sailor as she refilled her wineglass. I wished I could have a taste, but took a sip of my Coke instead.

"I think I might let you guys meet him."

"I thought he was only here for a month. That's what you said in January and here it is summer." For some reason, I felt betrayed, as though Ma hadn't been keeping me up to date. She hadn't even mentioned him in a few months. How did she go from dating Batman to maybe we should meet him?

"He left in February, but it turns out the project is taking longer than expected and he had to come back. He'll be in town for at least another couple of months."

I wanted to ask Ma what she'd do when the couple of months were up and the sailor went back to his ship, or wherever he was before I'd ever heard anything about him. But Ma ended the subject of her boyfriend when out of the blue she asked me about mine.

"What about him?"

"Are y'all having sex?"

"No, Ma." I focused on the television screen in hopes she'd stop her line of questioning. It didn't work.

"Because I told you before, I'm done raising babies."

"You told me a million times, I know."

"Well, now I'm telling you for the million and one time. Don't bring any babies into my house that you can't raise yourself. If you can't keep your legs closed, I'll take you to my doctor and get you on the pill. If you're too scared to tell me, then get over to the free clinic. You worked right there, so you know where to go and what you need to do."

"I know, Ma."

"Okay, then. That's all I'm going to say about it."

"For now."

Ma just rolled her eyes at me and went back to looking at a fashion magazine she'd bought just for the trip, a luxury she rarely had a chance to enjoy at home.

"You don't need to worry about it anyway. He broke up with me a couple of days ago." I must have looked like I was going to cry when I said it, because Ma put down the magazine and switched from "take-no-shit" mother to "I've been there" mother.

"Why didn't you tell me? Is that why you've been moping around the house? You want to talk about it?" Ma rarely asked single questions, they usually came in twos or threes, and without a space between for an answer. All the answers had to come at the end. I figured it was her way after making a living out of interrogating people, so I didn't mind.

"Not really. But it's funny you're having the birth control talk with me now. He dumped me because I *did* keep my legs closed after two years of his asking. But the girl across the street was more than willing, from what I hear. That's probably where he is right now."

Ma wasn't surprised by what I'd said, and made a sound that was full of disgust. "That's why I don't date cops. Not anymore."

"What about the sailor? He was a cop."

"He's an officer, not a sailor. And like you said—he *was* a cop."

"Kevin's father is the cop, not him."

"Same thing. Some things just rub off."

Like us, I thought. *It works that way with female cops and their daughters too.*

"I thought you loved cops."

"To watch my back, not to give my heart. They're too messed up, got too many problems."

I wondered whether she included herself in this appraisal, or if she was only referring to the men. Either way, it was one of those mother lessons that stuck with me well into womanhood. When my husband, who spent ten years in civilian management on a police force, suggested he might want to be a cop, I didn't need to consider my response. I told him if he became a cop, I'd leave him. It didn't matter that ours was a happy marriage, there was no way I'd live with a cop again. Once was enough.

It wasn't so much my mother's long-ago warning about cops as lovers, though I was certain she was right. How could cops see the craziness and sadness that was a part of their job every day and not be a little off? What terrified me was the thought of going through nights of worry if he was half an hour late getting home. Afraid to answer a late-night phone call if he was working the graveyard shift. Having my heart jump if a patrol car pulled into my driveway and he wasn't driving it. The prayer in the morning when we'd part that I'd see him again that night. The hardness he would learn to wear, necessary to survive the job but difficult to remove at the end of the day, even with those who love him. I wasn't willing to do it, though I felt guilty, and still do, about preventing him from trying.

It wasn't that I'd sought to bring another cop into my life intentionally. When I met my husband in college, he was a die-hard pacifist, couldn't understand why I was getting a graduate degree in national security policy, and shook his head at the books on my shelf with titles like *How to Make War,* even after I told him the real lesson was in how *not* to make war. When we moved in together, he asked me to return my .38 to my mother, her housewarming present when I left home and got my own apartment, along with my first set of crystal wineglasses, because "two things a woman needs to know how to do is protect herself and entertain well."

When I returned the gun, Ma said, "I don't see why you need to move in with any man when you're only twenty-four, unless what's-his-name is planning on putting a ring on your finger."

"You know his name is James. We've been together three years. I'd think you'd have it down by now."

"And I think he'd have married you by now."

"Whatever. Here's your gun." I handed it to her holding it by the barrel, the way she'd shown me so many years before.

"So can Jim protect you better than a .38 will?"

I ignored the fact that she still wasn't calling him by his name. "Don't worry about me. I'm your child, I know how to take care of myself."

Back then, before my husband had ideas about becoming a cop, he had refused to live anywhere near a gun. Years later, I refused to live anywhere near a cop. I figured we were even.

Chapter 13

A week before the Task Force was created, the eleventh child, nine-year-old Anthony Carter, had gone missing while playing a late-night game of hide-and-go-seek in his West End neighborhood. He was found dead the next day behind a warehouse less than a mile from home. The tired line that the mayor and the police department were sticking to—that the murders were not serial—had begun to work the city's last collective nerve. Parents called the police inept, and cops fired back with questions like, *Why is a nine-year-old playing hide-and-go-seek on city streets at midnight? Where are the parents?* It was becoming a cops versus parents battle, when both sides really wanted the same thing.

One group of parents in particular was most vocal, led by Camille Bell, mother of nine-year-old Yusef, who was found in November 1979. As early as her son's disappearance, she'd raised the possibility that the murders were related. In April 1980, she and a few other mothers had joined forces with some local church leaders to create a group called the Committee to Stop Children's Murders with support from some religious leaders, called STOP for short. By mid-July, they had forced the mayor to action.

Despite the grassroots spread-the-word campaign launched by STOP, despite the announcement of the formation of the

Task Force in mid-July, despite the murder of the eleventh child just a week before that announcement, there was still scant media coverage. I recall thirty-second spots, maybe they were a minute, on the evening news, but not much else. When I compare this to the media madness surrounding the murder of JonBenet Ramsey, the six-year-old beauty queen from Colorado, I find it hard to reconcile.

In the early summer of 1997, I turned into the parking lot of the Boulder Police Department to pick up my husband for a lunch date. I couldn't find an empty space because they were all taken by sports utility vehicles painted with logos of local and national news shows. The street was lined with television trucks sprouting satellite dishes and antennas. All of this to cover the investigation of a child who had been murdered six months earlier, a crime that, despite what the girl's parents said, the police felt was not random and had announced long ago there was no reason for parents to fear for their children's safety.

Even though the investigation hadn't generated any more than scraps of information in months, the media still covered the story as though it had broken that morning. I ended up parking two blocks away and walking back to the police department. When any officer above the rank of patrolman came through the glass doors, the media people swarmed from trucks and cars like kids freed from school on a warm Friday afternoon.

"Did something happen today?" I asked my husband as we walked to the car.

"Nothing new has broken in a month, but they keep waiting for something. And when there's nothing, they report on that too."

Ma had been going through case files on the dining room table, getting herself acquainted with the investigation. She had left the room for some reason, but didn't bother to put away her work because Bridgette and I had been told the dining room was off-limits. I found the *Kidnapped Child Bulletin* on Ma's stack of papers. It showed a picture of the still-missing seven-year-old girl, probably a school picture that came in assorted sizes meant for displaying proudly in a grandmother's living room and passing out to family for keeping in wallets. It had that look. She still looked more like a baby than a child, rounded cheeks still full with baby fat. The bulletin read, SHE SUCKS HER THUMB, AND HAS SLIGHTLY PROTRUDING TEETH. I couldn't tell this from the photo. All I saw was a little girl who looked so happy the day the picture was taken that the photographer probably didn't have to tell her to smile. I stared at the picture wishing for some sign, praying that she would send me a vision of where she was, who had her. No sign came. She just kept smiling at me from the photo, looking more like a baby than a child.

There were boxes full of reports and interviews, maps with little dots of ink drawn on them. I'd seen these things before, on other cases Ma had worked, which I'd sneak a look at when she wasn't watching. Until then, it seemed like something from TV, especially the hard-copy interviews between Ma and the suspects. When I'd read the words following Ma's name and a colon mark, I didn't believe she had actually said them. They belonged to the other woman, the hard-assed cop who didn't really care whether the bad guy was scared, high, or belligerent, he'd damn well better provide some answers. Just like TV.

Seeing the stories of the dead kids who'd become a part of my world, kids I hadn't given much consideration to a year ago, but who were now, and suddenly, *too close,* it no longer seemed like TV. Ma was going to touch these kids—through hearing about their last known actions, by talking to their still-grieving-like-it-was-yesterday parents. And through her, I'd be touched by them, even more than before. I wasn't sure it was something I wanted, not that it mattered what I wanted. I moved aside some of the papers Ma had scattered on the table, not looking for anything particular but hoping for something, and saw a photograph. It was of one of the eleven kids, I don't remember which. He was dead—not looking anything like a child ever should. The sight caught me, held me there too long before I let the picture fall back onto the table.

When Ma came to the door of the bathroom to see about the retching noises I was making, I blamed it on bad cramps.

I was still feeling the hurt of being dumped the month before. It was my first boy-caused sorrow, and I was certain I'd never get over it, and even more certain that there would never be another boyfriend. Kevin had been a shock to me, a sweet surprise, and I still wasn't sure how it had happened. Not only had he chosen me, but he was cute and popular. So what if I'd discovered he was a bit of a dog. I could reform him, even if that required a little reforming of myself. I'd get on the pill (when Ma said keep your legs closed, she always emphasized the not getting pregnant part, not the sex part). The pill would cover that concern. As far as the sex itself, only the nuns at church and the priests at school had a problem with that—and what didn't they have a problem with?

Now all I had to do was get his attention. The rumors that he'd taken up with the girl across the street had proved true. She was willing to go more than a few rounds on his basement sofa, or at least I was told. I was certain he was with her only for that, and he'd been with me for two years despite my unwillingness to provide that very thing. He'd have me back if I could produce what she could. It was a kick in the gut each time I saw him ride his bike up the street and instead of turning right into my driveway, he'd turn left into hers. Cassandra and I would sit on her porch, because she had the better view, and watch the way he pretended not to notice me. I'd curse him and tell Cassandra how it was a good thing I was done with him, and later that night, I'd cry myself to sleep.

But on the day I decided I'd finally give it up if that's the thing that would get him back, I was grateful that the new girlfriend lived across the street. It would give me an opportunity to see Kevin without being so desperate as going around the corner to talk to him at his house. On that summer day, I was off from work, so I laid out my plan. After a month of watching his visits to the girl's house, I knew exactly when he'd arrive; he and the girl must have timed his visits to coincide with the time her parents were out of the house. Luckily for me, Ma was at work and Bridgette was off somewhere, I don't remember where. I also had the house to myself.

Fifteen minutes before I expected to see his bike coming down the street, I put on one of my old white school uniform blouses that I'd bought when I first started at the school, the blouses that screamed cheap because of their sheerness. And because I'd grown from a B-cup to a C since I bought the blouse, it had become snug. I tied the blouse at the waist and neglected the buttons and my bra. I sat on my porch and waited, planning to run to the top of the driveway to check the mailbox when I saw him coming. The sheer white blouse would be the invitation to more inside my empty house.

But then I heard the slam of a screen door, saw Cassandra walking across her lawn to join me. I headed her off at the big pine tree that was the unofficial divider of our front yards, since there was no fence. If she made it to my porch, she might not ever leave.

"What's going on?"

"What's going on with that shirt?" Cassandra always got to the point.

"It's hot today; I wanted to wear something cool."

"It's hot every day and that never stopped you from wearing a bra. I can see right through that shirt, I hope you know."

I was thinking of a response that she wouldn't see right through as a lie when I saw Kevin rounding the corner of his street onto ours. Forgetting how I planned an air of cool, I ran up to the mailbox, bouncing all the way. I stood on the side of the mailbox that would allow me to see him coming, aware Cassandra was watching the whole thing. There was no way he could pretend he didn't see me now. But he found a way, and went on up the girl's driveway as if the mailbox hid me from view.

"So that's what's going on? You're out in public like that for *him*?" I hadn't heard Cassandra come up the driveway.

"No, I said I was hot." I stood there holding the mailbox open, watching him ring the girl's doorbell, watching him disappear into her house and could only imagine what else.

"Forget about him. If you stayed with him, all it would have gotten you is a bad reputation, or pregnant."

"What do you know about it? You never had a boyfriend." I regretted saying it immediately, but I was angry and needed to take it out on someone and Cassandra was available. Always available.

Cassandra stood there silent for a few seconds, looking at me. She should have slapped me, or ran off in a huff, or threatened to never speak to me again, but instead she said, "I just got some new nail polish. Want to come over and do manicures?"

That was the kind of thing that made me love Cassandra.

There was a slow moment at my register. The only time that happened was on Sundays, where in downtown Atlanta in 1980 the only traffic was people taking connecting buses through Five Points—people coming to and from church, or jobs that didn't close on Sundays, and the homeless for whom Sunday was just another day on a calendar. I went to the back of the restaurant to stand in front of an open freezer door. Even with air-conditioning it got hot in the front lobby, where the doors were always opening, and near the french-fry station, to which my register was the closest. I saw the supervisor and some of the kids taking a case of hamburger patties, along with all the necessary condiments, out the back door.

"It's for a party we're having," one of them said, explaining it as though it should be obvious to me. "You're invited."

I wasn't sure if the invitation was genuine or a form of hush money, but I declined anyway. I had too much guilt to enjoy myself at a party fueled by stolen food, but I didn't hold it against the kids for stealing the hamburger patties and buns. After I gave it some thought, I was almost ready to defend them to anyone who'd asked me why I did nothing about it (mostly I was thinking of Ma and the priests at school). The way I saw it, we got minimum wage to do incredibly tiring work. It didn't tax the brain, but it was hard business washing dishes in harsh soap, frying twenty burgers at a time all day over a hot grill in July, and being cussed out by customers who were probably cussed out at some point earlier in their day and decided to take it out on a sixteen-year-old making minimum wage.

Luckily, I had come to this way of thinking when some of them asked me to join them after work at a city pool that same week. I was able to join them almost guilt free. Since I wasn't scheduled to work that day, I lied and told Ma the manager needed me to come in, and that Bridgette would have to go to the sitter. I took the bus straight over to Adams Park in Southwest, relieved I didn't have to arrive smelling of Filet O'Fish, a scent that grabbed on to my uniform and refused to budge without benefit of extra detergent and fabric softener.

There was a boy I liked at work, and I thought him not only cute but sophisticated, probably because he was sixteen and I just didn't know any better. He reminded me of my first crush when I was seven, on a fourteen-year-old neighbor named Chopper. Like the boy at McDonald's, he had light eyes and sandy red hair, except that Chopper had a huge afro because it was 1973. He dated my babysitter and didn't know I existed, and for that I disliked my babysitter, even though her only fault was in being a pretty fourteen-year-old. I'd planned to tell Ma how Chopper came to our apartment, because no boys were allowed, until I realized it would mean I'd only see him in the parking lot popping wheelies on his bike, not close up in my own home.

I flirted with the boy from work all day despite my limited talent in that area. At one point in the pool, he pulled me against him, spoon style. To this day I can still remember my excitement in feeling him against me, and knowing that I could have that effect on a boy that I barely knew. The whole two years with Kevin I wondered why he'd chosen me and always expected it might end at any moment, even though it took me by surprise when it actually did. After being dumped, swimming with the cute boy from work was like therapy, knowing that I might excite other boys the way I did Kevin. I didn't know until later that it wasn't that difficult a thing to accomplish, but at the time, I was damned impressed with myself.

Chapter 14

When Ma was officially on the case I expected the kidnappings to stop. There was no logic to this thinking, other than I was a fourteen-year-old child who had that much faith in my mother's ability to make things right. But they didn't stop. At the end of July, Earl Terrell went missing. Like the last three, he was young enough for me to call him young, only eleven. He must have loved to read because he had seven books checked out from the library when he went missing. The last time anyone saw him alive, he was being thrown out of the pool at South Bend Park for misbehaving. South Bend Park was just three miles from my house.

The day after Earl went missing from the pool, his aunt told the Task Force that she got a call from a white man (she said she was sure about this) saying he had the boy in Alabama and would set him free for a couple hundred dollars. That little bit of money was enough to make your heart break. No amount of money can equal a soul, but to take a child away, to make his family ache for the hole his taking leaves, for two hundred dollars was just plain meanness. In my mind, this could only be someone who saw no value in the life of that child and wanted to make sure the world knew it, the way diners who've received bad service will leave a penny instead of no tip at all, to make sure the waiter gets the point.

No one knows how legitimate this ransom call was, but his body still hadn't been found going into August. The immediate effect his abduction had on the investigation was getting the FBI involved. Since there was a possibility he'd been taken across the state line, it was now a federal crime, and the FBI, which had long been reluctant to join the case despite pleas made by the mayor, didn't have any option but to get involved, though minimally. It wasn't until later that local cops began to wonder if it wasn't a mixed blessing.

Ma was working at the dining room table again. Even though it had always been reserved for Sunday dinner, we never ate there anymore. It was where she kept all her information on the case, where she worked long after Bridgette and I had gone to sleep, and where I'd find her when I woke up in the morning. Sometimes I stopped in to check on her, see if she needed some water or iced tea, but mostly I hoped to remind her that Bridgette and I were still in the house and among the living. On this evening when I checked in, Ma showed me a picture of one of the kids and asked if I'd ever seen him.

"Why would I have seen him before," I asked before I paid the photo any real attention.

"I spent all day riding his bus route between downtown and home."

"Which route number?"

When she told me, I understood why she asked me. His bus left from the same starting point, the same corner, as mine.

"No, I don't remember ever seeing him. Even if I had, what information could I have that would help?"

"If you'd seen him before, you could tell me if you ever noticed him talking to someone regularly at the bus stop, or if you ever saw him get into it with someone. Maybe another rider was ticked off with him or something."

I took the picture from Ma and stared hard at it, wishing I

could remember something, trying to will myself to recall some bit of information, but nothing came to me. I knew if I spent more time on it, my mind would likely conjure something up, that I'd eventually believe it to be true, and provide well-intended but false and misleading information like so many witnesses did. I gave it up and told Ma I'd never seen him.

Even though I couldn't remember the boy's face, I didn't doubt that at some point we'd stood on that corner together. The odds were good that we had; both kids in school with similar commuting hours, both standing at that bus stop on the weekends waiting for a bus home after a day of movies at the Rialto or hanging around the Omni Center, people-watching and meeting up with friends. It wasn't at all unlikely. I wondered why I hadn't noticed him. Certainly if he was my type, I'd have remembered him. If he was the loud and rowdy sort of kid who'd make a run for the back of the bus, I'd have noticed him too.

That made me think he was quiet, probably kept to himself and didn't make fun of the homeless people who hung around our stop like the kids who ran in packs did. He probably just minded his business like me, just trying to get home without much drama involved. I wondered if he had a favorite seat on the bus, too, where he could stay out of trouble but also not look like too much of a sissy. When I took a last look at his picture, I felt regret that we had never met. He probably would have been a good person to talk to, killing time until one of our buses arrived.

Ma turned back to the papers on the table, signaling that she was done with me. She shouldn't have asked about the boy on the bus because all it did was make me hope she had something, even a germ of a theory, when it was obvious she didn't. Instead of leaving her to her work, I took a chair and asked questions, because up until that point I'd asked so few.

"Don't you have any leads yet?"

"You sound like my boss." She laughed a little when she said it, so I knew she didn't mind me interrupting her work.

"We thought we had something yesterday, a *person of interest* the city had contracted to paint project apartments. Some of the kids lived in some of the apartments he'd painted."

"That sounds like a good lead."

"The tip came from a man who'd been inside the painter's house and thought his décor was a little strange. So Sid and I drove fifty miles into the country to visit this man. He's got the *White Lightning,* a Klan newspaper, lining the walls of his living room like wallpaper, with headlines about how white people need to seek vindication for all the whites who had ever been killed by blacks."

"That's crazy."

"Not as crazy as the black dolls he had sitting on top of doilies on every furniture surface of the house. Some dolls weren't black, but white dolls he'd painted black. In some cases, he'd ripped the heads off the dolls, so only the heads sat on the doilies."

"So you don't think he did it?" Surely, this was a clue.

"Being crazy doesn't make you a suspect. If it did, the jails couldn't hold all the people. We're still keeping an eye on him, but his alibis check out. I think he's just a crazy Klansman."

"Aren't they all?"

One more boy was found dead before the school year started, making him the thirteenth child abducted or killed. Clifford Jones was thirteen and not even from Atlanta, but in town visiting relatives when he was taken. The last time his family saw him, he was walking home from the grocery store with them when he broke away to search for aluminum cans. Like so many of the kids who would end up being abducted, he was just trying to earn a few dollars when he was taken. He told his family he'd see them at home, but he never made it home. Clifford was found the following day, left next to a garbage can behind a strip mall.

The only solace I could imagine for the families of the kids who were found quickly was that they didn't have to wonder where their child was for very long. They didn't have to see their hope dry up into despair. This wasn't any silver lining—there rarely is one when people die unless they were in terrible pain or very old and just plain tired of living—but I imagined that if I had a loved one missing, I'd rather know they were no longer in misery. There were still four kids of the thirteen unaccounted for, and I couldn't imagine the hurt their families were feeling.

People were relieved to see the start of school, hoping fewer kids on the street meant fewer opportunities for the killer to strike. When school had ended in June, I was certain the killer would have been found before it started again. To a teenager, three months seems a long time, more than enough to figure out who the killer was, especially with Ma working the case, I thought. But I was starting my second year of high school, riding buses in the dark again, and I was afraid.

In some ways, I took some comfort in the rich school. The economics of it made it safer to be in that part of town. I knew even then that crime didn't come from the color of your skin, it came from need, and in the neighborhoods where I lived and traveled, there was a lot of need. In Ashford-Dunwoody, I didn't see people running through the streets like they had stolen something because usually they had, as I did in downtown. I didn't hear people arguing over money on street corners, because in Ashford-Dunwoody, the two-car garages held two cars and housewives paid someone else to clean their houses, most everyone had enough.

Most likely the killer would stay away from there, because the kids he'd gotten so far had one thing in common: need. They needed to hustle a dollar to help their mothers with the rent. Maybe they needed a few bills to buy a Member's Only jacket because it was the style, and even though they were poor, they wanted to be part of what other kids were doing, and what's wrong with that? They needed to find an honest way to make a little cash because the alternative might mean jail time. Their need made them easy prey for a killer who knew the need existed and knew where to find it. Nowhere near perennially green and professionally manicured Ashford-Dunwoody.

In other ways, the school brought me nothing but bad feeling. One thing that didn't change in the new school year was the fact that there were no black teachers, administrators, or office staff out of more than sixty people. The only time I saw a black face older than mine at school was behind the counter of the cafeteria deli or on a riding lawn mower. At my old school, the teachers were black and white, mostly white with all the Catholic nuns who taught there. But they weren't like the white teachers at the rich school. Those teachers at my old school taught us pride in who we were, told us what we could achieve. They were as much for us succeeding as the black teachers.

Going to the new school made me question all that I knew up to that point: that I was valued, that I was equal. It was my first experience being a minority. Up to that point, I knew that I was but it hadn't really mattered. Now, it mattered. Even if it wasn't intentional (but I suspected then that it was), the message sent to me by the new school was that black folks were only good enough to cook the rich kids' food, not good enough to educate them in the classrooms, accept their parents' hefty tuition payments in the office, or coach them on the fields and courts. I was glad I'd spent three years with the teachers from my old school first, the years when kids start deciding how they'll think as adults, because if the rich school was all I'd known, I would have believed the world was full of white people who didn't really give any thought to me at all, even the ones who were paid to.

I was lucky enough to get to the downtown stop just before the bus pulled in five minutes early, which meant I'd have my choice of seats. There was a psychology to selecting a seat on the bus. In the very front sat the old and infirm, or the people nervous about being on the bus in the first place. The middle of the bus was, appropriately, the middle ground—not as dangerous as the back, not as pathetic as the front. The back was the domain of juvenile delinquents or future inmates, hustling card players, and folks who normally wouldn't sit back there but are forced to when there are no other seats left. Depending on the route, I would see people stand rather than go to the back. I was never that pitiful.

My preference was somewhere between the front and back doors on the route from downtown to home. On the route from the suburbs to downtown, I always sat as far back as possible, figuring I was as tough as any of the riders on that route—mostly older black women who worked in rich white folks' homes, or immigrant laborers working on all the construction that was going on in north Atlanta who made it a point to blend in and stay quiet. The back of the bus was where the kids from the high schools along the route liked to hang out, along with the kids who got off the bus in front of the projects, so I tried to stay as clear of them as possible.

About halfway through my first year at school, they finally tired of commenting on the crested navy blazer and plaid skirt of my school uniform. More than once, I'd considered changing into regular clothes before I left school, but as chickenshit as I was, I still wouldn't go that far. It's true what they say about bullies—once they know they have you, you'll be gotten good. Sitting midway between the front and back doors meant I wasn't such a chickenshit that I needed to sit up front near the bus driver for protection, but it gave me enough distance for the project kids to miss my existence.

I was first on the bus, but people were trickling in behind me. I was trying to get a head start on a homework assignment when a woman said, "What's going on out there?"

"Looks like some kind of fight," said the man in the seat across from her. They both stood up and leaned toward the front of the bus, as if that small movement would give them a better view of whatever was happening fifty feet ahead of our idling bus. I still didn't move to get a closer look, but watched our bus driver, who I always thought was far too smooth to be driving a bus (though he was still driving the same route when we left the neighborhood five years later). Somehow, he always seemed to have the "laid back but I don't take no shit" attitude that would have served him well as a cutthroat businessman, nightclub bouncer, or high-end pimp. He didn't shift his position in the driver's seat—one foot propped up against the rail alongside the money-drop machine, wearing his ever-present sunglasses, his mouth slowly but stylishly working a toothpick. It appeared to me he was watching the same scene the rest of the bus was watching, but he was unaffected by it.

He closed the doors of the bus and made that noise that must have something to do with the brakes as air is released, a sound I still associate with my old bus route no matter what city I live in, or the bus system I'm riding on. People continued to stand, hoping to get a better look when our bus passed the commotion. The sound of sirens made the driver pause and made me finally join the gawkers on the bus while admitting I was no better than them. The crowd that had gathered around the fuss made it clear right away that it was a fight—someone was fighting someone else right in the middle of the street.

The driver pulled into the far left lane to let the police cars through. I could hear through our open windows that the crowd was cheering on whoever was winning, saying what I thought sounded like "get her, get her." A catfight no less. It had to be between two women—who would cheer for a man over a woman? The crowd got louder in its support as the police cars pulled in, making me wonder what made them choose one stranger over the other. The bus slowly made its way past the fight, and as soon as I caught a glimpse of the fighters, I had my question answered. It wasn't a catfight at all. It was a man beating a woman, and the crowd was indeed throwing its support behind the man. She was wearing the deep navy uniform of the Atlanta Police Bureau.

I never got to see what happened next, but I imagine the cops in all those cars that had just pulled in probably beat holy shit out of the man, not particularly concerned about who saw it. Or more likely, they took him away and did it privately since they were greatly outnumbered by the frothed-up crowd. There wasn't a lot of love for the department during that time; the city was tired of the killings. But that scene frightened me, took me by surprise in a way not much else has since.

The whole ride I thought about Ma as a rookie cop and the time she came home after a night in the hospital because she was beaten by a perpetrator. Being only eight, it didn't make much sense to me. My idea of cops and citizens then was what I'd been told in classrooms. Officer Friendly was always surrounded by adoring kids in those coloring books they handed out. People were grateful when the cops on *Adam-12* showed up, ready and willing to save the day. Ma's beating was the first time I realized that a lot of people hated cops, though they complain or cry lawsuit when they need one and that patrol car doesn't appear within a minute of them calling for help. I wondered if people stood around and watched, cheering on a man who likely had a few inches and fifty pounds on Ma. The thought made my stomach turn, and I couldn't shake the idea of it for several days.

Chapter 15

The second week of September, the medical examiner finally confirmed that the second boy to go missing, the one who was on his way to the movies downtown, was one of the bodies found at Niskey Lake last summer. His name was Alfred Evans. When those first two boys arrived at the morgue at the end of July 1979, the medical examiner had said one of the boys died of a gunshot wound, the other died from an overdose "or something like that." I wondered if over the year that he spent working on dead children's cases, this boy's case in particular, if he'd come to care more about what had happened to them than that statement from his original report would indicate. I imagined he had, it would be impossible not to, as I learned while watching Ma, noticing how working the cases began to change her.

She was assigned as a lead investigator on Alfred Evans's case now that it had been officially ruled a homicide instead of a missing person case. She still worked on some of the other cases, but mostly in how they tied to her assigned child. That's what she took to calling him after first naming him Victim Two, "My child, my boy." It seemed to me Ma was forgetting the rules about keeping some distance from her cases when she started saying things like, "My child."

Sometimes she talked out loud while going over case files.

I thought it was because the information was just too much hurt to keep locked in her head, that by speaking the words she was filtering some of the bad out of them. I could hear her reading a report from the Fulton County Department of Family and Children's Services while I loaded the dishwasher. "It says they have 'no record on this child other than a pauper's funeral.' I guess that's something, at least there was no cause for DFACS to ever be a part of his life before he died."

It seemed sad to me that the boy, even though I knew his spirit was gone and he was really just a body, had to lay in the cold morgue all that time with no one to claim him, no one to cry over him and mourn his passing for more than a year. Surely his mother cried, first when he went missing, then when she finally gave him up for dead, if she ever did. But I don't imagine it's the same thing as when you cry for someone you know in your heart of hearts is gone for good because you watched him be lowered into the ground and you threw a handful of Georgia clay onto the casket, maybe a white flower because children's funerals always seemed to have white flowers.

So I asked Ma what took so long.

"I don't want to talk about it."

"Because it's top secret?"

"Because I've been asked that question a hundred times already, and a hundred times I didn't have the answer people wanted to hear."

"If you answer me this one question, I'll leave you alone."

It was a lie, and we both knew it when the words left my mouth. I wanted to know all about the kids—what they did for fun, what places they went to, and mostly, what made them trust the person who would steal them from their families—kids who lived lives that would have made them a bit more suspicious than most. Or maybe that's what made them more willing. What made them go away with this person when they knew kids were disappearing? I wanted to know so I wouldn't fall into the same trap. Without me explaining this, Ma knew the reason for my questions. And most times, she answered them.

"For one thing, he'd been in the woods for three days. In July. The police accurately matched the missing person report on a boy who had disappeared about the same time the boy in the woods had probably died. They asked the parents who had filed the report to identify the body from the woods." The look on Ma's face let me know she was uncomfortable telling me this, but my look let her know I'd nag her until I got an answer. "The parents tried to identify him but couldn't positively say it was their child, given what the heat and the animals had done to him."

This didn't make me squeamish, little did. But it made me wonder if a parent can see a child's face look any other way than the way it did the last time they set eyes on it. I wondered if maybe they thought it could be him, but their hope was stronger than whatever power it would take to accept that their child was lying on cold metal in the medical examiner's office. Did they say, *No, this can't be my child,* when they thought maybe it was? Did it hurt to know that for three days he'd lain out in the woods, exposed, away from the care they'd surely have given his body if they'd known where he was?

There wasn't much Ma could tell me about the boy's life that might help me understand why he trusted the person who killed him, why he got into the car or turned his back on his killer, or was willing to go inside his home. What I did learn only showed me how often my world intersected with the boy's, despite our worlds being so different. The clothes he was wearing were bought in a shop just on the other side of Central City Park from where I caught the second leg of my bus ride to school. His family bought their groceries at the Big Star on Memorial Drive, and we'd shopped there before. His sister, like the boy whose body was found a few hundred yards away, skated at the same roller rink I did. MARTA was his main source of transportation. He liked to go to the Omni for the wrestling matches, and I went for the movies and the video arcade. There was nothing in this information that taught me what to watch for, only that I'd better be watching.

Ma said she had another "person of interest" she was checking into, the last person to have seen him alive, a man who'd said he'd given the boy a ride to the bus stop so he could catch the bus and make his movie on time. I didn't know it then, but that man's name would be forever in my memory. For six months, it was spoken around our house during the one-sided phone calls I overheard, quietly spoken words that I eavesdropped on from my bedroom door.

"Are you anywhere close to catching him?" I asked.

"It isn't about catching him, we know where he is. It's about being certain that he even had a thing to do with it."

I wished that he did, that Ma would discover this was the person who had made kids afraid to hang out past dark, made parents put their children on lockdown for more than a year. Like everyone else, I was ready for it to be over.

"I don't think I like Ma's boyfriend," Bridgette told me while we watched *Gomer Pyle* reruns. Even though school had started, the days were still long and hot, and watching reruns on TV after school made it feel like it was still summer. And Ma wasn't there to make us do our homework.

"We haven't even met him yet."

"So what. I don't need to meet him to know I don't like him."

I thought maybe I should pretend I was Ma and make Bridgette do her homework and get started on my own. But school hadn't been in but a week, and I hadn't shifted my thinking from summer to school just yet. So I didn't move from the couch.

"What don't you like?" I asked.

"How Ma is always going on dates with him."

Bridgette was a Mama's girl and didn't like any of Ma's

dates, except for the cop who broke both their hearts when it didn't work out. She wanted Ma to herself and she got most of what was left of our mother at the end of her days of working two jobs. She had no desire to share that small amount with me, much less a man.

"That's what it is to have a boyfriend," I said. "You go on dates."

"Yeah, but all the time? She's either always at work, or always with him."

"Not always." I wondered why I was defending Ma when Bridgette's words were mostly true.

"Oh yeah? Then where is she now?"

"Maybe it's time to grow up. You don't see me crying 'cause Ma isn't home every night. You keep saying you're not a baby, so act like it."

"What's your problem? I'm just saying she should be home sometimes." Bridgette tried to sound suddenly disinterested, but she looked like she was about to cry. I felt bad for what I'd said, but I didn't take it back.

When Ma told her she couldn't afford private school anymore, Bridgette was happy. Toward the end of the school year, she'd gotten into it with one of her teachers and had told the principal that the teacher was ignorant and couldn't pronounce certain words correctly. It was true; the woman would say "streen" instead of "screen," or "ax" instead of "ask." And we were paying good money to be in that school. Bridgette was only ten, but she was like a small grown person in some ways. She didn't take anything off anybody, including teachers. This was an admirable trait, and even though I'd have her on my side in a fight any day despite her being four years my junior, it made life more difficult for her than it had to be.

Anyway, the teacher had called Ma and said Bridgette didn't have any home training if she could question a teacher that way. Being that Bridgette got her ways straight from my mother, Ma went down to the school to have a few words with the teacher *and* the principal. After that, Bridgette was enrolled in the Atlanta Public School system. This was okay by her because she hated Catholic school. There was too much structure, too many rules, both of which made Bridgette nervous.

Ma used the Minority-to-Majority transfer to get Bridgette into one of the best schools in the system, which of course meant it was way across town in a white neighborhood. Even then, I knew that the best of everything—unless it was something that only black folks had any use for—was always located in the white neighborhoods. This included the grocery stores with the freshest produce, libraries with the best reference books for school papers, hospitals where there were enough doctors and nurses and beds to go around. Bridgette was going to a school that sat right in the middle of it, on Peachtree Street between the Brookwood and Buckhead neighborhoods. Between old Atlanta money and even older Atlanta money.

I'd left the West End a year ago, and I still missed it—the cadence of voices similar to mine, a few notes of loud and familiar music from passing car windows, and the store across the street that sold candy like Mary Janes and Now and Laters instead of the Skittles and Starburst that were popular with kids at my new school. I knew Bridgette would miss it, too, but I was glad I wouldn't have to worry about her being in the same neighborhood that the killer was finding his prey.

My relief that she might be safer grew every time a child went missing, including the fourteenth child, ten-year-old Darron Glass. For a few hours after he disappeared, there was a scant bit of hope that he might be found. He was last seen on a Sunday in mid-September, and a few hours later, his neighbor went running next door to get the boy's foster mother, who had no telephone. Someone was on the neighbor's line claiming to be the boy. By the time the foster mother reached the phone, it had gone dead. It was hoped that he might call again, but he never did. Still people hoped, because Darron's brother told the police that Darron had threatened to run away from his foster home to a relative's house, but he never showed up there, or anywhere else. His lasting mark on the investigation is that to this day he's the only child who was never found.

He was last seen at Second Avenue and Glenwood Road in Southeast, an area straddling the Fulton/DeKalb County line and less than a mile from his home. The intersection of these two streets, if you were to look at it on a city map, bordered the East Lake Country Club. What most folks think of country clubs, and the life of those whose travels take them past one daily, would likely not match this particular country club or the lives of the people who lived nearby. Not in 1980, anyway. There was a time when well-to-do Atlantans and nationally famous players golfed there, but by the time the killings began, white-flight had long ago changed the economics. By the time kids started dying, the East Lake area was known not for golf but for the housing project that was built to fill the space left by white people fleeing the city for the suburbs.

Back then, East Lake Meadows, when spoken of by people who didn't live in the projects or within a mile of it, was something foreign and barely imaginable. In 1980, it was in a section of Patrol Zone Five where drugs were traded, violent crimes committed, and gunfire rang out with such regularity that it earned the nickname "Little Vietnam." It made me grateful that when Ma was a beat cop, she was assigned to Zone Four, far from safe, but at least it wasn't East Lake Meadows. For Atlanta, it represented one of the neighborhoods that exists in all cities of decent size, a part of town where no one who didn't have to be there would ever go anywhere near. The second child killed, Alfred Evans, lived in those projects. Sometimes when my bus passed the projects near my neighborhood, I'd remember seeing the lady cop beaten up downtown and wonder how Ma's day was going while she questioned cop-hating, child-grieving people in the Meadows.

Chapter 16

I decided to make the best of my sophomore year. Besides, Ma had warned me that I'd better not have a bad thing to say about the school since I had a chance to get out and didn't. Especially since it was costing us good money when I could be getting the education that her tax dollars were already paying for. There was a school dance at the end of September, and I figured it was an opportunity to call my truce with the place I couldn't stand being but was too afraid to leave. Ma agreed to drive me out to the school and pick me up afterward. I didn't concern myself with how she'd spend the two hours in between, which provided too little time to go home and come back. She only said, "I'll be here at 10:00," and I just assumed she had somewhere to go.

As my first year at the school went on, I'd tried to fit in, not because I wanted to, but because I thought it would make things easier. I was more careful with my grammar, though the cadence of my words still echoed with the voice of a black girl raised in the South by black folks who once lived in the North. At home, my record collection was still disco, funk, and R&B, but at school I pretended to like Queen, though I'd never go as far as feigning any love for the southern rock that my classmates seemed to think was the end all, be all of music. And though I'd toned down my fashion sense a bit, I figured when it came to parties, I still knew what was going on in the world of style.

That's why I was so surprised at the reaction I got when I walked into one of the gyms wearing an outfit I'd bought just for the party: a cotton blouse in hot pink woven through with silver thread, a wide leather belt in the same shade of pink but with a metallic finish, and skintight BonJour jeans. Across my body, I'd slung a purse that was hot in those days—a disco bag, a leather pouch made to hold only the essentials so it didn't get in the way of dancing. It matched the belt, and when I went shopping for it downtown with some of my friends from my other life, they said it would be the piece that would set off the whole outfit.

I wished those friends were the people at the party, because all I got for my coordinating efforts were questions about where could I *possibly have found that outfit* from girls wearing plaid blouses with bow ties and matching vests. Or below-the-knee plaid skirts with cowl-neck sweaters. The boys wore jeans topped with plaid shirts. Didn't they get enough of wearing plaid during the school day? None of my school friends was there either, because they were the studious kids who didn't go to school dances. My efforts in trying to talk Dana into coming had been met with opposition: "I don't like to dance. Who wants to hang out with those kids anyway? I don't want to ask my dad to drive me." In response to the last argument, I'd offered for us to pick her up and drop her back at home, but she couldn't be persuaded.

Now I was thinking she was the one with good sense. I wanted to run from the place where I was clearly not meant to be, but where would I go? Ma wouldn't be back for two hours. So I stayed there, and danced with the cute blond who'd grabbed my butt the first year but who I was certain by the second year was gay but in denial. It wasn't until later that year that I finally figured out that his attraction to me wasn't sexual or platonic—it was safe. He was a rich white boy who would one day inherit his family's construction empire and would never actually bring home a black girl from the Southside. His flirtation with me was for show.

After a few dances, he went back to join the group that I'd never be a part of, or wanted to be, a group that included the girl from the badminton incident. The other kids said something to my dance partner when he rejoined them, laughing and making me wonder if he'd asked me to dance on some kind of dare. But he'd always been nice to me, and I was sure he understood being the outsider even though he was popular, so I figured it was something else. A few months later, when Ma gave me a rabbit jacket for Christmas, the kind with a patchwork of different color fur, I wore it proudly until I overheard some girls say it looked cheap. The following week, the rich boy's younger sister arrived at school in the same jacket. I liked to think of it as his way of defending me, though it was more likely I had not figured at all in the purchase. All I knew was they were one of the richest families at school and could have afforded mink if they wanted.

The DJ put on Queen's "Another One Bites the Dust," bringing kids to the dance floor, and all I could think was how the tune was ripped off from Chic's "Good Times," anthem of the disco they all hated so. I found a chair in a quiet corner when I grew tired of pretending I belonged there. My feet hurt from standing for hours in my Candies knockoffs, reminding me I had to work the next day. I wondered how many kids at the dance would wake at five on a Saturday morning and be reconstituting dried onions and brewing coffee in a Bunn-o-Matic an hour later.

When the two hours finally ended, I went outside, hoping Ma wasn't late like usual, and was surprised to see the car parked in the same place it was when I got out. She was asleep, head against the window and mouth open, as though she'd been in that position for a long time. I knocked on the glass softly so I wouldn't startle her because I knew never to surprise a cop, then opened the door.

"Am I late?" I asked, knowing that I wasn't.

"What time is it? No, it's a few minutes before ten. I guess I fell asleep."

"Where'd you go?"

"Go?" Ma looked as if I'd spoken some language she didn't know. "I've been here. Where would I go?"

It was only then that I noticed the little cooler on the backseat that she took to work on long days of watching some suspect's house, and the paperback on the dashboard spread spine side up to hold the page. I wanted to thank her and say I wished I'd known because I was having a hateful time in there with the construction company heir and the music that was never meant to be danced to, but instead I spent the whole ride home telling her about the fun I had.

"He was found this morning in a trailer park."

One of my coworkers was talking about the latest child to be found dead, twelve-year-old Charles Stephens, who had disappeared the day before. It was a Friday night, slow in the restaurant once the after-work-trying-to-get-home crowd had come and gone, and there was nothing to do but talk. I leaned against the counter, watching for signs of the manager coming out of his office so I could run a wet cloth across the counter in feigned industry if he appeared. He was always threatening to fire anyone caught slacking off.

"That makes, what, the fourteenth?"

"No, fifteen," I said. Since I'd finally let on that my mother was a cop, my coworkers looked to me for the most recent developments and statistics. I told them only what they could have found in the newspaper and ignored their repeated requests for more.

"I hate that I have to catch the bus home now, not that I felt so safe before," said the other cashier, a girl who seemed to be always scratching her scalp, then studying her nails for content. I wondered why the supervisor never made her wear her cap, and I never got into her line to purchase my half-price meal during my dinner break. I liked her despite her questionable grooming, mostly because she was sixteen, had a baby, worked full-time, and still managed to stay in school. I admired her for that, and she made it hard for me to complain about anything.

"You're lucky your mother comes to get you," the girl said.

"She has to. My bus stops running at 7:00."

"Still, you're lucky you get a ride."

It was true. If I had to ride the bus home at 11:30 at night, it would mean not having a job and not going to the private school. For my fellow cashier, it meant not being able to pay the rent. As if reading my mind and to calm her own fears, she said, "At least the killer doesn't want girls. Not much, anyway."

I wanted to tell her what Ma told me, that the dead girl and the missing girl shouldn't have been included on the official list, but that was one of the things I couldn't discuss outside the house. Instead, I just agreed with her and hoped Ma was right.

Ma was assigned a second case, another missing person report that turned into a homicide. A search team gathered in Northwest, near the Hightower rail station and not far from the day-care center where an explosion killed four children and a teacher earlier in the week. It reminded people of the Klansman who put a bomb under a pew in a black Birmingham church in 1963 that killed four girls, and made us wonder if the murderer had decided to kill on a bigger scale. That memory was still warm because the Klansman, who originally had been fined a hundred dollars and six months in jail for possessing dynamite, had finally been brought to trial and convicted of murder just a year and a half before children began dying in Atlanta.

That was on people's minds when the search team set out that morning looking for the body of seven-year-old Latonya Wilson, whose picture I thought looked more baby than child. She'd gone missing in June when someone, according to her parents and one witness, snuck into her home through a window, found her sleeping in her bed, and carried her away through the back door. People in her neighborhood were frustrated that four months had passed since her disappearance and she still hadn't been found. They held out hope that she might still be alive, but not much. In the four months since she'd gone missing, five children had been found dead. The city councilman who had sponsored the search team, and the people he represented in his district, didn't feel the police had done enough to locate the girl's body.

A small group broke away from the rest of the search party, two teenagers and an adult, and walked along the railroad tracks that led into the rail station. Where Sewanee Avenue and Verbena Street met, one of the children crawled through a hole that had been cut into a chain-link fence, crossed into an open wooded area, and found what appeared to be human bones. One of the children ran to the main search group and radioed for the police. The detective first on the scene was certain they were a child's bones, and two days later, the medical examiner confirmed it was the body of the seven-year-old girl the search party had set out to find. The parents were brought in to identify what they could—the elastic hair tie with green plastic balls and the white full-length slip she was last seen in. After four months, there was little else.

"People must be relieved they found the girl," I said to Ma. To myself, I wondered if the parents regretted that instead of having a final memory of their little girl being alive and happy that night before she went missing, they'd now have to remember her from a tattered hair tie and a muddied slip.

"Only for a minute. Now they're back to questioning the police, demanding to know why it took a bunch of frustrated parents and fearful teenagers a few hours to do what the police couldn't in four months. I can't say I blame them."

Whenever Ma said "the police" instead of "us," I knew those were the places in the investigation that she didn't agree with what was going on. She'd never admit to doubting the Blue in public, and when people from the outside asked what went wrong, Ma ran through a list of things that could have hindered the search:

> *"It was so hot on the June day that the search began, the dogs couldn't pick up a scent."*
>
> *"The mounted police doing the search were probably too far from the ground to see beneath the underbrush. . . ."*
>
> *"There were so many tips coming in from concerned citizens that the detectives on the case were overwhelmed. Remember, the Task Force wasn't formed until a month after the girl went missing."*

It was no lie about the number of tips received, and all had to be checked out. Some were of the crazy and futile variety—seers and dreamers telling of visions they had over that morning's bowl of cereal. But there were also the tips that made enough sense to give the detectives a bit of hope in the early days of the girl's disappearance. A father who reported that the morning before the girl was abducted a black man had entered his own child's bedroom window just a few miles away, but had been frightened off by the man's wife. A woman who called in with a partial license plate of a car she thought she saw the girl riding in on the same day. Three days after her disappearance, a MARTA police officer stopped a man carrying a young girl in his arms at the Hightower rail station. Like the other tips, this one didn't lead to anything either. It turned out the man and his daughter had run out of gas on the freeway and were taking the train home.

It wasn't as if the city didn't try. Five days after her disappearance, the police department even enlisted the help of the civil defense team to assist in the search, but their search area didn't go out wide enough apparently, or the girl wasn't dead yet, or hadn't been placed in that location at that point. Either way, it was clear that the body had been there for some time, and it still should have been found.

Everybody who knew Ma was a cop demanded an explanation—neighbors, family, the carpenter who was turning our garage into a rec room because Ma's work had spilled off the dining room table and was threatening to take over the living room. She had ready explanations for them, snapped out with a hostility that belied her usual cool. In private, she had as many questions as the rest of us. People had decided the police were either inept or just didn't give a damn, but either way, this discovery only widened the gap between community and police, two groups that needed each other more than ever if there was any hope of solving the crimes. Ma was thrown right into the middle of this battleground, inheriting the anger and resentment that came along with the boxes of case files.

"Now I'm responsible for figuring out who killed Victim Two and Victim Nine."

"They aren't numbers. Can't you call them by their names?" I asked.

"If I did that, I don't think I could get through each day."

Depending on how her day went, Ma might call them by their names. If the day held no discovery of a body, no names to be added to the list, she could say their names. If a parent needed to be interviewed, or calmed, she could say their names: Alfred or Latonya. On the days when a signal forty-eight came across on her Motorola in reference to a child, or when something about a victim made her think of Bridgette or me, it was easier for her to call them Victim Two or Victim Nine.

Chapter 17

Even though I was two months from turning fifteen and had stopped trick-or-treating a few years back, I still looked forward to Halloween because it was my job to go around the neighborhood with Bridgette. Because I'd stay out a lot longer than Ma ever would, throwing a wider net than the ten houses on either side of our own and back home again, Bridgette got a much bigger haul and was willing to share it with me. I was too old to suffer the embarrassment of being caught almost fifteen and still trick-or-treating, but I wasn't too old for candy.

We were in K-Mart when Bridgette started begging for a costume.

"There won't be any trick-or-treating this year," Ma said.

"Why not?" I sounded as disappointed as Bridgette looked.

"There's a city curfew, no kids out after dark without an adult, and I'm not sure I'll be home from work early enough to take you."

"What kind of fascist regime is this?" It was something I'd just learned in school, but it was wasted on Ma because she just rolled her eyes at me.

"Write a letter to the mayor; it's his idea. He's just trying to keep kids off the street and away from you know what." This code-speak was for Bridgette's sake, but she was busy picking out the costume that Ma wasn't going to let her buy.

I wondered if my classmates paid any mind to the mayor and his curfew, whether the little kids in their neighborhoods had to give up trick-or-treating. Probably not, because the killer wasn't hunting kids on the Northside. They were safe from the killer and from having to give up the things that made us children. They had mothers who didn't have to work, who picked them up from school and took them trick-or-treating after cooking a nice dinner. They had mothers who had time during the day to make costumes from scratch, instead of going to K-Mart to buy the cheap polyester kind with the sharp-edged masks that gave you a paper cut if you weren't careful and made your face sweat.

"Bridgette's too big for Halloween anyway."

It wasn't true that being ten was too old. Halloween was one of the last child things left before the time when adults began admonishing kids with *you're getting too old for that mess, act your age,* and *you need to be more responsible now*, and now it was being taken away from us, too.

The curfew didn't work. The day after Halloween, nine-year-old Aaron Jackson went missing. He was last seen at a shopping center on Moreland Avenue, part of the route Ma sometimes took to get home from the north. We'd sometimes stopped for groceries in the same shopping center. It was just three miles from home, and I couldn't help but think about how close the killer was getting to my sister and me. He was moving back and forth between Southeast and Southwest, but it seemed he was beginning to focus mostly on Southeast, in areas that my friends and I might be anytime because he was working only a few miles away from where we ate, slept, and played.

It was true that while the victims were close geographically, our worlds were still different. The victims went to the same places I did, like the Moreland Avenue Shopping Center, to hustle a dollar because they were poor, while I was going to spend the dollars I had because I wasn't. They were more likely to get into the car of someone who offered twenty bucks for a few hours' work. I made $70 a week frying burgers and didn't have to get into the cars of strangers and pray they weren't the killer. Being a girl, I was naturally more wary than a boy might be of grown men offering me anything. And as the child of a cop, I rarely trusted anyone.

But this difference in our day-to-day lives made sense only if the killer was actually luring the kids with something they were hard-pressed to turn down—money or the promise of a way to make some quickly. If that wasn't how he was stealing these children, if he was somehow forcibly taking them off the streets, the fact that I had a job, that I lived in a middle-class neighborhood, or that my mother was a cop didn't make a bit of difference.

The next day, a Sunday, we went to church in the West End where Bridgette and I used to go to school, and where we still attended Mass. It was the feast of All Souls, the day Catholics officially remember their dead. Our parish marked the day with a special remembrance of all the children who had been killed, and the church was packed with people come to say good-bye to kids they didn't know, come to understand how such a thing could happen to innocent children, come to pray for the killings to stop.

Representatives from all kinds of community groups were there, including groups born of our crisis, one led by the mother of a victim. Priests from all over the Atlanta diocese were joined by non-Catholic clergymen representing Baptist and Episcopalian churches, and they prayed with us, over us, and for us. One of them said something like, "Remember, sisters and brothers, the killer is also someone's child, and we should pray for his redemption as well as his capture."

I felt no guilt in having un-Christian thoughts while I sat on the hard pews, crushed on either side by the people who packed the church, the body heat making it feel like it was

July instead of November. I was thinking that no matter whose child he was, I wished him dead.

Later, after the Mass remembering the dead children, after having our postchurch Krispy Kreme doughnuts and stopping by the grocery for Sunday dinner, we learned that Aaron Jackson had just been found. The discovery of this child's body is the one that stays with me most because he was found on my street.

When Ma got the call that he'd been found, it was hard for her not to walk down the street to the scene. The case wasn't assigned to her; she didn't need to be there. I asked her not to go. It was enough knowing that just a short walk from my home, a murder investigation was beginning. I didn't need to wonder later that night as I tried to make sleep come what Ma had found there, so close to the place I thought was safe. Home.

I didn't ask Ma for the details because I didn't want to dream about them that night. But I read them in the paper the next day. The boy had been found beneath a bridge that spanned a slow moving creek. He died of suffocation, and was left "stretched out on the bank of the South River," which to me sounded strange, as if he had lain down there to rest himself. He'd been friends with the tenth victim, a ten-year-old boy who had until then been the body found closest to where I lived, about a mile and a half away. This latest boy had been killed somewhere else like the others, and his body left just a few yards off the road, tossed over the bridge.

There was a long stretch of houses along the three or so miles of the street, with the final quarter mile on the north end being empty of houses, only a junkyard filled with rusted cars that never seemed to leave the place once they were parked. The junkyard was a strange sight against a backdrop of green pine, a seemingly thick and endless forest that hid Lake Charlotte, or maybe it was the sign of things to come—

five years later, the city turned the whole area around the lake into a landfill.

My house was on the north end, not far from where the woods began. That green and houseless stretch was my favorite part of the street, though I had to work hard to ignore the junkyard in order to see the prettiness in the rest of it. This stretch was where as a kid, before public transportation grew my world to places beyond my neighborhood, I'd ride my bike fast downhill, imagining I was flying through a forest. Even as a fourteen-year-old with a bus pass, I'd still pull out my ten-speed occasionally and pump hard up that hill until I had to get off and walk the bike, then ride back down, arms stretched out instead of holding the handlebars, and pretend I was flying.

That all changed. Soon after the boy's body was found, someone—maybe his mother, an angry and powerless grandfather, or a weeping aunt—placed a white wooden cross on the side of the road, marking the spot. I rode my bike up there, wanted to see if there was any clue that would tell me the boy had not died painfully, that his last place on earth was a good one. I didn't want the kind of clues that cops look for, physical things that told secrets of the flesh. I wanted to feel something move through me in that place, maybe God's presence, or something bigger than me, or the boy, or all of the people whose hearts were broken when his body was found. I wanted to know if maybe the pine and greenness of the place sent him off with something of the feeling I had when I flew down that hill, past the place he lay just days before. Nothing came to me but a great hole that was filled up by sadness.

He went missing on a Saturday, was found on a Sunday, but it wasn't clear exactly when he was left on my street. It seemed likely that it happened Saturday night, but it could almost as easily have happened during daylight. There were no houses down that way, and most people left the neighborhood through the south end of the street, heading toward I-75 and I-285. Traffic was light through that part of the street most times of the day. For days I wondered what exactly I was doing at the moment he was left there. Was I drifting off to sleep in my warm bed, lulled by the far-off sound of a train's horn? Was I giving Ma a hard time about not wanting to start dinner, *Why do I always have to make dinner?* Maybe we drove past the killer on his way to our street when we took that route to church Sunday morning. Maybe I was down the street shooting basketball in the yard of the boys who had the net and was like a magnet for kids on the weekends. We probably all felt safe, nothing on our minds but making the shot, while the little boy was being tossed aside like somebody's bad mistake a quarter mile down the road.

That Tuesday was voting day. Ma was getting off work early to vote and wanted me to come with her. When the next election came, I'd be old enough to vote and she wanted to make sure I understood the importance of it and didn't waste the privilege. My family wasn't very political, but there were two things that were taken seriously: supporting the unions and voting. My great-grandfather, who was born a decade after Reconstruction to a freed slave, visited with us for a month each year, and he'd tell me stories of how I came to be. And always he'd say, "Girl, don't you know men and women swung from ropes for a hundred years so you could vote?"

I got off the bus from the suburbs and met Ma at the Task Force building, which everyone just called the Task Force because those two words came to represent a place, a group of people, and a mission all at once. Located between Spring and Williams Street on the northern edge of downtown, it was once a car dealership but sat empty until the owners donated it temporarily to the city. Even full of desks, cops, witnesses, and ringing phones, it still felt like it was designed for selling cars. The space, with its floors bare of carpet, caused an echo in the early days of the Task Force, when there were fewer desks, cops, and witnesses to fill it.

The first time I asked Ma where the bathroom was, she warned me it wouldn't be pretty. Clearly, it had never been intended to be used by women, probably because back when the dealership was open, women didn't work as car salesmen or mechanics. The lighting was almost as bad as the smell, and there were no metal boxes that sold Kotex or Tampax for a dime. Ma and the other two or three female cops, along with the secretaries, decided to fix the place up themselves rather than asking the bosses, because in 1980, the majority still didn't believe women should be anywhere near a police department wearing a badge and a gun. From their own pockets, they made sure the soap dispensers stayed full, put a bottle of hand lotion on the sink, and kept a supply of feminine hygiene products handy.

But I didn't mind the Spartan conditions, the bleakness of stark walls or the chill during the cold months. When the secretary's high heels clicked along the concrete floor, making the place seem especially desolate, it didn't bother me much. Being there made me feel like I was part of something that was the biggest something in the city. Mostly I'd sit at Ma's desk during my visits, listening to her one-sided phone conversations. She sounded very much like a cop, using military time instead of *o'clock,* talking about the *alleged assailant* and referring to some person unknown to me as the *subject.* In these moments, she turned into the other woman without warning.

After we left her office and picked up Bridgette from her after-school program, we went to the high school in our neighborhood that I would have attended if I wasn't going to the private school. Ma said she was trying to help President Carter stay in Washington for another term, though the price of gas and the Beirut hostages made reelection seem unlikely, even against an actor-turned-politician.

She made Bridgette and I stand outside the voting booth

even though I'd tried to convince her to let me in. We had mock elections in civics class, but all we did was darken circles on a bubble sheet at our desks. There was no blue curtain to hide our decisions, or special cards to punch holes into. Bridgette and I just stood guard outside, hearing the rickety booth rattle every time Ma punched a hole into her cards.

On the way back to the car, we saw a man on the ground in the middle of the parking lot. He was convulsing and didn't seem to have any kind of control of himself, his arms thrashing about in a way that reminded me of the robot on *Lost in Space*. Then he started to throw up. My first thought was that he was crazy; the next was that he was on drugs. Beyond that, I wasn't creative enough to come up with any other possibilities. My experience in this area was limited to what I'd seen on MARTA or at Grady, and in most of those cases, drugs or plain craziness was behind most strange behavior.

Luckily, Ma had more sense. She dropped to the ground like this was something she saw happen every day and tried to get the man to lie on his side.

"We have to keep him from choking," she told Bridgette and me while she looked through her purse like the answer to the man's problems was hidden in there. I half expected her to pull out a syringe full of something, or a bottle of pills. I was disappointed when all she came up with was a scarf.

"It looks like he hit his head when he fell, there's blood. And he's starting to seize again. Run into the school and call an ambulance."

I didn't move, just stood there watching her lift the man's head and put the folded up scarf under it. She repeated her instructions, this time using a few cuss words so I'd see the urgency in the request, and I took off running.

When I returned to the parking lot, my task completed and some of the polling workers following me, Ma was still on the ground trying to get the man on his side again when he started having another attack. That's when the ambulance arrived. We got out of the way and let the paramedics take over, and I watched Ma talking to one of them, explaining how the man's seizures came in succession. The rest of the evening I wondered when I told my friends what happened how many of them would be able to say they helped their mother save a man between school and dinner. I was certain not one of them could.

Chapter 18

After the dance that had gone bust, I decided to treat school like a job—put in my eight hours and get out. There were no extracurricular activities that might keep me on campus a minute longer than required. My friends would be better described as acquaintances. The only way I'd survive those eight hours was to keep my two lives separate, be two different people like Ma. Unlike her, I enjoyed only one of my personas, and one didn't complement the other. At home and with my real friends, I was me—comfortable, still street enough to be respected despite the plaid skirt and crested blazer I wore. Black. At school, I found a new group of friends who worked hard at not fitting in. They were white, but not quite rich. A few of them had part-time jobs. They talked about antiestablishmentarianism, and on the weekends sprayed their hair purple, wore black nail polish, and stuck safety pins through their cheeks. I liked how much they didn't want to belong, and they took me in.

We went to *The Rocky Horror Picture Show,* where I learned the lyrics to "The Time Warp" and the matching dance steps, and the right time to throw toast at the screen. These new friends introduced me to yet another new music by groups called the Ramones and the Sex Pistols. Like all the other music, it had no beat I could move to, but it sounded angry and I was angry—at rich kids who didn't have to work to afford tuition, and at white kids who didn't have to understand me though I had to try to understand them. At a child killer who took my mother away from me for an hour, a night, a weekend at a time until there was little of her left for me. And at the weakness that kept me in a school I hated.

When I was with my new friends on the weekends, I painted my nails black (but only the pinkies), I turned safety pins into accessories (but only in already pierced ears), and I sprayed my hair purple (only the bangs). Nothing too radical because it all had to be changed back to my regular self before I reached downtown, where such a look would surely result in a beat-down on the bus ride home. The black polish was peeled off on the bus from the suburbs into town, the safety pins replaced by earrings, the purple hairspray brushed out of my bangs.

I spent more time trying to fit in somewhere—at home where my friends and I straddled the line between being street and being middle class; at work where my friends lived in a world that included housing projects and raising children, though they were only children too; and the unreality of school—so that more each day it seemed to me that I fit nowhere at all.

In between classes, I made my usual stop in the girls' room to slick on lip gloss and fix my hair. I couldn't find my hair pick in my purse. When I realized I must have left it in the gym locker room, I headed that direction but was stopped short by what was happening in the second floor hallway. My hair pick, the plastic kind with a handle shaped into a black power fist, but by 1980 was a grooming tool more than a cultural statement, was being passed around by a group in the hall.

The group was made of boys and girls, all white. They were putting on impromptu skits with my comb as a stage prop, taking turns pretending to be some TV version of a black person, the only black folks they knew save me and the other seven black kids in the school.

"Dy-no-mite!"

"Well, we're movin' on up, to the East Side, to a deluxe apartment in the sky . . ."

"Whatchu talking 'bout, Willis?"

When they saw me, they didn't stop the comedy show even though they must have known that the odds the pick was mine was one out of eight. I was embarrassed that it was my pick, and even more embarrassed that I did nothing about it, and instead just walked on by like I didn't notice them. Throughout the day as I went from class to class I saw the pick in different hands, white hands where the black power fist looked so foreign, but still I said nothing.

At the end of school, after I'd killed my usual twenty minutes in the library instead of the cold street corner waiting for the bus, I saw that they'd finally grown tired of the game. In a trash can on the bridge connecting the library to the main building, I saw my pick laying on top of soda cans and potato chip bags. I felt a sudden surge of rage toward the kids for being ignorant, but mostly at myself for doing nothing about the modern-day minstrel show they'd put on. As I walked to the bus stop, I made a mental note to stop by McCrory's on the way home to buy another pick.

Ma still had her doubts about what the FBI would bring to the investigation, but she had to admit she was relieved to have them join, not so much because the Task Force cops couldn't do the job, but because there weren't enough of them, or enough money. She was spending crazy hours at the Task Force building, and often I'd be down there spending some of them with her. My bus home stopped running before seven o'clock, and on days when I had to stay after school to study in the library, or when traffic was really bad from school into downtown because of an accident on I-85, I'd miss the last bus home. I didn't have a choice but to hang out at the Task Force building until Ma was ready to go home. Sometimes this wouldn't be until after eight o'clock.

Bridgette sometimes slept across town at her friend Nadine's house in Northeast where she was going to school, because Ma couldn't always pick her up early enough. Unlike Bridgette, Nadine wasn't on the M-to-M transfer and actually lived in the same district as the school. Her mother told Ma not to worry about Bridgette staying over so often, it was more important that she was safe. She said she was glad to know her own daughter had someone to walk home with after the school bus dropped her down the street from their apartment complex.

Most times I didn't mind killing time at the Task Force, and luckily for Ma, her bosses didn't mind either. They understood that there was just her. They knew that while she was working sixteen hours a day, one of her children was waiting for a bus home at the same bus stop one of the victims did. Her other child used to go to school two blocks from where one victim was last seen. A child had been found dead just a few hundred yards from where her children and their friends lived and played every day. While she was talking to a victim's mother about what route he took home, she was wondering if her own child had made it home okay. So her bosses knew they'd better understand when her daughter showed up at her desk, doing homework in the seat reserved for possible witnesses, tipsters, and people who had official business with the Task Force.

The cops didn't seem to mind me being there. I either went unnoticed or provided a brief diversion. I liked to think I helped them in a small way by being there, especially those who didn't have children. Maybe it was a good thing for them to be around a kid who they could get to know in person and not through crime-scene photos and interviews with grieving parents. Sometimes they made food runs and would ask me for my order because Ma was out on a call or in some office taking a report. A detective might look over my shoulder at my homework and ask what I was studying, but then be off toward his desk and a mountain of work before I could look up and answer.

Sometimes when I was hanging around the Task Force, the detectives included me in their work, making me feel as though I was helping them find the killer. While I sat at Ma's desk practicing my French verb conjugations, she or some other cop would ask me whether a kid would do this, might a kid try that.

"If you really needed some extra cash and a regular rider on your bus offers you twenty dollars to help him with a small job, would you get off at his stop instead of your own?"

No, I'd figure it was a con. Besides, Ma would kill me if I did that.

"Let's say you're walking along Martin Luther King Jr. Drive near Ashby Street, and it's raining hard and you forgot your umbrella, and a white man pulls alongside you and asks if you need a ride. What would you do?"

How many white men do you see hanging around MLK and Ashby? I'd know right off it was a scam.

"What if he said he was a cop and he thought someone was after you?"

I'd look for the Motorola antennae on his car. I'd check the make—Is it a Crown Vic, or some other model police departments like to use? I'd wonder why he didn't show his badge right off the bat. I'd run. You should ask another kid that question, one who wouldn't know the difference.

I stared at the *Special Bulletins on Missing Children* tacked on corkboards, memorizing the faces because I thought trying not to forget them was the least I could do. Maybe I thought I'd see one of those faces one day, the ones still missing, staring from the back window of a car as it pulled away, begging me to do something.

Other times, being at the Task Force made me feel like any other kid in the city, afraid and no more protected than they were. As a break from Algebra II formulas, I'd walk around the building, looking at the maps that someone with a steady hand had drawn symbols on showing where each child lived, went missing from, and was found dead. No matter where I started searching the map, my eyes would eventually stop at the red circle on my street. Red circle for *found dead.* In map space, it always appeared the circle had been drawn square on top of my house.

In the second week of November, the seventeenth child went missing. Taken just a month before his sixteenth birthday, Patrick Rogers, who loved Bruce Lee movies and planned on being a singer when he grew up, was the oldest child to make the official list so far. Patrick was last seen on Thomasville Road in Southeast, just two miles from my house. I hadn't had a decent night's sleep in the week since the boy was found on my street, wondering how he died and whether I'd ever passed him in a grocery store aisle at the Big Star, or saw him playing Space Invaders in the video arcade on Jonesboro Road. When I did get to sleep, the boy was still able to sneak inside my dreams and eventually frighten me awake. Knowing the killer was still nearby didn't help.

Another child going missing right after the mayor kicked up the fuss with the FBI just increased the pressure on all the agencies working the case, local and federal, and it also instigated fighting among the agencies.

"The FBI acts like they're gonna save the day," Ma said, her anger so easy to raise up now. "So far, all they've done is dredged up old theories about drugs and gangs."

Drugs and gangs was just the twentieth century version of a centuries' old belief in this country, at least in the South—that any evil that befalls black folks, we must have brought it on ourselves, including slavery. Didn't work hard enough, didn't get enough education, waited for someone to help us instead of helping ourselves. All our problems were self-inflicted, no matter that slavery was a hundred years fresh, access to voting and desegregated schools just fifteen years young. The part I didn't understand was that the lead agent in the FBI's Atlanta office, a black man, was also blaming drugs and gangs. Maybe he'd been in the FBI too long. Or as one victim's mother kept saying, the FBI had no business working the case in the first place because they didn't know Atlanta, didn't understand its people or its ways.

The FBI didn't help Ma's second case by saying publicly that it was imminently solvable, basing this statement on what had turned up so far in the investigation—the possibility someone in the girl's family knew what happened to her.

"Of course we're looking at the family. You always start with family. I don't appreciate them working off the same knowledge and theories that I am, and saying they're about ready to solve the case if only they had more FBI agents to put on it."

The first thing that struck Ma about her second case was that the *modus operandi* was so completely different from that of the other victims. With one exception, the other sixteen victims to date had been boys. All the other victims were taken off the street at least a few blocks from home, except for the only other girl, who was last seen near her home. Latonya's parents said the girl had been taken from her bed while her family slept, that the abductor had climbed through her brothers' bedroom window, which was found open the following morning. But once inside, the killer would have had to walk past the sleeping boys, into the hall, and past the sleeping parents, past a third brother sleeping on the living room sofa, lifted the girl from the bed she shared with her sister, then gone out the back door, undetected.

From the beginning, Ma regretted the girl being added to the official list of Missing and Murdered Children because she didn't believe the child's case was related to the other abductions and murders. She didn't believe the girl was a random victim. If there was any truth at all to the abduction-from-her-bed story, it had to be someone who knew her, someone who'd been in the house before and knew important details about her family, such as the layout of the apartment and who slept in which room. Because the kidnapper passed over the two boys in the first room, and the third brother sleeping on the sofa, Ma concluded it wasn't the same person who'd killed or abducted the seven male victims up to that point.

She didn't like to question the parents of a child victim. It was a hard thing to do but still had to be done. In the beginning of any investigation, no one wants to believe someone the child loved could have been the reason the child was dead. Sometimes when we had tested her very last nerve, Ma would threaten Bridgette and me with the line, "I brought you into this world, and I can take you out," but no one ever expects that a parent could lift a hand to do it, and yet it happens every day. Like other detectives on similar paths in their own cases, this didn't do a thing for her popularity in a community where parents were mistrustful of the cops. Where parents were certain there was a conspiracy to deflect the city's inability to catch the killer back onto the victims' families, all wrapped in the now familiar cry of *cover-up*.

Chapter 19

It had been a week since Thanksgiving and the last time we'd had a regular dinnertime, one where Ma got home early enough to cook dinner and all three of us were sitting at the table. I was happy to have things back to normal, even if I knew it was probably just for the night. Ma was taking a meat loaf from the oven, Bridgette was adding sugar to the Kool-Aid, and I was slicing tomatoes for a salad when the phone rang. Ma answered, and I could tell from her side of the conversation that it was something about work that was going to delay our regular dinnertime.

"Tell him I'll talk to him tomorrow. I'm just putting dinner on the table. My kids are waiting for me."

When she got off the phone, she said, "Okay, let's eat," in a too-cheerful way.

"It's almost 7:30. Why they have to call you so late?" I asked, knowing the answer—cops don't work nine-to-five.

"Another detective and I arrested a man yesterday on an outstanding warrant for a theft charge, but we think he might have something to do with my first case. He was the boy's neighbor. We told him since he was the last person known to see the boy alive, he was at the top of our list of people that needed to be polygraphed. His mother tells me if her son has to take a polygraph, she knows a guy in Decatur who'll do it, like she's referring me to a hairdresser. I told her that suspects don't get to make that choice, and she got all riled up. Then the suspect jumps bad and tries to fight us."

This was the part of Ma's stories about her day I didn't care to know the details of, the violent parts, but I didn't tell her that.

"Good thing we'd called some uniforms to assist before we got there. Turned out we needed them. Now this man's telling the deputy at the jail that he needs to talk to me. But I told him it'll just have to wait until tomorrow."

"Remember you said we can pick up my viola this weekend," Bridgette said. She was old enough now to understand how fragile Ma's promises to us were becoming, and she saw in the phone call from the jail that her weekend plans might be slipping away. "Practice starts next Monday, and I'll be the only one in class with no instrument."

"I might be too busy this weekend; we'll have to see."

Bridgette looked at me and rolled her eyes, being careful not to let Ma catch her.

"Nadine's mother took her to get her violin, and they already bought the outfit we're supposed to get—black pants, white shirt. See?" Bridgette produced a piece of paper from her book bag, but Ma didn't pay it any attention.

"Kim will have to take you over there on the bus. I'll call in the morning and give them my charge card number, and you can pick it up Saturday."

Saturday morning I was planning on doing nothing but waking up late and watching cartoons because I still liked them and it had been forever since I'd seen any, then maybe shoot some hoops if it wasn't too cold. Before I could tell her Saturday morning was my only free time on the weekend, that I had to work Saturday evening shift and all day Sunday, the phone rang again.

"All right, give me half an hour."

While she pulled on her coat and looked around for her keys, she told us she had to go. The man in jail was demanding to see her right away. The deputy said the man was going off, acting crazy, and wouldn't shut up about having to talk to Ma. So she went down there, just like that, as if it were the Queen of Sheba requesting her audience instead of some repeat offender who had resisted arrest the day before.

"Will Sid or somebody meet you down there?"

"The man is in a jail cell, cuffed." Ma rolled her eyes when she said that. "I might be late, so don't wait up. And make sure Bridgette eats her broccoli or she doesn't get a Popsicle."

After she left, we took our plates and Kool-Aid to eat in front of the TV in the rec room. I told Bridgette she didn't have to eat her broccoli and I gave her both sides of the Popsicle, instead of banging it against the edge of the countertop into two pieces the way Ma did. When she asked if I'd take her on the bus to get her viola, I told her I would.

"I'd rather have your promise to take me, anyway. Otherwise, I'll never see that viola."

The next morning, as an apology or an excuse for leaving dinner, I wasn't sure which, Ma said the suspect had given her some good information that she needed to follow up on. She didn't look up from the stack of mail she was going through, mostly bills. She reached the bottom of the stack and then went through them again as if there would be fewer bills the second time.

"I have to go out of town tomorrow and follow up some leads the suspect gave me."

"Where?"

"It's a town three hours south, which means I'll be staying overnight."

"Who's gonna watch us?" Bridgette asked.

"Kim will."

And pick up Bridgette's viola, do a shift at work, and finish my class project.

"But what about the killer and the boy they found down the street?"

"You do what Kim says. She'll be fifteen in a few weeks." She ignored Bridgette's question about the boy down the street, and she sounded like she was trying to convince herself that leaving us would be just fine as much as she was trying to convince Bridgette. "This came up too quickly for me to arrange for someone to come over. Maybe I can ask Mrs. Willis if she'd keep you."

Mrs. Willis was Cassandra's mother, and still used Mrs. even though her divorce had been final a couple of years ago. Ma would say Mr. Willis was strange because one time she went over there to borrow something and he answered the door wearing only his underwear. I figured things like that probably had something to do with their breakup. Mrs. Willis and Ma were worlds apart in everything but being the single mothers of two girls, so she and Ma looked out for one another, though you wouldn't exactly have called them friends.

Even though Cassandra was my best friend from the neighborhood, and her sister was Bridgette's best friend, we didn't do sleepovers with them. We stayed over there once when Ma had to go out of town, and they had roaches like I couldn't believe—on kitchen counters, in the bathtub, even in the refrigerator—and I made up excuses for why we couldn't eat their food. I didn't sleep the whole night for fear of a roach crawling into my mouth.

So I told Ma that I was old enough to stay home alone, old enough to look out for Bridgette. Normally this would have been the truth, but because I was thinking of the flimsy white cross planted in wet riverbank soil just up the road, I didn't believe my own words. With the growing pressure from her boss to make an arrest in her cases, Ma had enough trouble without me giving her more. But I couldn't help but wonder if she didn't care more for the dead kids than she did Bridgette and me, considering she was willing to leave us alone overnight, and just a few hundred yards from where a body had been found, and where the killer had spent some time, even if only long enough to put his still-running car into park, lift a dead boy from the backseat, and toss him off the bridge. Maybe Ma sensed what I was thinking, or maybe it was the guilt I hoped she felt, but she said she'd get Mrs. Willis to look in on us before bedtime, and that we should call her if being alone didn't feel right. Mrs. Willis could be over in half a minute.

When I went to wake Bridgette for school the next morning, I found a letter on her nightstand. Despite all that was happening, and though she was about to turn eleven, Bridgette still believed in Santa Claus. I don't think she stopped believing completely until she was well past the age that most kids give it up, thirteen maybe. I envied her ability to hold on to childish things since I never could.

Santa was an early sacrifice for me, when I was six or seven and had stayed up late one night handing Ma the parts to a Big Wheel she was putting together for Bridgette. Ma hadn't intended for me to find out then, but I was a light sleeper and could hear her in the living room. She tried to come up with some story for why she was putting together the bike instead of Santa, but when I admitted I'd had my doubts for a couple of Christmases now, she told the truth, made hot chocolate for us, and asked me to help her while Bridgette slept, no doubt dreaming of reindeer on the roof.

Maybe it was because I had to let go so early of so many things that Ma tried to help Bridgette hold on too long, to the point that her friends teased her. But teasing still wouldn't shake her faith in childish things. Maybe that's why I supported the charade same as Ma. I couldn't hold on, but Bridgette could. That's why it was like finding out there was no Santa Claus all over again when I found this letter she'd written:

Dear St. Nick,

How are you? Fine I hope. I sometimes think your not real but sometimes I do. How is your wife is she fine to? I must be wasting my time on this I might not. Well I guess your busy now. Thanks a lot.

Merry Christmas,
Bridgette

I took the letter from her nightstand (and still have it today, which is why I know every word), and when Bridgette asked about it, I told her I mailed it to Santa, that it was a good letter that needed to be mailed. I told her Santa understood that kids had their doubts and wouldn't mind that small and temporary breach of faith. Bridgette believed for at least two more Christmases after that—in the face of so many reasons not to.

It took longer than usual to get home because I had to take a bus to Bridgette's latchkey program, pick her up, and then go to the music store to get the viola, which thankfully wasn't far from her school and along the bus route we'd take home anyway.

"Thanks for taking me," Bridgette said on the ride home.

I was wondering if people on the bus knew the value of a viola and might jump us for it, but no one seemed to notice the gray case propped between Bridgette's knees.

"That's okay. You'll owe me a favor now."

"Like what?"

"I'll let you know when I think of something."

"Not something *too* big. It's not like it wasn't on the way home."

Bridgette was no longer the kid who could be easily convinced the slightly taller, skinny glass of Coke was a better deal than the shorter, fat glass when Ma made us share a can.

"I still need the white shirt and black pants." Again she produced the sheet of paper from her book bag that Ma was too busy talking about her trip to read.

"It says here you don't need that until your first concert, and that's not for a couple of months."

"Nadine's mother already bought her outfit." She folded the paper carefully and put it in her knockoff Trapper Keeper, as though she hadn't already memorized everything on the sheet.

"That's because Nadine's mother works at Neiman Marcus, and all she had to do was take an escalator ride on her lunch break to get it."

"I bet Ma'll make me get mine from the JC Penney Outlet Store."

This was true. One of my favorite things about having a job was no more shopping at the JC Penney Outlet where it was apparent that cost, not style, was the appeal.

"Nadine's mother has a store discount, that's why she can buy her all those nice clothes." I offered this as an apology, but Bridgette was staring out the window and clearly didn't want to hear any excuses—not for me playing proxy for the viola shopping trip, not for our inability to afford clothes from Neiman Marcus, or for Ma's seemingly waning interest in her baby girl.

As we headed for downtown, I worried what I'd do if traffic was bad and we missed the last bus home from town, but I had a list of phone numbers of people I could call to come get us while we waited at the McDonald's where I worked. We made the bus okay, but Bridgette was fussing the whole walk home from the bus to the house about it being so dark, and how we were out past the city curfew, and how the killer could be cruising the street. I told her to hush, but halfway home she'd scared me enough that I suggested we run the rest of the way, her viola case slapping against my leg.

"Are you scared?" Bridgette asked while we ate a dinner of Hamburger Helper.

"No, why should I be?" I looked at the orange and yellow daisies on the wallpaper instead of Bridgette. Even if I was scared, she didn't need to know about it. She stared at me for a second.

"You are too. But that's okay, who wouldn't be? Ma should be here."

I didn't disagree.

After I let the dog in for the night, grateful that he was the meanest dog around and fearless, too, I double-checked all the locks. I knew where Ma kept her extra gun, which she left behind, only mentioning it like it was an afterthought when I knew that it wasn't. Wasn't this the reason she'd taught me to shoot? To respect what a gun could do, and to be willing and able to use it if I ever had to? I took the gun from her closet shelf, pulled it from its holster, and checked the chamber before putting it into my nightstand drawer. Once our neighbor called in her last check of the night, and Ma called to make sure we were okay, I got Bridgette out of her bed and told her to sleep in my room. I told myself that if something should happen, she should be close to me, but really I was just being a chickenshit. I tried not to wonder what I was dreaming the night the killer dropped a boy off the bridge not far from where I was trying to sleep tonight.

Ma called the next morning. "How did last night go?"

"Okay."

"Good. Well, I'm getting some good interviews down here, got a few more to do."

"That's nice." I hoped my lack of enthusiasm flew through the phone wire.

"How's Bridgette?"

"Okay." I decided I'd give her as little as possible. If she really wanted to know how we were doing, she'd be here.

"What's she doing?"

"Watching TV and eating cereal. You want to talk to her?"

"No, she'd just ask me to come home now and I can't just yet."

"She'll be mad she didn't get to talk to you." And why couldn't she come home now? She'd said it would only be overnight, that she'd be home by dinner.

"I'll call again later. Look, I need to stay over one more

night to get these interviews done. You think you could manage another night?"

I wanted to say no. No, because if I said yes, leaving us alone would become easier for her. No, because those weren't your kids and we are. No, because those kids were dead and we weren't. But I didn't say any of those things because Ma expected me to say, *Yes, it's fine, Bridgette and I will be okay and I'll take care of everything*. Which was exactly what I did.

Chapter 20

Until the summer the killings began and I got the volunteer job at the hospital, I'd spent all my summers in Cleveland with my grandparents. It gave Ma a chance to be a woman instead of a mother. She tried to pack all her fun into those three months—pool parties, dating, and whatever else she could get into because Bridgette and I weren't there.

When we were younger, Ma would throw house parties that Bridgette and I would sneak out of our bedroom to watch, hidden by the darkness of a hallway: people blowing crayon-colored whistles that Ma gave out as party favors and singing Parliament's "Tear the Roof off the Sucker"; people yelling out "Bullshit" while they played a child's card game made more interesting by rum and Coke; and later in the evening, couples slow-dragging to Marvin Gaye's "Let's Get It On." Even at seven or eight, I knew that song had everything to do with sex, without understanding, or even listening, to the words. The next morning, Ma would give us a dollar each to help clean up the mess, which I thought unfair since I was four years older. I complained under my breath about that injustice while pouring plastic cups of stale wine and flat beer into the kitchen sink and Bridgette tossed ashtray remains into a garbage bag.

But when we got older, Ma must have figured we'd understand too much of what went on at the parties and thought it best to have them when we weren't around, so she'd wait until summer and send Bridgette and me to stay with our grandparents in Cleveland in an effort to keep us out of trouble and allow her to get into some. Ma didn't know that between my grandparents working full-time, the rough neighborhood they lived in, and the kids I hung out with, there was more opportunity for me to get into trouble there than back home in Atlanta.

If she had the money, the day after school let out Ma would put us on a plane where the stewardess would look after us, or Grandma and Granddad would drive down to get us. I always preferred the plane over driving because in the southern half of the trip, we couldn't use the bathrooms unless we were in some sizeable town, and those were scarce along I-75. My grandparents knew the route well, and if we were asleep in the backseat, they'd wake us up and say, "Last bathroom stop before Whites-Only country." If we had to go after that stop, which one of us always did because it's difficult for a small girl to hold her water through two states and four hours, we had to take the roll of Charmin and squat in a ditch off the side of the road. Even today, I don't much care for road trips that are long enough to require a bathroom stop.

My grandparents always put us into some kind of summer program because they still worked full-time during the day and they wanted to make sure we stayed out of trouble. Bridgette went to a church-run day camp, and I took art classes at a place called the Supplemental Center. Kids called it the Sup Center for short. I don't remember why it was called that, but it was the perfect name. For me and many of the kids who went there, it did a good job of filling in the empty places: a father who'd left; gaps in education because of too many moves that were the result of paying the rent late too many times; the wide-open boredom of having nothing else to do. My twelfth and final summer spent in Cleveland, I'd take the bus downtown for a day of watercolor or batik class after my grandmother scrounged up enough change for the bus, sometimes having to resort to the tithing envelope meant for the collection plate come Sunday.

Sometimes my grandfather would sneak me a little extra, which I'd use to buy a hot dog and root beer from a street vendor after class, having my lunch on a park bench before catching the bus back home. I kept this a secret, because Grandma would have likely given him hell for such an indulgence. "We have good food at home, she can carry a sack lunch," she'd say. The good food at home sometimes wasn't that great. Grandma was a cook in the public school system and sometimes came home with some cheese and canned beef, the latter conspicuously government issue with its label-free shiny aluminum can, generic black lettering, a silhouette of a cow and USDA stamped across it. I was grateful my grandfather was a soft touch with us grandkids and I didn't have to carry chipped beef sandwiches to class every day.

My grandparents lived off Eighth and Superior. I didn't know until I returned in my late teens that it was truly a bad part of town. I was unaware of the danger during those summers I spent running errands to the A&P alone through back allies, or joining my cousins (who also stayed with my grandparents each summer) to fight another group of kids who allegedly had looked at one of us wrong days earlier. Bridgette, my cousins, and I would sit on the porch playing poor kids' games like I Spy and That's My Car until all hours, trying to figure out the song a car horn played as it went by. It was the thing back then in that neighborhood, if you were a player, for your horn to play a few notes from "Superfly" or "Shaft," and for you to sound your horn as you approached so everyone knew you were coming and could stand on their porches and watch you drive by as you gangster lean on your armrest, left hand casually resting on the top of the steering wheel, in a shiny Lincoln Mark IV or a Buick Deuce and a Quarter.

The summer I was nine or ten, I went to a day program at

my grandparents' church and had to walk the mile there alone. I was slightly afraid of the walk, and made a weapon out of a stick with a piece of rope tied to it, the other end of the rope tied around a rock. I know now that it would have been little help if I'd ever had to use it, but it made me feel safer then. I'd hide it in some bushes in front of the school until I pulled it out again before starting the walk back to my grandparents' house. Those summers in Cleveland I learned to fight because I had to, but I'd never associated needing to protect myself with living in a bad neighborhood until that return trip. It was definitely ghetto, and I knew four years couldn't have changed it. I'd changed, and saw things differently with my seventeen-year-old eyes.

The way the neighborhood was going down was the reason my grandparents considered returning to Georgia where they were born and where most of their children now lived. They decided to come spend Christmas week with us to get a feel for living in the South again after forty years. Life in Georgia for black folks in 1940 was the reason they'd left. Returning seemed like a step back somehow, but there had been no steps forward in Cleveland for longer than they could remember.

Now they were sitting in our living room on their first day in Atlanta, asking Ma about how things were going with the case.

"We've been trying to keep up with it in the news," Grandma said. "There's something about it now almost every day. Everybody keeps asking what I know, 'cause they know how you're a lady detective and all, working on the case."

"That's right, I tell folks at work how my daughter is working on this famous case, and how you're gonna find the killer any day now." My grandfather was as hopeful as I was when Ma first joined the Task Force, before I understood how difficult the task was.

"Well, Daddy, I think you've got more faith in me than I do."

I'd read in the paper that people were angry about the continued questioning of parents, including those in Ma's case. *Why don't they go and find the real killer, instead of harassing her family,* the people kept asking. I asked Ma the same question.

"We always look at the family, you know that. More times than not, it's the family."

I wondered if she wasn't wasting time while the *real* killer was walking around. I felt guilty questioning her, but I could see the logic in what the people were saying.

Because of the city curfew and because Ma wouldn't have let me hang out after dark whether there was a curfew or not, I had to celebrate my fifteenth birthday at home instead of at the mall, or in a video arcade, or if I was with my school friends, drinking beer while leaning against the car of someone who looked old enough to buy a six-pack. Ma promised we'd go see a movie instead after dinner.

She called to say she'd be a little late, go ahead and start making dinner and she'd be home soon. Grandma had cooked dinner, we'd eaten it, and the dishes were cleaned and put away when Ma called again to say she would be a little while longer because she was still working. She told me the details as if that would make it less wrong of her for not taking me to the movies on my birthday after keeping me from going out with friends.

She was still at the Task Force, interviewing a witness who knew the first two boys killed. The man once lived on Niskey Lake Road across the street from where the boys' bodies were found. He'd dated the sister of the suspect who'd last seen Alfred Evans alive. He'd given karate lessons to Edward Hope Smith, either at his house on Niskey Lake Road or sometimes behind the Greenbriar skating rink the victim and I liked to visit. She included me in that sentence, I guess to show that she was staying late as much to protect me as to find out who killed the boys. She was finding too many connections for her to stop the interview now.

"Just let me wrap this up," she said, "and I'll be home soon. Oh, and I told this witness I'd give him a ride to the train station after, so he'd agree to stay a bit longer and finish his statement."

A ride to the train station, I wanted to yell. Is she a taxi service now? Will she be in an unmarked car where she'll be protected from this witness by the thick wire mesh that separates front seat from back? We both knew she wasn't looking at this guy as a witness but as a suspect, whether the man knew it yet or not. Will her partner be with her when she drove this man to the station? And was this her version of soon, which I knew by now could mean hours turned into days, or my version of soon, which was now? But I said none of this and took my anger out on my grandmother, saying I didn't want a piece of chocolate cake *or* sweet potato pie, even if she had baked both because they were my favorites.

I knew I was acting like a child even though I'd just marked another year closer to being an adult, but I was tired of acting grown-up, asking no questions and just dealing with it. On my birthday, I wanted to be a kid. I didn't want to sit in my room watching the clock as Ma's *soon* turned into the hours I expected it would, wondering if the witness knew she was marking him as a suspect and had gotten her gun away from her, and had dropped her in some wooded place where animals would make it difficult for me to identify her weeks from now. Someone would show me her necklace with the gold Queen Nefertiti charm she always wore, and say, "Do you recognize this? It's all that was left." By the time I heard her keys in the front door late in the night, I was thanking God for getting her home safe and hating her for missing my birthday all at the same time.

As a peace offering, Ma said we could redecorate my room. I'd been begging her to since I moved out of the large room Bridgette and I shared and into the small guest room two years before. It was hardly a guest room as much as it was like a room in a boardinghouse, with one of Ma's sisters or brothers passing through for a few months each during the first two years we lived there. Ma was the first of her siblings to leave Cleveland, and our place became the way station as all the rest followed, one by one, until all five had relocated to Atlanta.

The room started out as mine when Ma first bought the house, the first time I'd had a room to myself since Bridgette was born. But I was only in it a month or two before the first aunt showed up and stayed for a few months until she could get her own place. I'd move into Bridgette's room for those few months, move back into my room once my aunt left, and just as I'd get comfortable, here came an uncle to move me out again. When it wasn't an aunt or uncle, it was a girlfriend or a cousin. Always someone. When I was twelve, the last of the boarders had come and gone but we didn't know that at the time, so I decided it was easier to stay put in Bridgette's room than to keep moving all the time, getting my hopes up that it would finally be my room. When no one had called asking for a place to stay for nearly a year, I moved back in without asking Ma, who had taken to calling it the guest room instead of Kim's room.

When I moved in, the dresser was cluttered with leftovers from all the sisters, brothers, girlfriends, and cousins because each would always leave something behind—a mirror, a tube of lipstick, those springy things that men squeeze to build their forearms that as a child I couldn't squeeze even using both hands and all my might.

After I cleared away their things and replaced them with mine, it still didn't feel like my room. I could smell one aunt's perfume still lingering in the bedspread even though it had been washed several times and she'd been living in the Middle East for two years now. I could detect another aunt's cigarette smoke still hanging in the curtains regardless of the fact she'd gone away to the Air Force a year earlier. The rug smelled of the aftershave that one of my uncles must have spilled there. So I'd asked Ma if she'd let me redecorate, but that was almost two years ago and we still hadn't done it.

So now after missing my birthday, Ma said yes, and this time she promised, and despite seeing how some of her promises had lately fallen victim to crime scenes and witness interrogations that simply had to be done, I believed her. I looked forward to the shopping she said we'd do come the weekend. She said we'd have lunch at the Chick-fil-A Dwarf House afterward, and I was certain we would.

One night that week, Ma was home at a reasonable hour but still working because she was in the dining room. Bridgette and I weren't supposed to bother her there, but we did anyway.

"We're hungry," Bridgette said.

"There's nothing to eat," I added. I enjoyed whining like this when she was home to hear it. If she wasn't home, I'd have gone into the kitchen, looked through the cabinets and refrigerator, and scared something up—an omelet using chopped-up hot dogs and whatever vegetable I could find shriveling in the back of the fridge, a can of pink salmon fried with onions and an egg, served over rice, and if the grocery shopping had really been neglected, Vienna sausages with saltines and mustard. But Ma was home, and I expected her to cook.

"I know there's *something* in there you can eat," she said without looking up from her work.

We just stood there watching her, willing her to pay us some mind.

"All right, we'll figure something out."

Bridgette and I followed her into the kitchen to see what miracle she could perform that we hadn't thought of. While she opened and closed cabinet doors without taking anything from them, Ma said, "I think I might want you two to meet Pete."

Pete was the sailor, and I knew Bridgette had no interest in meeting him because it meant things were getting serious and she already knew she wanted no part of him. I only wanted to meet him to see if he was as cute as Ma made him out to be.

"I think he's getting serious about me. I might have him over for dinner."

I crossed my arms over my chest, and asked, "Shouldn't you do some grocery shopping first?"

Ma gave me the evil eye, so I didn't say anything more.

I decided to sneak a look at Ma's notes when she left them on the table to go pick up the Chinese food order that she'd phoned in. I turned down making the food run with her, but she took Bridgette along. Bridgette was probably grilling her about the boyfriend the whole ride, something she could get away with because she was the baby, but I never could because I was supposed to understand. Them leaving gave me a chance to snoop around in Ma's files, a bad habit I'd taken up since she started on the Task Force. I read notes on the main suspect in her first case.

> *He was still the last person known to have seen the boy alive. He said he took Evans to the bus stop and watched him get on the bus, but we can't find a single person who remembered seeing the boy on the bus. The suspect said he never saw the boy after that because he left town that day for a job in South Georgia and didn't return to Atlanta until January of 1980. He offered as proof a speeding ticket he'd received on his way to his new job on July 26th or 27th, which still doesn't explain away the fact that Evans was seen with him on July 25th—it's only a three-hour drive—he left Atlanta on the 26th. I learned that the job didn't start until November 1979. He had gotten a speeding*

> *ticket, but it was dated November 4th. And as far as his being out of town until January 1980, in the last three weeks of August 1979, he was on a maintenance job in Atlanta. He also was in town to turn himself in on an outstanding rape warrant on December 12, 1979.*

Ma doubted every word out of his mouth. After interrogating him, he changed his story. He had returned to Atlanta four days after Alfred Evans had gone missing, which is when he learned of the boy's disappearance, when his mother asked if he'd seen the boy since the day he'd given him the ride to the bus stop. He also admitted that he had lied about the car he was driving when he gave the boy a ride. It was a Chevy, not a Ford. He didn't buy the Ford until August. Ma told the man his growing list of lies was making him a prime suspect, and he requested a polygraph to prove his innocence.

Just as I was getting to the good part, where Ma began catching the suspect in his lies because she'd had surveillance on the homes of his alibi witnesses, checking out his stories, I heard her car in the driveway, then quickly tried to put her papers where I'd found them.

Ma decided against having the sailor over for dinner, and he took us out instead. She seemed nervous while she got ready, something I rarely saw in my mother. I sat on her bed while she went back and forth to the bathroom mirror, asking me, "Is this too much blush? Is this lipstick too loud?" as though it were a blind date and she'd never met the man before.

"I really hope you like him," she said. "This dress looked a lot better in the dressing room. Maybe I should just wear my tan wrap dress."

"That dress is fine, Ma. If you keep changing, you won't be ready when he gets here." Not that I cared about him having to wait, I just didn't want to have to make small talk with him when he arrived.

Bridgette came into the room, still wearing shorts and a T-shirt. "I'm not feeling good; I don't think I can go, Mommy."

Ma wasn't having the baby routine, and said, "If you don't get in there right now and put some clothes on . . ."

Bridgette became well, understanding the implied threat.

It turned out the sailor was as handsome as Ma said, cute wasn't the right word for him after I saw him wearing that Navy uniform, standing 6'4" if he was an inch, and heard his voice that was nearly as deep as Barry White's. I could see why Ma was acting like a schoolgirl about him, though I didn't approve of it. You would never think she was a cop who made life-and-death decisions for pay. On the way to the restaurant, she let him do all the talking. At dinner, she let him slide out her chair and order our food.

"But I don't want steak," Bridgette complained. "I want spaghetti and meatballs."

"You always want spaghetti. Try something different," Ma said, smiling at the sailor all the while.

He asked Bridgette and me the usual questions: How's school? What are you studying? Are you thinking about college yet, Kim? Our answers were equally uninspired, but we remained civil at least. When the food came, I ate mine because I rarely turn down any food, even if it isn't my first choice. Bridgette picked over hers, only showing some enthusiasm when the sailor asked her what she wanted for dessert.

Other than the sailor's looks, the dinner was unremarkable.

After dinner, he dropped us off at home but wouldn't come inside because *the girls need to get their sleep*. Was he already trying to talk like a father?

"So, what did you think?"

"He was all right." Bridgette and I said the same thing at the same time. Ma looked disappointed there wasn't more.

"Well, you'll have to get to know him more. I think he might ask me to marry him."

How did we go from dinner at the Ponderosa to a marriage proposal? But I didn't ask that. I said, "And where would we live—on his boat?"

"It's not a boat, it's a ship. And, no, we'd be stationed on a base and he'd be there sometimes, and sometimes he'd be at sea."

Bridgette and I weren't buying any of it. We didn't want Ma to marry the sailor, or anyone for that matter. As it was, there wasn't enough of her for the two of us.

"We'd live in Hawaii. Y'all love the beach. We'd live four minutes away instead of four hours."

"What about my school?" I asked, grasping for something that might bring her to her senses.

"You don't even like that school. If it means that much to you, we can see if they have one in Honolulu. They have those same schools in other states, there's probably one in Hawaii."

Bridgette still hadn't said anything, but her lips were poked out a mile.

"And what are you thinking, Miss Bridgette?" Ma asked.

"I'm thinking that food he bought us made me sick." She left us then, and a second later, I heard her bedroom door slam.

Two weeks had come and gone since the weekend Ma and I were supposed to go shopping to redecorate my room. I finally reminded her after seeing that two weeks' worth of pouting and giving her the silent treatment had gone unnoticed.

"Whatever happened to us going shopping for my room?"

"What?" Ma was sitting on her bed filing her nails and listening to the news. I wasn't sure if she was in her news-watching trance or if she really had no idea what I was talking about. But she cleared up my confusion. "Oh, I forgot all about that. That was supposed to be last weekend, right?"

"It was supposed to be two weeks ago." I felt angry not only because making my room *my* room nearly five years too late wasn't the priority for her that it was for me, but she hadn't noticed how cold I'd been to her lately, hadn't even detected my disappointment.

"Look, I won't be able to get to it this weekend either. Hand me my purse over there." I passed it to her, noticing from the weight of it that she hadn't taken her gun out like she usually did when she got home from work. So many of her routines no longer were. "Here's fifty dollars. You can buy yourself a nice comforter set with that."

"What about paint? I don't know anything about buying paint. Plus, that'll be too heavy to carry home on the bus."

"We'll figure it out." She said that all the time now, but *we* rarely did anymore. Mostly I figured it out.

I ended up taking Bridgette along with me to the mall to buy new bedding—a reversible blue/green comforter with sheets and a dust ruffle in a floral pattern that was far more frilly than my usual tastes, but it was on sale. I used my own money to buy an extra set of sheets to make curtains from, courtesy of sewing lessons from the Singer store at the Greenbriar Mall that Ma enrolled me in when I was eleven. She was big into me being well-rounded and was always making me take lessons of some kind—sewing, art, music, judo (this last one I believed was more for Ma than me, because she was interested in the instructor at the time).

She learned this from Grandma, who made Ma do the same thing when she was a girl. I understood Grandma's reasons; she was from the old school, raising her daughters at a time when the goal was to marry as well as possible, though for a black woman back then, marrying well didn't mean she wouldn't have to work. It only meant she wouldn't have to work as hard. I wasn't sure what Ma was grooming me for because she'd told me she didn't buy into the idea that a man was necessary to live a life (though I was never sure she truly believed this). I always figured it was a way to keep me busy on weekends while she worked extra jobs and Bridgette stayed with a babysitter or at a neighbor's house. Bridgette escaped the weekend sewing classes and etiquette training because just as she was getting old enough to start becoming well-rounded, kids began dying, and Ma was taken up with those kids instead.

"You think I can buy a decent-looking purse with three dollars?" Bridgette asked.

"Probably not. What do you need a purse for, anyway? You have a book bag."

"What about when I'm not going to school?"

She had a point. I tried to remember when I got my first real purse, one without cartoon characters on it and made of something other than pink vinyl. I supposed eleven was a good age to start carrying a purse, though I wondered what she'd put in it.

"Well, maybe you can get an okay-looking purse with a little more. I'll loan you a five."

Bridgette found a small white canvas purse with a red pleather strap for five dollars because it was out of season. I pointed that out to her, but she didn't care about the no-white-after-Labor Day rule. She loved that purse immediately. I let her keep the rest of the money, which she used to buy a wallet that opened and closed noisily with Velcro, some strawberry-flavored lip gloss in a tiny bottle with a rolling ball applicator, and some Tic Tacs. The lip gloss she applied everywhere but her lips from what I could see. She thought she was grown.

Before we left the mall, we ate lunch in the food court instead of at the Dwarf House, and it was an unworthy substitute. Instead of a cute and colorful house that, from the outside anyway, could have been taken from a Grimm fairy tale, we ate from plastic trays amid screaming kids and worn-out, yelling mothers, neither of whom could drown out the too-loud elevator music raining down on us from speakers in the ceiling tiles. By the time we started the walk to the bus stop, Bridgette and I were both tired from me going store to store looking for the best deal to make the most of the money Ma had given me.

The comforter set was light but bulky, so it was still an awkward package for transport on the bus. I had to share a seat with it, requiring Bridgette to sit alone in the seat in front of me, something I never liked her to do in case some freak sat beside her. I made her sit in the outside seat, which was one way to make people walk past you in search of another seat. When the bus got too crowded to take up two seats, and a man asked Bridgette to move over, I pushed the comforter into the seat beside her and told the man to take the seat next to me. The bus continued toward home while I watched Bridgette's head occasionally bob in a myoclonic jerk. I wondered how it could be that I was eleven, same age as Bridgette was now, when I started taking the city bus myself.

That night, Ma came home with a can of paint in a shade of blue that was closer to her favorite color than mine, which was emerald green and not blue at all. But it still matched the bedding I'd picked out, and the following weekend, she was able to help me paint one wall before she was called away by some captain or lieutenant who claimed it was urgent.

Chapter 21

A couple of months passed between disappearances. Maybe the killer took the holidays off, which always made me wonder if he wasn't a regular family man with kids at home himself, who had to work extra hours to cover the Christmas bills, who was affected by the holiday spirit the way most sane people were. An almost-regular man who had some kind of crazy hatred of black boys. Maybe the cold kept kids off the streets, making them more difficult to steal away, but it was just like the winter before when we had a four-month break in the killings. Unlike last winter, there wasn't the hopeful feeling that it was all over. People knew not to get excited just because it was the new year and the last child went missing in mid-November.

Sure enough, the killer justified keeping our guard up. Three days into 1981, fourteen-year-old Lubie Geter went missing from the Stewart-Lakewood Shopping Center in Southwest. When he wasn't found in the next couple of days, the city went through the played-out routine of suggesting there was hope he was alive, even though by now most folks didn't expect as much. A Missing Child flier went out showing his picture, looking for all the world like a boy I might know. He was just a regular boy like all the others, trying to hustle a few dimes by selling Zep Gel car deodorizer in front of the shopping center.

* * *

When I walked through the doors of the Task Force, the place was jumping. Something about the latest disappearance seemed to mobilize the community more than the others. Maybe it was because the boy was the first to go missing after a two-month break. Maybe people realized we were starting yet another year with the killer still loose. It seemed half of Atlanta had a tip to share on the latest abduction, because the desks just inside the front doors were full. The building sat close to the street, and everyone knew it was the home of the Task Force, which meant everyone and their mother was able to walk in and share premonitions, eyewitness accounts, what they saw in a dream last night, and psychic revelations.

The desks in the front were manned by recruits, trained by the detectives to do triage of the tipsters, separating the "probables" and "maybes" from the just plain crazies. The first two groups would get a chance to tell their story to a detective, while the crazies were told "thank you very kindly for your help," and sent on their way. That day, it appeared the recruits were outnumbered by the people sitting in chairs and leaning against the walls, waiting for their chance to help catch the killer.

I headed toward Ma's desk, weaving through the people, watching the eagerness on their faces to tell what they knew and feeling the energy of people charged with new hope and fresh anger. When I found Ma at her desk, I wanted to ask if something new had happened to bring people in, but I knew better than to discuss the case while she was at work. She looked up at me, surprised.

"I didn't know you were coming in today."

"I hadn't planned to, but I had to stay late in the library, and I-85 was a mess so the bus was late getting into town. Now it's almost dark."

The latest rule from Ma was that I couldn't take the bus home if it meant I'd be walking the half mile from the bus stop in the dark. In the short days of the winter months, that meant I usually spent an evening a week hanging around the Task Force waiting for Ma, depending on what time I left school. Almost daily, there was a new rule meant to keep us safe, though we knew by then that staying safe was really just a matter of gender, luck, and timing.

"Well, it'll be another hour at least; I've got an interview in a few minutes. I asked a detective working a lead up north to swing by and pick up Bridgette from latchkey. You can make sure she stays out of trouble if I'm still in the interview when she gets here."

"All right," I said, sounding put-upon, but really I didn't mind. Now I'd have someone to kill time with while Ma did the interview that would last at least an hour longer than she said it would.

"You hungry?"

"A little."

"Well, go and ask Sid if he'll pick something up for you. I heard him say he was going out for some dinner in a minute. And order something for Bridgette too."

"It'll be cold by the time she gets here."

"It'll be food when she gets here. There's no telling how long my interview will go. We might not get home until late."

That I knew for sure, so I went looking for Sid to put in a food order after Ma gave me a ten-dollar bill. I was glad he was going to Church's because cold chicken was just as tasty as hot, and that way I could wait and eat dinner with Bridgette. After talking to Sid, I returned to Ma's desk and pulled out my copy of *Catcher in the Rye,* required reading that I would have read without being told. The sounds around me had become background noise—the clicking of reports being typed, Ma's end of a telephone conversation, leather-soled and high-heeled footsteps, and last names spoken all around me because the cops rarely used first names. Except Ma, who sometimes called her partner Sid by his first name. Once in a while, Sid called Ma *Chevonne* instead of Yvonne, but I never knew the story behind that. She called everyone else by their last names, and the other cops called her Fuller.

A woman's scream pulled me away from Holden Caulfield's world with a shock, and the volume of the background noise was turned up loudly in my ears, but it seemed nothing else had changed in the building. Ma looked up but continued on with her phone call. The detectives at nearby desks stayed in their seats. At the front of the building, I saw a couple of uniforms talking to a woman who, from my vantage point, looked insane—her arms flailing in some kind of fit, her unkempt hair going every which way, her voice shrieking nonsense. They sat her down in a chair, and a few minutes later, led her out of the building.

When Ma got off the phone, I asked, "Did you hear that woman scream?"

"Yeah, I heard it." She was writing on a yellow legal pad, I assumed notes from her phone call.

"What do you think was wrong with her?"

"Who knows. We get all kinds of madness in here."

"Is she a victim's mother?"

"No, the families are sometimes the calmest of all the people who come in. I think they've made peace with their loss, even if they haven't made peace with us."

"They took her away."

"Probably had to call the paddy wagon for her." Ma looked up then, because she knew how I was. "Nothing to worry about. Wherever they took her is probably where she needs to be."

A recruit appeared at the desk, telling Ma that her six o'clock was waiting. Ma said okay, and a few minutes later, I saw the recruit leading a woman toward the same conference room Ma had gone into. I wondered if she was a victim's mother, and if I'd be sneaking a look at the transcripts of Ma's interview with her weeks from now. Sid returned with the food, and when I told him Ma had gone into the conference room, he went in that direction. I wondered who would play the good cop, and hoped that if the woman was a mother, they'd be kind, whether they thought she was suspicious or not. But the woman could have been anyone—a suspect's girlfriend, a landlady who had seen something shady, a victim's math teacher.

When Bridgette showed up, I asked her the questions that Ma would have asked if she wasn't in the interrogation room: How was school? Did your presentation on reptiles and mammals go okay? Are you hungry?

I left the desk for a minute to buy two cans of soda from the machine with change from Ma's pencil cup, Sprite for Bridgette and Coke for me. I spread napkins out on Ma's desk as place mats, found the paper plates she kept in her desk drawer, and began dishing out the food.

"I can fix my own plate."

"You have to eat a piece of corn and a little cole slaw. You can't make a meal of just chicken and biscuits. And slow down, the food isn't going anywhere."

After we'd taken the first bites of chicken and sips of soda, I became Bridgette's sister again, and told her all about the screaming woman who had to be taken away in the paddy wagon.

At school, my Winds and Weather class was standing around outside, supposedly studying cloud formations but mostly wishing we'd thought to wear our coats because our blazers weren't enough against the cold of January. The school was built on pillars to create a covered, outdoor walkway linking buildings on the campus. When the wind blew through the arcade, it felt even colder. People not from the South don't imagine it gets very cold, but Atlanta just missed being the southern end of the Appalachian Trail, sitting nine hundred feet above sea level. Factor in humidity and forty degrees can seem closer to thirty, making you wish you'd worn a coat outside over your school blazer. I was trying to remember the difference between a cumulus cloud and a cirrus when some boys standing nearby began telling jokes. They huddled together the ways boys do, as if what they were saying was something all the world would want to hear but shouldn't. Soon, one boy's voice got louder, and it was clear I was intended to hear this joke.

"Yeah, I was watching TV last night, and this one guy told a hilarious joke. I can't remember exactly how he said it, but he was wondering how black people know when their asses are clean after taking a crap. You know, because it's the same color as their skin."

The other boys laughed because the boy telling the joke was popular, the kind who wore his letter jacket everywhere and no matter the season, and because I was standing in earshot. For teenage boys, a joke is always better when it has a victim.

I called him an idiot but nothing more. I was tough with a girl on a badminton court, but a group of racist boys scared me. I wondered if I went to the principal with it, which of us would get the demerit. My experience told me I'd come out on the short end, so I tried to bury what they said with all the other things I'd heard in the halls, on the quad, in the arcade. He *was* an idiot, as if my skin came off with the tissue. Did his come off when he wiped his ass? How did they let such an idiot into this school, because I was certain he'd made the joke up, that it wasn't something he'd heard on TV. Imbecilic as it was, the point had been made. He was comparing me to shit.

The boy last seen selling the car deodorizer at the Stewart-Lakewood Shopping Center had been missing nearly a week. On the fifth day, the sheriff of Rockdale County—officially considered part of the metro area but what I considered the country, namely, because I'd never been there before—got a call from an unidentified white man claiming responsibility for all the murders and giving a location on Sigman Road where the latest boy could be found. The man sounded believable enough for the Task Force to conduct a search, although at that point, the Task Force was following up on leads that sounded implausible, too, no one wanting to be the detective who missed the lead that would turn out to be *the* lead. The amount of wasted time and work generated by tips provided by the well-meaning, the crazy, and the just plain evil were enough to make even a cop with the patience of Job a little upset.

Ma didn't have anywhere near the patience of Job, so when she got the call to go on another search the following day, she said, "I don't know how much longer I can do this—having hope, losing hope, looking for alive kids and finding them dead." But she went anyway because she had no choice; no one did until the killer was found.

She told me that evening, after the day had worn her down and she'd come home to sleep it off, that the Task Force decided to concentrate its search in the area where the boy was last seen, and amassed a search team of nearly 275 patrol officers, detectives, and FBI agents. They were still feeling the sting of being called inept after the girl was found dead by a citizen search party, and the Task Force wanted to make certain there would be no repeat. Nearly everyone in town who wasn't working the case, and therefore didn't know any better, had an opinion on whether the Task Force knew what they were doing.

On a Friday morning that was a bit cooler than usual, and felt cooler still because the humidity always hangs in the Georgia air regardless of the temperature, an army of cops fanned out across the search area lined up like ants, backtracking each other's paths so as not to miss a clue. Ma was one of them, her feet crunching over dry leaves and pine needles the color of brown paper bags, searching for something she hoped and hoped not to find.

After four hours of searching, they found the skeletal remains of a small child in a wooded area off Redwine Road. The search team then began a tighter search, combing the area for clues to how and when the child was killed. They were surprised to find a second set of bones. Neither set was the child they were looking for, who had only been missing six days while the two bodies found had been out there a long time. Ma said the thing that stayed in her mind the most when she saw each of the bodies was how their size made it clear that they were only children. Everyone knew right away, and after they had their own private moment of grief like cops do sometimes, so quick the rest of us wouldn't even notice it, they became hardened detectives again and got to work on the crime scene.

It was clear that a killer was using the area as a dumping ground, much like he had around Niskey Lake when the murders began. The area around Redwine Road where the latest two bodies had been found was also where the third victim was found back in November of 1979. The discovery of these bodies only cemented the belief that the seventeen murders committed to this point were for the most part committed by the same killer, or someone was copying the first killer's MO, leaving bodies in places the original killer left bodies a year and a half earlier.

The following day, the search continued because the victim they'd set out to find had not been found. As of early January, there were five children on the list still considered missing, including the boy who was trying to make a little change selling car deodorizers. A week later, the medical examiner would identify the two bodies: one was Christopher Richardson, the first of three kids to go missing in June 1980; and the other was Earl Terrell, who had disappeared at the end of the following month.

Chapter 22

Ma seemed to be going further into her own world as she pressed harder into the investigation of her two assigned cases, paying less attention to us when she was home, even paying less attention to herself. Unless she had a date with the sailor, her hair was always just thrown into a ponytail as she ran out the door, and her nails went unpolished. And it seemed that since that dinner at the Ponderosa, the dates had fallen off and she no longer broke into the spontaneous smiles that gave away when she was thinking of him.

Even though it made them unpopular with victims' parents and their groups, Ma and Sid continued to watch, interview, and check the stories of the parents in the Wilson case. They were still convinced that the MO on the case was too dissimilar from the others. The night the girl disappeared, a neighbor corroborated the parents' story, saying she'd seen a man come out of the window holding the limp and sleeping girl in his arms, accompanied by another man. Both men were black. But another neighbor said she'd seen the victim and her brothers and sister go in and out of the same window that night. The neighbor said the kids used the window as a door all the time, and that she'd spoken to the mother several times about it, but was ignored. According to the neighbor, the children were often left alone while the parents went out at night, and her son had told her he'd heard screams coming from the apartment in the early morning hours before the girl was reported missing. So the parents were still suspects.

Ma repeatedly read her notes from her interview with the parents of what happened that night, hoping to find some inconsistency: The parents and the girls spend the afternoon at the West End Mall. Get back home around 8:00 P.M. and have tuna sandwiches for dinner. Mother's cousin had two of her boys for the day, and was surprised he hadn't brought them home yet since it was now 8:30 P.M. Mother wants to go downtown to the Rialto to see a movie; father isn't interested. Father drives mother to the MARTA station around 9:00 P.M., taking the girls along for the ride, and she gets on the train alone. She left the movie at 12:15 A.M.; husband meets her at the train station for a ride home. Oldest boy is outside playing—*why is a child outside playing at one in the morning?*—she checks on the other kids and finds the two younger boys and the two girls are asleep in their beds. Parents go to sleep about 1:30. Mother wakes up at 6:00 A.M. and finds the girl missing. *Somewhere in here I'm going to find inconsistencies.*

Ma wondered if maybe the mother, who admitted she'd had to whip the kids a couple of evenings earlier in the week because they'd been acting up, had been angry about something and took it out on her kids. Ma knew how that could happen, having done it to her own kids once or twice, like the time I was seven and she sent me to the corner for the evening paper because she'd lost her job that day and needed the latest want ads. But I came home with the morning paper, and she whipped me—not because I'd gotten the wrong paper but because she'd been fired. So she knew from experience how it could happen.

In an interview taken five months after the girl disappeared, Ma asked the mother about the movies again, and why the husband didn't go.

Mother: What I had planned to do was get (my oldest son) to keep all the kids while (my husband) went to the movies with me. I don't think he wanted to go to the movies anyway, because he was tired. He had worked all week, he was saying. I said I sure do want to go and see the movies. I just be wanting to get out of the house some. I don't go to places very much. I don't care for clubs. Only place that I go mostly is to the movies. If I do go to the club, me and my husband go together.

Ma: Wasn't it your birthday? Did you just have a birthday?

Mother: That Sunday when my daughter was missing it was my birthday.

Ma: You wanted (your husband) to go with you to celebrate your birthday?

Mother: Yes, that Sunday. We were going to go out that Sunday, my birthday wasn't until that Sunday. I had been wanting to go out for a good little while and I said that Sunday he was going to take me out to get a drink. I don't really drink. Just go out every once and a while to have a mixed drink. When I got up, she was missing. I didn't even get a chance to celebrate my birthday.

Ma: Hers was that Monday.

Mother: Didn't get a chance to celebrate hers either. I had planned to take her down to the Omni so that she could play in the game room, eat a ice cream cone, eat at McDonald's, and do different things. I was planning on taking them all to the Omni . . .

All Ma's hard work, and the work of everyone on the Task Force, still didn't keep the killer from killing. The third week of January saw the murder of a boy who was just a couple of months older than I. Last time anyone saw Terry Pue, he was getting off a bus on his way to watch a basketball game. His mother didn't report him missing until she heard the description on the radio of a dead child who had been found the following day in Rockdale County off Sigman Road. The boy's body lay just a mile from where the unidentified white male caller had told the sheriff where Lubie Geter could be found. Police didn't find that boy when the first search was done, and didn't find him when the latest discovery prompted another search of the area. But now the Task Force had good reason to believe the unidentified caller wasn't just another crazy person claiming responsibility.

The boy's mother must have wondered whether it was her child or not since he was found in a county that was nearly all white and twenty-five miles from where he lived. But when she heard the description of the dead child's clothing, she knew it was her son. He was wearing a blue jacket with the word *KIM* on the back. Because I was Ma's child and was forever looking for signs in everything, I wondered what KIM was—a designer, a girlfriend, an acronym—and whether it was an omen I should heed.

It was strange to me that his mother waited until she heard the radio news before she reported him missing. How could it be that after a year and a half of murders, parents would still wait to report a missing child? My friends knew they couldn't be late getting home from anywhere, and if they were going to be, they'd better call home and let someone know about it, because parents were ready to call the Task Force if a child was just a few minutes late showing up wherever they were meant to be. If a parent couldn't escort a child personally, they'd take him as close to the destination as possible, then arranged for their child or some adult on the other end to confirm that he'd arrived.

So when I heard that this mother had waited until the following day to report her child missing, and then only after she heard his description on the radio, I wondered what could make her wait so long. When I found out she had eleven other children at home, I thought maybe it was just too hard to keep up with them since Ma had a hard time trying to spread herself around with just two. Maybe she thought it wouldn't happen to her kids even while she watched some mother on the evening news saying, "Why? Why my child?" as if they too believed it could never happen to their child. I also wondered if the grief in that family's home, with so many people to mourn for the dead boy, was more than their house could hold.

"Didn't Ma say she didn't want you messing around with that?"

"She won't know if she isn't here to see it, and if you don't tell. You owe me one, remember."

I was heating wax on the stove, getting ready to batik some cloth, a craft I learned during a Cleveland summer. The last time I batiked, I got hot wax everywhere, melted crayons and paraffin that hardened on the countertops and floor that took forever to clean up. After that, Ma told me not to do it again. Most times I did what she told me unless I was absolutely certain I could get away with it. It was early morning when she left for work, and I knew she wouldn't be back until late, giving me plenty of cleanup time. Besides, as much as she was away lately, I felt like I ran the house.

I left the wax heating on the stove to go dig through my closet for the cloth I planned to use, which must have taken longer than I'd expected because I still hadn't found it when I heard Bridgette scream my name. I ran to the kitchen to find the pot of hot wax on fire. Bridgette was holding a pot of water, and before I could stop her, she threw it on the flames, which only angered them.

"Get out, get out," I yelled at Bridgette.

"Call the fire department!"

"Just get out, in the yard." I gagged on the smoke that yelling at Bridgette made me inhale in gulps.

The flames were still contained over the stove, and I was

afraid to call for help, afraid Ma would kill me if she found out a fire truck had been to the house. I threw dish towels over the flames, then ran to the pantry where we kept big boxes of baking soda, our poor man's substitute for raising alkalinity in the pool water. I ripped open box after box of soda and threw it at the fire, certain it would never work before I ran out of soda and that I'd have to call the operator. But I started getting the better of it by the second box, and had put it out by the fifth.

I realized then that Bridgette had never gone into the yard as I'd told her, and had watched me from the front door.

"Why didn't you leave?" I yelled, my fear and frustration misdirected.

"You might have needed my help."

I looked at the mess on the stove—the ruined pot, the blackened hood, and singed cabinets—and I began to cry. The tears were probably long overdue from so many other things, but there was something fresh in them too. Fresh guilt because I was the responsible one and could have killed Bridgette and burned down the house. Fresh fear because although Ma hadn't whipped me in a long time, I remembered well when she did, could feel the sting on my thighs and the red warmth spread across my skin. And I never knew what mood she'd be in anymore; it didn't take much for Ma to get mad lately. So I cried while I filled a cardboard box with the ruined pot and wax pens, and while I buried the box at the bottom of the Herbie Curbie trash can. I was still crying, low and quiet, while Bridgette swept baking soda from the floor and I opened every window in the house, trying to get rid of the smell.

We worked for hours to scrape up hardened wax, but there was nothing to be done about the stove hood and cabinets. When I heard Ma's car pull into the driveway, I readied myself to take whatever came. Bridgette waited in the kitchen with me, and together we listened to her key turn in the lock, the door open, her first words.

"What the hell . . ."

Before I could say anything, Bridgette ran to her. "Don't be mad, Ma. All I tried to do was cook some fries and the grease caught on fire."

"Are you all right?" Ma's anger abated to worry.

"I'm okay. I remembered what you said about putting baking soda on a fire."

"That was smart." She turned to me. "And where were you? You know better than to let this girl near hot grease. Why didn't you cook the fries?"

I was about to explain that there weren't any fries, but Bridgette stopped me. "She was studying in her room, so she didn't know until the fire started."

Ma went into cop mode then, beginning to question the story. She looked at the singed cabinets, opening them as if the truth lay inside. Would she notice the oil can still full or the unopened bag of fries in the freezer? But those clues would be useless to her because she hadn't cooked much lately. Could she smell burned wax in the air?

"All this from a little grease fire? The flames must have gone pretty high. Why didn't you call the fire department? And how long did it take you to realize the house was damn near on fire?" These questions were for me.

"I threw water on it before I remembered about the baking soda," Bridgette said.

"Good Lord. Can I not leave y'all here alone anymore? Isn't it enough I have to worry whether you made it home okay, now I got to worry about you once you get home? Kim, I'm holding you responsible for this; you're the oldest."

Usually I hated hearing that line, but in this case, she was right. I deserved whatever I'd get, and I knew how bad it would have been if not for Bridgette taking the rap.

Ma took a beer from the refrigerator. "If it's not one thing, it's another. I'll think of something good for you, but for now, you don't leave this house except for school and work.

And don't think you're getting off either, Miss Bridgette. You know better too."

When she left the kitchen to put away her gun and change out of her clothes, I knew the worst of it was over. She wasn't going to resurrect the whipping belt.

"Why'd you do that?" I asked Bridgette, grateful for once that she was still treated like the baby.

"Because she would have given you the belt. And I owed you. Now I'm paid up for a long time."

A few days later, Ma told us she'd quit night school. She said it was so she could be home one more evening a week, giving us fewer opportunities to burn down the house and more together time. But I knew that extra evening would just be spent looking at case files. She was letting go of her old life, the person she was before the Task Force, a piece at a time.

Ma told me about an interview she had with a boy who was trying to thumb a ride the summer before. Someone stopped for him, and the boy got into the car because he recognized the man behind the wheel as a gypsy taxi driver who hung around the A&P in the West End. The boy sometimes delivered groceries to cars for tips at the same A&P, as did the victim in Ma's first case. When the boy reached the place he wanted to go, he asked the man to let him out, but the driver wouldn't stop the car. The kid asked again and again to be let out, but the driver wouldn't say so much as boo to him and kept right on driving. The boy got scared and jumped from the car when it slowed down enough. He was afraid the man would come back for him, but he never did.

Ma went to check out the boy's story with the manager of the A&P and confirmed what she could, the part about the gypsy taxi driver. In the summer of 1980, sure enough he'd hung out in the parking lot selling rides to people loaded down with groceries looking for a lift home. The manager didn't know the man's name, but he hadn't seen him since last summer because he'd had to run him off for stealing groceries from his store. The manager didn't remember much about the driver, other than him being a little strange, soft spoken, and mild-mannered. And black.

This last description was the one that stuck with me. I knew that Ma and the cops were looking at everyone, had to look at everyone, but like so many other black folks in town, I believed in my heart it was a white man doing the killing. Especially after the Sigman Road caller. Even without all the scientific talk I'd overheard at the Task Force and on the news about most serial killers being white men, it just never really flew with me that a black person would do this to so many of his own, especially children.

I'd long ago let go of the silly idea of a hooded Klansman coming down from Stone Mountain, or driving in from Douglas County and going unnoticed cruising through all-black neighborhoods picking kids off, but I still believed it was a Klansman. The quiet type who didn't wear his affiliation where you could see it. The dangerous kind no one paid much attention to when he drove utility trucks into black neighborhoods, delivered mail, painted project apartments. I suspected the smarter breed of racists, the closet racists I later learned to detect as an adult, those who worked next to me every day, smiling and asking about my weekend, all the while wishing I worked somewhere else.

One day after school I was waiting at the bus stop wondering if the creek that bordered the school was going to flood its banks again and turn the soccer field into a marsh, which always happened after a good rain. A man drove past slowly, looking at me hard as if he knew me, but we both knew he didn't. He was white and not one of the teachers from school, so I knew we didn't know one another. But I wasn't afraid of him or the way he slowed when he drove past me, not the way I was afraid of the black man on my street who'd done the same slow drive-by. For one thing, the man on my street didn't scare me until he came back around again, because I thought he was just making some play on the first pass, the way men do when they call to a girl from passing cars: *What's up, shorty?* or *Hey, slim*. And in the moment I saw that man's car crest the hill to make the second pass, I thought of the killer and how his victims didn't live so far from me.

But the killer didn't come out to this part of town; it was far away from his hunting ground. If the killer was black, he'd be an easy mark around here. And if he was white, he'd know black kids who needed to hustle for the day's dinner and were willing to get into a stranger's car were scarce in Ashford-Dunwoody. I knew right off that this man was watching me because he wondered what I was doing in his neighborhood where the only black folks were gardeners and twice-a-week maids. I knew he'd move on once he took in my uniform and realized I was no menace, just buying a piece of his world for eight hours of the day. He'd notice the fact that I was standing at the bus stop on the side of the street that took me away from his neighborhood and not farther in. Then he'd speed up and drive on. And I was right, because that's just what he did.

In late January, Ma told me that the Task Force was going to be doing surveillance of certain shopping centers around Atlanta, looking for cars driven by black men with black boys riding with them, or being picked up by them.

"I thought the killer was a white man. What about the white man that claimed he killed that boy in Rockdale County?" I asked. Had my guard been up against the wrong people all this time?

"That didn't turn up anything concrete, but we're still looking into it. We have enough witnesses who last saw the boys alive in the company of a young black man."

"Can you believe these witnesses?"

"Right now, it's all we've got."

The shopping centers to be watched were places where some of the boys had disappeared from, or visited, or tried to make a little money at, or had been found dead. There were several victims who fit into one of these categories, and just as many shopping centers. These were run-down strip malls with vendors providing services and selling products that the people in the neighborhood needed: grocery stores that took food stamps and WIC coupons; beauty supplies so a relaxer and manicure could be done on the cheap in the kitchen instead of the beauty salon; payday check cashing and money orders, both of which lessened the sting from the difficulty of opening a checking account when you never had enough for the minimum required deposit, or because the only jobs you could get didn't last long enough to create an employment history. Ma told me the place on Moreland Avenue where I bought my hair supplies was on the list, and now I couldn't go anymore unless she was with me. I knew that meant I'd never be going to any of the places on the list because Ma and I hardly went anywhere together anymore. It seemed she never had time.

On top of watching boys in front of shopping centers, the Task Force enlisted the help of boys who fit the victim profile, using them as decoys at the shopping centers in an attempt to catch the killer while surveillance officers sat in cars watching the boys just a few feet away. This stirred up all kinds of controversy among citizens and police alike, and so didn't last very long. The mayor also made the curfew from the previous fall permanent on the first day of February. He may have had good intentions, but in the few months the curfew had been in place, it still hadn't stopped the killer. Five more children had either been killed or abducted. We kids figured it didn't matter whether we were off the streets by dark or not. If the killer really wanted to get us, the curfew wasn't going to stop him, even in broad daylight.

Chapter 23

Even though the list of things I hated about my school seemed to grow daily, I couldn't deny there were some things about it I'd come to like, things I'd never experienced if I'd gone to school in my neighborhood. They were small things, but still changed some of my perceptions: an appreciation of music I'd never bothered to listen to because it was supposed to hold no interest for me; the realization that rich white people had problems, too, although they didn't always look like mine.

Some of this discovery frightened me, made me wonder if I hadn't crossed over as some friends had suggested I might. As a direct result of going to the school in the suburbs—at least this is what I blamed it on because I could find no other reason that made any sense—I found myself with a crush on a white boy. When I started going to the school, Ma would say in a teasing way that made it clear she wasn't playing around, "Don't come home with a white boy. There's nothing but trouble and heartache in that." I was told by older women in my family that white men were blue-eyed devils and didn't mean me anything but harm in the end, no matter what sweet things they said. As a young girl, I didn't pick up on the conviction they used in giving me this advice, a nuance I later decided must have come from some firsthand experience, some firsthand hurt. Ma warned me about the white boys' underhanded ways, collectively, even though we'd once had a white woman as a roommate before Ma was a cop, a friend of my aunt's who needed a place to stay for a few months and ended up becoming Ma's friend too. When I reminded her of this, Ma said that was different—she was a woman.

That must explain why I played it safe and had my first crush on a white boy I had no chance of ever meeting, although I gave it a good try. The guinea pig for my cross-cultural adventure was Jimmy Baio from *Soap,* a TV show I loved, which I also blamed on the influence of my white friends. Before knowing them, I'd never have considered watching a TV show about rich white people with a black butler and ridiculous problems that black folks didn't have time for because we were busy just trying to get by. But I gave *Soap* a try because even though *Good Times* was one of my favorite shows (finally, a show about *us* I thought when it first aired), I had to admit if only to myself that sometimes it was just depressing. Sometimes it's enough knowing in real life that your family is just one paycheck between having a warm bed, lights on, phone working, and food on the table and not having those things. Sometimes it's too much watching another family going through the same worry on TV.

I'd read that Jimmy Baio was staying in a hotel downtown. Sitting in my health class, I imagined him inviting me to dinner in a fancy restaurant that Ma could never afford. My fantasy had me pointing out which buildings made up the Atlanta skyline since I knew downtown like it was my second neighborhood. He'd take me up on my offer to show him the city the next day. He'd be happy to join me in my first-time skipping of school. He'd help me explain it all to Ma when the school called to say I'd cut class. I'd ask him if I was his first black girlfriend.

I made up some illness to get me out of my last two classes and took an earlier bus downtown. My plan was to stake out the hotel lobby and wait for him to walk by. What I'd do then I wasn't sure. When I visited the hotel that time with Ma, I didn't feel out of place. I never felt out of place anywhere with Ma because she could make it seem like we owned wherever we were, were born simply to be there, no matter how inhospitable. Walking around the hotel lobby alone, I felt like I was being watched. *What's she doing here?* I imagined the front desk clerks wondering. When I walked past the concierge desk, I was glad I'd learned the word in my French class, in the chapter where the American girl takes a trip to Paris. Speaking a little French made me feel less like an intruder.

When I finally settled on a leather sofa with a view of both the front doors and the elevators, I made a big production of taking off my coat. I wanted the concierge and the front desk clerks to see my plaid, private-school skirt. I hoped the distance blurred the cheapness of my jacket but gave them a good view of the fancy crest on the pocket. Yes, I was a fifteen-year-old black girl sitting in a fancy hotel lobby where the only other black folks I saw were opening the front doors and pushing luggage around on carts, but I belonged here. See my uniform? Here is the proof that for at least eight hours a day, we travel in the same circle.

I studied the elevator doors, not only looking for Jimmy Baio but also hoping it would provide an explanation for my presence, that I was waiting to meet a friend, someone with no concept of time who was willing to make me wait for hours. Each time the doors opened, I hoped I appeared expectant to the hotel staff, because I was. There was a shift change during my wait, for which I was grateful. For all the second shift knew I'd arrived in the lobby just minutes before they had.

To pass the time during my elevator watch, I imagined what my life would be like with Jimmy Baio. When we went to fancy places like this, no one would question whether I belonged. Shopping trips to Lenox Square would end with me buying more than a pair of socks. When he introduced me to his parents, they'd say, "Oh, Jimmy, she's so *articulate,*" and I'd have to pretend I took it as a compliment and not an insult. In time, I'd get used to the incongruity of pale white skin against warm brown when we held hands. But I wouldn't have to worry about him being caught by the killer.

At school, I'd become instantly popular. The whole time the other popular kids smiled in my face, they'd be asking themselves why Jimmy Baio chose me. The girls would toss their corn-silk hair and smile at him, then at me, and wonder what he saw in me with my kinky hair. Some of the racist kids would probably be thinking *nigger-lover* while asking him for his autograph. When he left my side to talk to a group of boys (only briefly because he couldn't stand to be away from me for too long), one might ask him what it's like to be with a black girl, because they'd heard how easy we were, how wild in bed, and *is it true?* The minute Jimmy told me that it wasn't going to work out, him living in Hollywood and me in Atlanta, the popular kids would forget about me. I'd go back to being part of the group no one invited to parties, and I'd be even more of a mystery to them than before.

At home, people would change the way they talked around Jimmy and me. They'd start talking "proper English" the way some black folks will do instinctively around white people because they already think we're illiterate, and why give them any more reason? I'd have to stop calling Keds tennis shoes "White Girls," which is what all my friends called them even though we wore them too. At Thanksgiving dinner, I'd have to explain to him that chitlins are pig intestines, but they're so tasty, especially when sprinkled with a little hot sauce. When some crazy news story came on TV about people in England jumping off bridges while attached to a bungee cord, or a parachute failing to open when someone jumped from an airplane, we'd have to stop saying, "Only white people."

Because they didn't watch *Soap* either, I'd have to tell my friends who Jimmy was, that he was a celebrity. They wouldn't be impressed until I explained he was the cousin of the boy who played Chachi on *Happy Days;* even then, only mildly so. I imagined trying to join a pickup basketball game with Jimmy in tow. To be polite, David might choose him for his team, but would wonder what I was doing with a white boy. Since I was going to that fancy private school, was I no longer interested in black boys? One of my girlfriends would ask me how rich he was. He must be rich, or why else bother with him? Another would ask what we talk about, "Do you have anything in common?" Cassandra would say, "I knew this was going to happen." Ma would say, "Nothing but trouble in that." And Grandma would add, "And misery too."

I hung out in that lobby for hours, not noticing I'd missed the last bus from downtown to my house. When I finally gave up on ever meeting Jimmy Baio, it was dark, cold, and I didn't have cab fare. I probably never even considered a cab then, having never been in one and certain I'd never seen one go down my street. All I could think to do was run like crazy to the Task Force and hope Ma was working late like always. The nine or ten blocks gave me time to make up some lie about why I missed my bus. I don't much remember the lie or Ma's reaction, or even the disappointment of missing Jimmy Baio. Even though it was just a fantasy, I realized dating him would have been too much work. Trying to manage him within my two worlds likely would have brought nothing but trouble and misery, just as I'd been warned.

Most things about my home life I didn't share with school friends, including the dead boy found on my street, even though dreams of him still kept me up an hour or more each night. I wasn't proud of the reason I'd never told, but it didn't keep me from thinking it just the same. Though I never expected it to really happen, I always left open the possibility that I'd one day introduce my school friends to my other life, when I got to know them well enough to bring my two lives together, if only for a short time. But I knew that they'd never leave the comfort of the suburbs to come hang out with me on a street where nine-year-old boys were dropped over bridge railings like nothing, even if I was dating Jimmy Baio.

* * *

When I told my friends at work I wasn't going to a black college because the business world was white and there was no sense in putting off that fact for four years, they said I'd turned. I never believed this for a second, but just being suspected of it hurt. First, my friends made comments about how my speech had changed, how I "talked white." No, I talk right, was my response and all the rational conversations I had with myself about it didn't keep what they said from hurting. Now my goals were being questioned, the future I'd planned for myself didn't sit right with the folks who, at the end of the day, were the people I came home to.

This is what I was thinking about while I sat in a Lit class taught by a man I had some sort of perverse attraction to even though I was certain he was a racist. Maybe it wasn't so much an attraction as a mission to make him see his ignorance, that whatever grievance he had against me was misplaced. I worked on being an attentive student, tried to get the best grades, as if I had to prove something to him. Now he was talking about significant American writers and poets. Suddenly I didn't appreciate the fact that he didn't include a single black writer on the list—no mention of Baldwin, Wright, or Hurston—writers I'd learned about at my old school. As usual, we were insignificant at this school, and whatever it was I thought attractive about him had faded away. Right in the middle of his sentence, I stuck my arm in the air and began talking before he could acknowledge me.

"Don't you think we should include some black writers in the discussion? They made a lot of contributions to American Literature." Even I wasn't sure where the voice was coming from because it surely wasn't something I'd say, definitely not in the middle of a classroom where mine was the only dark face.

"Say what?" I wasn't sure if he hadn't heard what I'd said or if he'd heard but like me, didn't believe I'd said it right in the middle of his lecture.

"I was just thinking we should cover more than just the

white writers. Maybe we should cover Richard Wright or Langston Hughes." I was saying the words, but with each syllable I could feel my resolve leaving me, though I never knew where it had come from in the first place. I looked around at the class for the first time and saw that they were looking at me the same way they did that first day I arrived on campus to buy my books. *Where did she come from?* It was clear that no one in the room wanted to discuss black writers any more than the teacher did, and that before my little episode, they'd only been counting the minutes before they were released from the last class of the day. And as strange as my behavior was, it still didn't hold more interest than whatever plans they had for Friday night and the weekend beyond.

When the bell rang, they all rushed from the room, leaving me there staring at the teacher. I still wasn't sure why I hadn't followed the herd, but I guessed it could be the voices of my friends from work still playing in my head. *That's some fucked-up thinking.*

"Don't you have another class to get to, Kim?" He'd dismissed me long before the bell had rung, long before the class had even started. Dismissed me and all the people and effort that helped me to reach that moment in his classroom.

"All I was suggesting is that maybe we can include *all* the significant writers. They're a part of American Lit too."

"I teach the class according to the lesson plans, not the students' wishes."

I felt lonely and separated from everything that made me certain there was a place for me.

"Apparently, it's only one student's wish."

I left before he, or I, could say anything else.

The next day, I got a ride home from school because Ma had to meet with the principal about the demerits he'd given me for disrupting a classroom. Father had brought in my teacher for backup, which he probably didn't realize he truly needed until he met Ma.

I was already in the office, had already been given a sermon by Father, when Ma arrived. The first thing Father seemed to notice about her was the gun on her hip. Ma was used to this, and always tried to put people at ease, so the first thing she said was, "I'm a cop."

"Oh, we weren't aware. I don't think we've met."

"Once," Ma said, shaking his hand, "when we first came here to check out the school."

"I guess you haven't been here since, then."

That was the line that got Ma's anger up. It didn't take much these days.

"And why am I here today? I should be out finding a serial killer right now, so I'm assuming this meeting is extremely important."

Father said nothing, surprised as he was by this response, so my teacher tried to fill the dead air.

"Kim was disruptive to my class, and the standard punishment for that is ten demerits. We ask parents to join us for a discussion of the problem, to ensure parents are aware of what's going on with their children in our school. And we'll also need you to sign off that you've been made aware of the infraction." His thin mustache and brown hair pressed against his head made me think of Hitler.

"What was the infraction, exactly?"

"I thought Kim would have told you." Father stared at me, attempting to give another sermon telepathically.

"She did, but I thought she must have left something out. I was certain that what she told me—asking about black writers in an American Literature class—wasn't all there was to it."

"That is precisely what happened."

"Are you sure? For something that trivial, I know you wouldn't ask me to drive twenty-five miles up here from the Southside where I should be working a crime scene. I know you wouldn't have brought me or my child in here on some pissant charge like that. So what's the real problem?"

I could tell from the look on Father's face that he'd not run into a parent like Ma before, cop or no. The teacher didn't know what to make of her either, so he just slid the piece of paper across the desk toward Ma and offered her a pen.

"We won't take any more of your time then. If you'd just sign here, please."

"I'm not signing this. Kim had a legitimate question. All you needed to do was answer yes or no. How did she disrupt the class? Did she scream her question? Did she start an argument with you?"

"No, but we follow a prescribed curriculum—"

Ma cut him off, dismissed him by turning to me and asking, "Are you done with classes for the day?"

"Yes." My first word since she'd arrived.

"Then let's go. I've got work to do."

She didn't say good-bye, didn't acknowledge the paper. I wanted to look back to see the reactions of the principal and my teacher, but I didn't dare. I had to be back there Monday. This performance wasn't a surprise to me. Ma was like this anytime she got rubbed the wrong way, anytime she felt even an inkling of an attack on her kids or herself. Most times, I'd cower in embarrassment while she set straight the fancy department store clerk who followed us around expecting us to steal, or the front desk clerk at check-in who discovered suddenly that there were no more rooms even though we'd made the reservations weeks ago. Even though she was right in most cases, and I longed to have her nerve, I'd still be embarrassed. Couldn't she fight back with a little more grace? But this time I was glad Ma was the way she was, even though I was certain I'd feel the repercussions next week.

Now she was moving through I-285 traffic in her usual way, as though launching a tactical assault on the beginning rush hour, so I wasn't sure if she was angry or just driving normally.

"I don't have time for this mess," she finally said.

"What mess? All I asked was if he could talk about black writers."

"Not that. You heard me defend you to that pompous ass. I'm talking about the whole thing. You hate the school, you complain about it all the time, and it's costing us a ridiculous amount of money. I don't get it. And it isn't like I got time to come way out here to West Hell to deal with these crazy priests over stupid shit."

Maybe Ma hadn't studied the map with the circles and squares in a while, hadn't done the math, but I had. The number of miles between my school and the home of the nearest victim was twenty. The child who lived closest to our house had played ball, hung out with friends, slept, did his homework, and watched TV less than two miles from where I did the same things. One boy may have died only footsteps, not miles, from where I did those things. But I knew Ma wouldn't understand this was the reason I wanted to stay in a school that made me feel like I'd walked into the wrong door every single day, so I said nothing, and wondered what it would be like sitting in American Literature class come Monday.

I was glad I had a house party to go to that night. I didn't want to think about school, how much I hated it, or what Monday would be like. It was a birthday party for the girl whose house provided the table and chairs for our Spades games. Cassandra and I walked down together after I spent half an hour convincing her to go.

"You know I don't like to dance."

"So don't dance, just talk to people."

"I don't know what to wear."

"That looks nice what you have on. And look how it matches your new manicure."

Even a few houses away, I could smell the smoke from the pine burning in our fireplace, thought I could feel its warmth.

I could see Bridgette in front of the fire, putting too many marshmallows on a stretched-out wire hanger, and not letting them toast for as long as Ma taught her. Then she'd complain that they wouldn't smash right when she put them between the graham crackers. I knew that Ma had watched through her bedroom window as Cassandra and I left her house. Without looking back, I knew she had slipped out of the house in her robe and house shoes and was watching us now, and wouldn't go back in until we'd arrived at the party, because you just never know. Bridgette was going to have one of those nights in front of the TV on Ma's bed that she missed, and I had a brief moment of regret that I wasn't home.

At the top of the driveway, we could hear Kurtis Blow's "These Are the Breaks" coming from the house, and I wondered when the birthday girl's parents were going to come from their bedrooms and tell her, "Turn down that music before somebody calls the police." Even though the night was cold, kids were hanging out on the front porch, trying to cool off from dancing inside a house packed with people. Inside, the party was already going strong. Having to coax Cassandra out of the house timed our arrival just right; that awkward moment when no one knows what to do or say had already passed. Now kids were doing the dance inspired by Chic's *Le Freak* despite the record being a couple years old, because it was a dance even the most uncoordinated could pull off. I wanted to join them, but we couldn't just walk into a party and start dancing. So Cassandra and I made the rounds, checking out who was there, both of us carrying cups of soda because holding something always helped quell our nervousness at parties.

"Look," I said to Cassandra, barely nodding in the direction of a boy across the room. "Who's that?"

"Like I know."

After some investigation that I hoped appeared nonchalant, I learned that the new boy was a visiting cousin of one of the neighborhood kids. I spent most of the evening trying to work up enough nerve to introduce myself to him, and never would have if his cousin hadn't called me over to them.

"Kim will tell you, she knows," said the cousin, a girl from the next street over who I didn't hang out with much.

"What do I know?" I couldn't help but stare at the new boy, who was introduced to me as Mark, because he had blue eyes, something I'd never seen before on a brown-skinned person.

"I was telling Mark about the dead boys, how he'd better watch out while he's in town. The killer is looking for boys just like him. Am I right? Kim knows 'cause her mother's a cop."

"It's true. One of the victims was from out of town, just visiting family like you, when he was abducted." I wished I sounded like a girl interested in a cute boy instead of a cop or TV reporter. I wished I'd said something that would make him want to stay in Atlanta forever, instead of making him want to catch the next bus home. But I kept talking like a cop or TV reporter. "His body was found the next day."

Despite my morbid conversation, he asked me to dance. His eyes weren't blue like the boys at school, an icy blue that made me think of watching the sky through a frosted windshield in winter. Mark's eyes had heat, the warmth and color of the deep end of my pool at dusk, when a full day of summer sun had knocked off the water's chill. He would have been beautiful without the blue eyes, but the shock of them made it even more so. We started out dancing to Gary Numan's *Cars*, but someone put on something slow and I was glad he didn't run like most boys would. I didn't dance with him the way I danced with Kevin, but it was nice.

Chapter 24

On Monday morning, I played sick. Even though I began building my case Friday night, complaining that something I ate at the party didn't sit well with me, on Saturday blaming it on cramps, and by Sunday turning it into a stomach virus, Ma didn't buy any of it. But I was smart enough to wait until the last minute to tell her, when she was already running late and needed to get Bridgette to school and herself downtown, so she let it go.

At the dining room table, I finished the homework I'd put off over the weekend, giving me an excuse to look at Ma's files. There was no one in the house to catch me, only my guilt. Ma would likely kill me if she knew I was snooping around her papers, but by now, I felt like I was as much a part of the investigation as she. It was my helping around the house, watching Bridgette, taking over the budget and bill paying (which I had to do after Ma got so caught up in work that she forgot to pay the light bill the month before) that made it possible for her to spend nearly every waking hour on the investigation. She was working more closely with the FBI now on the Wilson case, using their hypnotist and victim profiles to help with the traditional police work she and the Task Force were used to doing. I read her notes from an interview with the hypnotized neighbor boy who said he'd heard screaming coming from the girl's apartment in the early morning hours when she had been allegedly abducted.

The boy had brought his date home to watch some TV a little before midnight. Before going into his home, he saw two males and a female leaving the girl's apartment. He thought the female might have been a young girl. They disappeared from his sight. He saw what might have been an ice-cream truck in the driveway. The boy then went into his apartment with his date. He heard what he thought was the sound of someone getting a whipping. The boy thought he heard the victim's sister yell out "Stop," after which he heard no more sounds.

At about one in the morning, the boy left his apartment to walk his date home, and saw the victim's mother sitting on her porch. He greeted her but she ignored him, which was strange because she was usually friendly. The boy thought the mother seemed upset. He noticed the victim's younger brother playing in the front yard.

The end of the report was missing, and I had to use my imagination to fill in the rest.

Going back to school on Tuesday wasn't as bad as I'd expected. I realized I'd given myself too much credit as far as the impact I had on my classmates. Three days had passed and they'd forgotten about my call for a more complete literature lesson, and they'd probably forgotten it the minute they hit the door Friday afternoon. My teacher was smug as usual, more so since he'd won this particular battle and I now had only twenty demerits remaining of the thirty allotted per school year before being expelled.

After school, Grandma was waiting for me in the pickup circle out front. Ma had convinced her to take some time off for a couple of weeks in January to come back to Atlanta to help around the house and look out for Bridgette and me. Two weeks into her visit, she decided to make her temporary stay permanent, and quit her job while my grandfather stayed in Cleveland another two years to finish out his time with Ohio Bell so he could collect his entire pension. Grandma moved into my aunt's house, left empty when she joined the Air Force, and immediately found a job cleaning the house of a rich white man who had no kids or wife. She'd had the job for a week before we discovered how close her employer lived to my school. We planned that on Tuesdays and Thursdays she'd give me a ride home and save me an hour off my commute. I was especially grateful that Grandma had started her job in cold and dark January.

We still get a laugh from the fact that I increased our trip by twenty minutes because I knew the way into downtown Atlanta only by following the bus route, unnecessarily making Grandma go down side streets, do switchbacks *(Why are you sending me in a circle, girl?)*, and travel through residential neighborhoods when the on-ramp for I-285 was just a couple of miles from the school. But the bus route was all I knew, and I didn't discover how far out of the way the route took us until long after Grandma had quit that job.

I'd been to the man's house a couple of times in the first few weeks she worked there. When she didn't get everything done before it was time to pick me up from school, we'd go back to the house so she could finish up. Being in the man's house gave me a glimpse into how my classmates must have lived. I usually referred to them as classmates more often than friends—our connection lasted only as long as the school day. I'd never been invited into any of their homes, and I was told little about their lives outside of school, though their questions about how I lived (really, how *all* black folks lived through my single interpretation) seemed never ending.

So I had to piece together what their worlds must be like when they weren't at school. Since the man's house was only a couple of miles from the school, I imagined many of the kids lived in neighborhoods and houses much like his—huge plantation-style houses full of columns and hanging ferns out front, azalea bushes manicured by professionals, grass that seemed to stay green straight through winter. And always the older black women walking the mile from the bus stop into the neighborhoods where their day's work lie. They made me grateful Grandma had a car, and once she got to know some of them, she'd offer a ride instead of just passing by.

Grandma let me raid the rich man's refrigerator, justifying it by saying the food would just go bad anyway since the man traveled and was never home, causing her more work by having to clean out the refrigerator. Besides, it was sort of like her food since she was the one who ran around to the three different gourmet stores that he specified, scrutinizing shelves looking for the foods on his list, many of which she couldn't pronounce and had never heard of, despite her having been a school cook for fifteen years and a housekeeper for a rich woman in Cleveland. The doublewide refrigerator was always stocked with things I wished we had at home but never did. A shelf full of different flavors of soda. New York-style cheesecake bought from a bakery, not from the Winn Dixie and thawed from frozen. All kinds of deli meats and cheeses that didn't require the removal of red plastic from around the meat or clear cellophane from the cheese. I'd make a big sandwich and eat it while marveling at the size of the man's kitchen.

The kitchen, like everything else in the house, was just too much, though I could imagine living this way if I ever had the money. There were two ovens, one on top of the other, which seemed extravagant except during Thanksgiving maybe, when it might come in handy. Ice and water were dispensed through the refrigerator door, and shiny, expensive copper pots hung from the ceiling. There wasn't a single cast-iron skillet, well seasoned by generations of cooks. No aluminum cookie sheet gone black with age and use, despite careful scrubbing. I got the biggest thrill out of the microwave oven—something I knew about but had never used. It blew my mind that I could warm through cold pasta in only seconds. We'd gotten a dishwasher only a couple of years earlier, so it didn't take much in the way of appliances to get me excited.

His bedroom alone was bigger than the three bedrooms in our house combined. It had two fireplaces. I'd never seen a fireplace in a bedroom, and two just seemed greedy. It was my first look at a jetted tub. Each time I went to his house, I wondered what made a man with no wife or children, who was rarely in town, buy such a house. Eventually I realized it was because he could, the reason rich folks do many of the things they do. Each trip to his home distanced me further from my classmates, whose homes I imagined were just as excessive, making it difficult to see any connection between their lives and mine.

On the first Thursday of February, when the air was still cool enough for a jacket but spring seemed less an impossibility, a caretaker of some land near Vandiver Lake in Southwest was out destroying rabbit traps on the property when he found the body of Lubie Geter, the boy last seen selling car deodorizer. When Ma called that night to say she was on her way home from the crime scene, I put a plate of food in the oven to get warm. Even though it was a school night, I'd wait up for her no matter how late she got in, unless she told me she'd be staying very late at the Task Force. It seemed so long ago that staying alone overnight had worried me, but it had been only two months. I'd been right the first night—it became easier for Ma not to come home after the first time. Fortunately, it became easier for me too.

On the nights she worked a scene, she always came home. And I always waited up for her because those were the worst days, making her feel blue in a way nothing else could, and I didn't want her to feel worse by coming home to a quiet house and nothing hot to eat.

"Animals had gotten to him and he'd been out there nearly a month, but he was still identifiable." She said this while I pulled off her boots, even though I hadn't asked her about the scene. "Thanks. Feels like I've been on my feet for a lifetime."

"These probably aren't the best shoes for police work, but

I know you gotta be cute. And look how muddy they are." My efforts to take her mind away from the crime scene with some teasing didn't work.

"We were in the woods. My heels kept sinking into the ground." She kneaded her feet with gloved hands. I didn't hear the usual strength in my mother's voice, which once calmed my worries with a few words. "He was only wearing his underwear, but like all the other boys, there wasn't any sign he'd been messed with. But they don't know for sure. There's not much for the medical examiner to go on by the time we find some of them."

"I got dinner warm for you."

"Let me wash up first."

Ma came back to the kitchen table, but the minute I pulled the plate from the oven, she had to run for the bathroom. She closed her door, but I waited outside until she finished. She was in there a long time before she told me to go to bed.

"I'll wait until you feel better."

"No, it's after midnight and you have school tomorrow. I'm all right."

I didn't believe her, but I left my post at the bathroom door anyway.

I grew up with superstitions taught to me by the women in my family, mostly from my grandmother and aunts because Ma said she didn't have time for that foolishness. I learned to burn my hair lest birds make a nest with it and bring all types of bad luck on me. I never put my purse on a floor unless I wanted to lose all my money. And I was careful not to swipe anyone's feet with the broom while sweeping because I didn't want to be the reason for any catastrophe that might befall them.

My greatest fear was Friday the 13th, because since I'd turned ten, I'd had some mishap on every Friday the 13th: slipped in the garage and fractured my arm (didn't matter that I was wearing flip-flops and hosing down the slick concrete floor, I was certain it was the date that doomed me); riding my bike down a hill, I crashed into a just-opened car door and went flying (didn't matter that I was riding on the wrong side of the street); electrocuted while plugging in the sewing machine (this turned out to be bad wiring in the apartment we lived in at the time). Each accident put me into the emergency room, but I'd survived them all.

So I waited for whatever was coming on Friday the 13th, February 1981. It turned out the bad thing wasn't meant for me this time. Two more bodies were found. One was the body of Patrick Baltazar, who had gone missing a week earlier from Piedmont Avenue in downtown Atlanta. The eleven-year-old, who had enough confidence and maturity to hold down a job as a restaurant busboy, had boasted to his friends that the killer would never get him. He was found in a ditch behind the Corporate Square office park just inside DeKalb County in north Atlanta. It had rained heavily on the Tuesday and Wednesday of that week, and the police could tell from his waterlogged clothes that he'd been in the ditch since at least Tuesday. He'd disappeared the Friday before.

I thought of this boy often when, a few years later as a college freshman, I got a job working in the same office park, in the same building near where he was found. I'd forgotten many of the details of the investigation by then, but this case came back to me the first time I walked past the ditch, and each time after. The memory wasn't vivid, it was just a fleeting realization that there had been a cool February day when a dead boy had lain nearby, that his killer had been there, and that Ma had been there, too, working the crime scene, slightly distracted, wondering whether I'd gotten home safely that day.

On the same day the boy was found in the ditch, Ma and the rest of the Task Force searched an expanded area of where other victims had been found, now considered one of the killer's dumping grounds, in some woods off Suber Road. That's where they found the skeletal remains of Jefferey Mathis, the ten-year-old boy who'd gone missing from the West End, just two blocks from my old school, in March of 1980. It was believed he'd been lying out in those woods for nearly a year. It took the medical examiner a week to identify the remains. His mother didn't believe, or maybe didn't want to believe, that it was her child they'd found, said it couldn't be her boy. But that must have been her heart and her hope talking, because there was nothing left of him that even a mother could identify with only her eyes. The boy's medical records were enough confirmation for the medical examiner and the cops, even if not for the boy's mother.

Chapter 25

The third week of February was a busy one for the Task Force and the killer. The city announced that it was making some headway in the investigation, that there were fibers found on Patrick Baltazar, the twentieth victim, that matched fibers found on five others. This meant that at least six of the victims had been in the same place to be able to pick up the fibers, possibly the killer's car or home. It also confirmed that at least six of the victims were linked. This may have seemed like obvious information to most people, but to the cops, it was something they could finally go on. If they could find the source of the fibers, they might possibly find the killer, or at least one of them.

This news that the police were getting closer didn't scare the killer at all. Two days later, thirteen-year-old Curtis Walker, who was last seen on Bankhead Highway trying to scare up an odd job or two at a gun shop, had gone missing. The last time people at the gun shop saw him was around five o'clock in the evening, past the curfew and already well into dusk. On the same day, the Task Force officially added Aaron Wyche to the list, the boy police originally said had fallen from a bridge over a railroad track.

In January 1981, a witness had come forward and said he'd seen Aaron get into a car with a black male, and gave a description of the driver similar to descriptions given by other witnesses in some of the other victims' cases. As a result of the tip, DeKalb County police reopened the case to investigate it as a homicide themselves, and didn't turn the case over to the Task Force until nearly the end of February and after the twenty-first victim went missing from Bankhead Highway. This was just one example of the difficulties the massive and sprawling Task Force investigation had. The sheer geographic size of Atlanta and its suburbs, the fact the killer or killers were operating in multiple jurisdictions when abducting the children and disposing of their bodies, made the case difficult for even the best cops in town to manage.

Ma was still tracking down information on the man who claimed he'd only taken Alfred Evans to the bus stop and nothing more, convinced he was the closest thing she had to a viable suspect in the second victim's murder. I found a transcript of an interview Ma and her partner Sid had with that suspect whose name seemed to be spoken in our house with regularity now, on phone calls, Motorola radio transmissions, and visits from other detectives working the case. Whenever I read the interviews, I had to imagine Ma taking on her cop persona to hear the words as she must have said them during the interview. I'd noticed a trend in the transcripts. When the person interviewed was a woman, especially a victim's mother, Ma's words sounded gentle, reassuring, like she was trying to be the woman's friend and confidante. The male partner in the interview, oftentimes Sid, played the impatient and insensitive cop looking for a confession. When they interviewed a man, it went the other way, Ma played the bad cop to Sid's good. I guess cops actually do that.

The dialogue may have sounded like some kind of hack TV cop show, if you weren't a person living in Atlanta and living with the reality of the murders every day.

> *Sid:* You take him out?
> *Suspect:* I wouldn't do something like that.

Sid: Somebody did.

Suspect: Yeah, somebody. I hope y'all hurry up and find that somebody too.

Sid: We want to resolve this matter. This whole thing has the city in an uproar.

Suspect: Not only the city, the people.

Sid: I meant the city, the people. Somehow, we've got to do something about this thing.

(Sid later leaves the room on some pretense, allowing Ma to interview the suspect alone.)

Ma: It's looking bad for you, real bad. I was hoping you would help us. You are still not being truthful to me.

This last line is not a stretch for me to imagine, because it sounds similar to the interrogations I'd get from Ma when I missed curfew or got into some other trouble.

Suspect: Yes, I am.

Ma: Just think about all the times you've changed your story.

Suspect: All you got to do is talk to _____, and she can tell you how screwed up my memory is.

Ma: She could tell you that, but I don't think that would help you in court.

Suspect: What do you mean, help me in court?

Ma: That's about where you're going, on your way to court.

Suspect: Yeah?

Ma: That's the way it looks. You haven't been charged with anything, I've tried to give you several opportunities to tell me the truth. But you know what? The more I work to prove . . . Really, I've been working to find your stories true. So I can eliminate you . . . I can't eliminate you. The more I work to prove you're telling me the truth, the more I find you are lying.

Suspect: No, I am not lying. Don't accuse me again.

Ma: Okay. What you want me to call it?

Suspect: I told you, I got a bad memory.

Ma: Okay. The more I find that you have a bad memory.

Ma wasn't buying his story, but a bad memory wasn't enough to build a case on.

The pressure only grew as the country finally turned its attention on Atlanta. At the end of February, Phil Donahue did a special show on the Missing and Murdered Children's Investigation. National morning news shows began carrying the story, updating viewers around the country with the growing death count. President Reagan gave one and a half million dollars in aid to the city. Vice President Bush sent his special aide to town to speak to the mayor personally and to find out what more Washington could do to help Atlanta. And Ma and Sid were chosen to go on the *McNeil-Lehrer News Hour* to discuss the Task Force investigation.

I'd seen Ma on TV before, but only on the evening news for just a few seconds while the cameras watched her make an arrest, or as she walked behind a reporter who was giving an update from a crime scene. This time she was going to be interviewed and the tape shown all around the country, although I remember wishing it wasn't being shown on PBS, a station I believed had only two demographics—preschoolers and old people. I figured not many of my friends would catch the *McNeil-Lehrer News Hour.*

Bridgette, Ma, and I sat on Ma's bed, our evening TV viewing spot despite having turned the garage into a rec room. We made a bowl of popcorn like we were in front of a movie, and watched the opening credits, excited about our brief moment of celebrity.

"When will they show you, Ma?"

"Hush, we'll miss something."

Then Ma appeared on screen with Sid, looking like herself and not whatever I'd imagined. I blamed my slight feeling of disappointment on too many fantasies of Ma as Christy Love, Coffy, and Foxy Brown. She looked regular, like any businesswoman, except she was trying to explain what the Task Force was doing and why they hadn't figured out who was killing Atlanta's children. Ma, Sid, and their bosses hoped to get two things from the national public, one spoken and the other not: getting help in solving the cases and generating sympathy for the maligned Task Force.

Charlayne Hunter-Gault appeared neutral, almost sympathetic I thought, to Ma and Sid during the interview. She didn't attack them the way I expected most journalists would if given the chance. But she was still an Atlantan and like every other person who called Atlanta home, she wanted to know what was being done to stop the killer. So she asked questions that Ma and Sid couldn't always fully answer, although they gave it their best shot, partly because doing so would compromise the investigation, but also because they just didn't have the answer. Especially to the questions about whether the murders were racially motivated.

But she asked questions I knew no one in town could fully answer. If they could, I'd have been watching *Perry Mason* reruns instead of PBS. I'd have gone to bed that night without fear that there'd be another child found dead in the morning. Bridgette would be sleeping in her own bed instead of mine, which she'd taken to doing after that night Ma spent away, sometimes even on nights Ma was home. And I wouldn't have been wondering whether the despair I saw in Ma's eyes on the TV screen was something I'd imagined, a trick played by television cameras, or something real.

Bridgette and Ma weren't home even though it was after seven and I'd already cooked dinner, cleaned the dishes, and checked the phone twice to see if maybe it was off the hook.

Just as I was about to call the Task Force to see if anyone knew where my mother was, I heard a car door slam shut. It was an unmarked car and I felt a little better until I saw Bridgette get out of the passenger seat and right away noticed she'd been crying. I wondered if this was The Moment, but no, the detective was smiling. Even Bridgette was smiling, holding on to a fast-food restaurant bag. *This isn't the moment,* I told my stomach and it tried to settle down.

"I'm Detective Hurst," he said to me. Right away, I noticed and appreciated that he spoke to me like an adult, though I'm not sure why he did or why I appreciated it. "No worries, your mom's okay." He was also a mind reader, or had family at home who also prayed The Moment never came, but were always prepared, or thought they were, if it did.

"Where is she?"

"She got caught up on a scene, so she asked if I could see to your sister getting home."

"Look, Kim, he bought us some dinner." She was only eleven, and whatever made her cry had been forgotten, replaced by the promise of a Happy Meal.

"Thanks for bringing her home, Detective Hurst. For the dinner too."

"No problem. You girls gonna be all right?"

"Yes."

"Your mom says she might not be home for a while yet."

"We'll be okay." I was immediately angry at Ma for not calling to say she'd be late, or to say a cop I'd never met would be bringing Bridgette home, or to tell me how long "a while yet" would be this time.

When the detective pulled out of the driveway, I noticed how cold the evening had grown. February was like that in Atlanta, the warm days could fool you into thinking spring had arrived, and the nights reminded you that no such thing had happened.

"Why were you crying?" I asked Bridgette as I hustled her inside.

"When?"

"Before. I can still see the streaks on your face from where you were crying. And your eyes are still red."

"Ma was so late. It was closing time and the day-care people were trying to find her. I was scared she'd forgotten about me. Then the cop came, and he scared me."

"Why did he scare you?"

"Anybody she ever had pick me up has been someone I already knew, some good friend of hers. I didn't know what to do 'cause I didn't know him and 'cause he's white, and Ma doesn't have any close white cop friends that I know about. And you know how they're saying it's a white man killing the kids."

"But he showed you his badge, right? And the day-care teacher saw his badge, right? And you know what an unmarked car looks like." Even though it was over and Bridgette was safe at home, it made me afraid thinking about what might have happened. I wanted to make sure she knew the right things to do next time, because I was certain there'd be a next time.

"That doesn't matter anymore. You know what the mayor said."

"About what?"

"That until they catch the killer, everybody's a suspect. And one of the parents of the dead kids was on TV talking about how it could be a cop, for all she knew. For all I know too."

"So what made you go with him?"

"He knew the code."

I'd long forgotten the code, mostly because I didn't have much need for it anymore. For a few years now I'd been responsible for getting myself home, it had been a long time since a patrol car came to pick me up from school because Ma couldn't get away from some crime scene. But back in those days when she couldn't always rely on a friend or family to pick me up, Ma had given me a code word. We had decided on *Mannix*, the name of my first dog and the cop show she loved to watch, never suspecting she would be running down bad guys herself a few years later. I could only get into the car of someone who knew the code word, no matter whether he was a cop or not, in uniform or not. Back then I thought it was cool, a secret that made me, in a small way, part of the Blue circle. Now, while I wiped Bridgette's face with a wet towel, it only made me angry.

"I can wipe my own face," Bridgette said, slapping my hand away, tears forgotten and playing the big girl again.

When Ma got home, the first orange in the sky was just beginning to show. I'd already missed the bus that would get me to school on time, but I couldn't leave Bridgette home alone.

"God I'm tired," she said as she hung her coat in the hall closet. "My feet are killing me."

I didn't say anything at all, just watched her from the kitchen table while she pulled off her boots, which I noticed were caked in mud again.

"What are you pouting for now?"

"You didn't call."

"I was in the woods on an investigation. I couldn't even get decent radio reception, much less get to a phone. I had to send a uniform into radio zone so he could call the captain and make sure someone could get Bridgette. I told them, 'I have to get my child. Either get someone to pick up my child or I have to leave this crime scene right now.' Didn't Hurst tell you I'd be late?"

"Yeah, but he didn't say *tomorrow*."

"I got a mother." Ma's tone told me that I needed to back down, but I was ready to fight until I noticed the expression in her face change from tough cop to someone I'd never seen before. Her eyes were wet and it scared me. I filed through every memory I had and realized that I'd never seen my mother cry. I thought I'd heard her cry late at night through the double layers of bedroom doors. But I'd never *seen* it.

Never, not once. I was afraid of what might come next and tried to leave the table before it did.

"You think this is what I want? You know what I was doing at the very moment I should have been picking Bridgette up from school?"

No, I don't, and please don't tell me. You're scaring me. At least the tears didn't fall. She'd pulled them back somehow and her record remained unblemished. I still hadn't seen her cry. But she looked as though she could at any minute.

"I was standing over another victim. I was looking at bones that I knew were once a child because of the size, but there was not much else to go on because of what time, the elements, and animals had done to him. I was wondering how his mother would react when we asked her to identify what little was left of him, once we figured out who he was. Would she just die right there on the spot?

"I was thinking, 'How can I be here in these woods standing over this boy's body when I don't know whether my own baby has gotten a ride home? When I'm not sure my other child is okay walking that half mile between the bus and home? How can I be here doing this now when I've got my own babies out there?' No, this is not at all what I want. And I don't need your attitude either."

Her eyes were dry then, and she'd gone back to be being tough again, but for the first time I fully realized how much of that was an act. So much of it *was* an act, and I wondered what I'd done to make her think she had to act around me too.

"It was okay, Ma. Detective Hurst even brought some dinner when he dropped Bridgette off. She liked the burgers a whole lot better than the chicken and rice that I made." Even to me the cheer in my voice sounded false, especially when I'd hoped it sounded like an apology. It didn't matter, she didn't hear me anyway.

"I always think I'm going to be prepared. After so many years being a cop, and after working nearly ten of these murdered children crime scenes, I keep thinking I'll know what to expect. It's always the hair and teeth that get me, the only parts ever left intact that might distinguish them from all the others. I expect it, but I'm never ready for it." She looked directly at me now instead of out of the window behind me where, until now, she had been focused on something or nothing. "Once, we found a boy wearing only his underwear, and they were the kind with cartoon characters on them. Underoos, I think they call them. They didn't have those when you were little. They're only babies, some of them. Just babies."

She left me then and went toward the back of the house, saying she needed to wake Bridgette for school.

Chapter 26

There was another reason for Ma's sadness. There was a point when I just knew things hadn't worked out for Ma and her sailor, even though she hadn't said anything about it. I knew because she stopped talking about him, she never mentioned again that I might find a branch of my school in Hawaii, she didn't talk about him, or much else, in future tense anymore.

Her male friends couldn't help her through this particular hurt. It was a moment that called for girlfriends, and Ma didn't have many. Her sisters and friends all seemed to have flown away just before everything began to happen and she needed them most. Aunt Marsha had married and moved with her new husband to Iraq, a faraway country she had to point out for me on the map. Aunt Deborah had joined the Air Force, surprising everyone when she quit her job as a flight attendant for Delta. Before my aunts left, one of my mother's girlfriends decided she needed to go back home to New England and stand up to whatever made her run to Atlanta in the first place. Another friend, a woman who seemed so innocent to me even when I was a young child, was attacked by a man one day while jogging, and even though Atlanta had once been the love of her life, after that happened, being there only made her sad, so she had to leave too.

So when Ma finally had to tell someone that her heart was splitting wide open, it was me. I brought her favorite food to her in bed: popcorn that I made on the stove old-fashioned style even though we had a hot-air popper, because this was no time to be concerned with calories, and butter pecan ice cream, which I always thought of as an old folks' flavor but Ma loved.

"He said I had too much going on in my life without him adding to it. He couldn't see where there was enough room for him."

On this point, I had to agree with the sailor. I was surprised that Ma couldn't see it was true the way Bridgette and I, and now the sailor, could.

"It's for the best, I suppose—he was too weak. The last thing I needed was some man leaning on me. Why can't I be the one to lean sometimes?"

"I know."

"I don't know why he made me think this was serious when he never meant it to be. And why ask to meet my kids? I didn't want him to until he was dead sure about us, but he kept insisting. Doesn't make any sense."

"I know."

I didn't know, but I couldn't think of anything else to say. I was still feeling some leftover hurt from my own first breakup, but I was learning that a young girl breakup was nothing like a grown woman breakup, and I didn't look forward to when it would first happen to me. And when she couldn't be stoic any longer, she'd send me out of the room, telling me I should go to the den and watch TV with Bridgette, and made me close the door. The den that used to be the garage was the farthest room from hers. Distance and a loud television would provide a cover. I knew she was in there crying, and I wished she wasn't so afraid to let me see that, because it's one of the saddest things in the world to cry alone.

* * *

I was walking down the driveway after checking the mailbox when Ma pulled in but didn't turn off the car. Bridgette had barely gotten out when Ma put the car into reverse, yelling to me that she had to get back down to the Task Force, and that she'd be home late. No news flash there.

I didn't wait for her to come home anymore in the evenings because I knew it could be anytime. Without noticing, I'd fallen into a new routine. On weeknights, I took the bus home and sometimes waited for some unmarked car to drop off Bridgette, but most often she'd stay with her friend on the Northside, so I was alone. I made dinner. If she was home, helped Bridgette with her homework. Did my own homework while Bridgette watched TV. Watched the evening news, hoping I could figure out what Ma was doing that night, where she might be working a scene. Listening to middle-class parents say they were sending their kids out of town to stay with relatives until the killer was caught, even though the killer hadn't snatched any middle-class kids but one. When they talked about another child missing, they'd pan across some housing project from the air, showing kids playing in what looked like a military barracks instead of a place children should grow up—no trees, no grass, just red dirt. Kids using a garbage can for a basketball hoop, or playing games I thought existed only in the old days, like stickball or keeping an old bike rim upright and rolling down the street with a stick. I wondered what happened to the rest of the bike, and felt guilty when I thanked God I wasn't poor.

If it was a Friday night, I packed my brown polyester uniform in my school duffel bag in the morning and went straight from school to work, and hoped Ma hadn't forgotten to pick Bridgette up from school or had arranged for someone to do it. Then I'd call Ma at home when the restaurant closed at eleven, waking her out of her sleep so she could come downtown to pick me up. While I scrubbed down the grill or cleaned the shake station or whatever task I was assigned for cleanup that night, I would hope Ma didn't fall back to sleep, and that when we'd finish the cleaning and the supervisor was ready to lock the doors, I'd see her car outside. Sometimes I'd see no car and would have to call her at home again because she hadn't gotten more than a few hours of sleep a night in months and she had a hard time staying awake. Sometimes, a coworker or the supervisor would wait with me for the fifteen minutes it took for Ma to get there, but sometimes they wouldn't. Those times I'd stand in front of the locked restaurant's doors wearing my "don't fuck with me" face, certain no one was buying it.

I thought Ma had forgotten about having to go to my school to discuss my demerits situation because she'd forgotten about so many other things lately, but I learned otherwise one morning as I fried up some link sausages for Bridgette and me. My favorite breakfast was fried sausages on white bread with some Miracle Whip.

"I want us to check out a public school," Ma said.

"Where is this coming from?"

"It'll either be the one in our district or something through the magnet program. You choose, but we're looking at one. I don't think where you are now is doing you any good. Don't think I don't know why you're always coming up sick on Monday mornings lately."

"But what about getting into a good college?"

"That line has grown tired. I'm more concerned about you not winding up on Grady's eighth floor. That's where you're headed if you stay where you are."

It was true I hated the school ninety-five percent of the time, but I didn't know where Ma got this idea that I was about to lose it.

"You think I'm crazy just because I'm not all the time happy about the school?"

"A mother knows."

A mother snoops, I realized, especially one who made a living of it.

"You've been looking in my journal."

I was taking a creative writing class that semester and the teacher made us keep a daily journal. It made my day when she left comments like "you have some obvious talent" or "nice use of alliteration" in the margins. Mostly I wrote poetry about racial injustice because I was at my militant stage, using English class to note the inequity of using black as a descriptive for bad, like *blacklist* or *black sheep*, and white to make bad more acceptable, like *white lies* and *whitewash*. I noticed on those manifestos there were never any comments in the margin. I also wrote angst-filled poems about how I hated school and my life, with lines like "I'm afraid that when I'm gone, no one will remember me. I'm afraid that I am lost, please take my hand so I won't slip away" that made my teacher write on that entry, "You've got to hang in with the hard part," and call me to her desk after class to ask if I was okay. These must have been the lines that made Ma think I was crazy.

Ma looked at me, trying to figure out whether she should lie or just come out with it. She decided on the truth, although she tried to justify herself first.

"Anything in this house is my property. I pay the mortgage around here. And I'm the mother—it's my job to make sure I'm doing the best by you."

"So, yes, you've been sneaking into my journal." I wanted to add that some months when money was tight, I helped pay the mortgage too. But I didn't dare.

"I don't *sneak* into anything that's in my house. *My house.* Believe me, between you playing sick to get out of school and all that depressing talk in your little diary about being 'miserable and lost,' this is a good idea. Your grades are down this year too. I'm not so busy with the investigation that I don't know what's what. If the load is lighter, going to public school might actually help you get your grades up so you can get into a good college. Besides, I'm tired of you blaming everything wrong in the world on that school, especially when it's costing a few thousand a year for you to be there."

The list of victims grew quickly in March. Altogether, five people went missing, and three were found dead. April was no better, with another disappearance near the end of the month. All those who went missing in March were found dead in April. By mid-April, the official number of Missing and Murdered Children was twenty-six.

It seemed the bodies were coming faster than I could keep up with. After a while, it was just expected. I woke up in the morning and wondered if anyone would go missing that day. Would Ma tell me that a body was found in some river, some stand of trees not far from a road where people went about their day like any other day, while across town some mother was crying because the cops had just left her door after giving the news? At dinner, would she tell me that some mother is angry because here comes Ma again with her questions?

The last three victims to go missing in March, and the victim who disappeared in April were adult men, young but still men, twenty, twenty-one, and twenty-three years old. They were included on the Missing and Murdered Children's list because the medical examiner and the cops determined that with one exception the adult victims had the physical appearance of children and because the MO was similar. Twenty-three-year-old Michael McIntosh was only 5'4" and 115 pounds. The murderer probably thought he was picking up a child.

The South River and the Chattahoochee had become a favorite dumping ground for the killer because he could easily stop along a bridge at night and throw the bodies over. As in the beginning, the killer was still just throwing bodies over bridges and down embankments as if the boys' lives didn't mean a thing at all, as if there wasn't some mother or father or friend somewhere trying hard to remember the last thing said between them. Probably something small and everyday because they never expected it to be the last time, and they hoped that whatever the words were, they weren't angry or hurtful or disappointed words.

As the body count grew in April, so did my mother's fear. The Task Force agreed with the FBI profiler who suggested one or two copycat killers might have committed some of the more recent murders. How could they catch two or three killers if they'd been unable to catch one?

Cassandra and I sat on the big boulders that the people who lived in our house before us had put in the front yard, beneath some white pine, oak, and dogwood trees. Our property was fairly big, like all the other houses on the street, and it took creativity to fill so much space when you couldn't afford landscapers. So mostly we just had old trees that were there long before the house was built in the fifties, which kept the house cooler in the summer, but created more fallen leaves and pine needles come autumn than we could ever seem to rake up. Around the boulders we had planted pink azaleas the color of dime-store lipstick, bright and noticeable.

I would have rather played basketball with the boys down the street on a pretty spring day like that one, but Cassandra never played basketball or softball (or dodgeball and kickball when we were younger). She always complained it was too warm and she didn't want to sweat out her hot press and get all sticky after just taking a bath. She was far more girly than I, which I thought was a wasted effort since she didn't have a boyfriend.

"I don't need a boyfriend to look nice," she'd tell me, a fact I didn't appreciate until I was well into my twenties.

We watched Bridgette and Latrice doing cheers on Latrice's driveway, clapping hands and stomping feet in time with the cheers.

Latrice sang, "Latrice is red hot, Latrice is red hot, Latrice is r-e-d red h-o-t hot, once I start I can't be stopped, Latrice is red hot."

Bridgette answered with, "Well, my name is Bridgette, hello, hello. And I'm a sexy, sexy Capricorn, hello, hello. I'm a sing and shout, hello, hello. Until I . . . turn it out."

"What do eleven-year-olds know about being sexy and red hot?" Cassandra asked, and we both laughed at that. After a while, they went inside, taking away our entertainment, so we just watched the occasional car go by and hoped someone would walk past and provide some excitement.

"Maybe we should check on Latrice and them. They've been in there too long and too quiet."

"And them" was only Bridgette, but that's what we used to say regardless of how many people we were referring to. The way "y'all" was mostly used for plural, but it could be used in the singular as well.

"As long as they aren't burning down the house, let them be. I get tired of seeing after Bridgette all the time." Only briefly did I consider my own close call with burning down the house. I was feeling lazy and didn't want to leave the cool spot beneath the trees.

"I know that's right."

Like me, Cassandra had to look out for her younger sister because there was only her mother, and that's what happens when you're the oldest and there's only a mother. Sometimes knowing each of us was in the same boat made things better for us, though Cassandra didn't know all the things I did about dead children and a mother who sometimes forgets you because all she can think about is her work, mothers who sometimes don't even come home at night anymore, so Cassandra got to be a kid more often than I did.

Just then Latrice came running out of her house, Bridgette running behind her, both of them screaming.

"Sandra, Sandra!"

"Oh Lord, what now?" Cassandra and I both talked like old women when we had to take care of our sisters, though we didn't notice it then.

Latrice's hair was wet, and some of it she was holding in

her hand, which wasn't a good thing because she didn't have much to start with. Bridgette was holding a bottle of Nair.

"What did y'all do?" I asked.

"A girl at school said Nair makes your hair grow faster," Latrice wailed, likely waking dogs all over the neighborhood.

"Didn't ya'll read the bottle?" Cassandra asked. "It's for taking hair off."

"But the girl said it works the opposite on head hair," Bridgette offered since Latrice was bawling and couldn't defend her poor decision.

Even though the tears were coming fast down Latrice's face, Cassandra and I looked at each other and burst out laughing at the same time. Then we went inside to see what we could do to save the rest of Latrice's hair.

Chapter 27

Ma checked me out of school after fourth period and we were on our way to the school I'd chosen. It was in Garden Hills, a neighborhood just south of Buckhead. Though I had no intentions of leaving the private school willingly, I figured if Ma forced me, I'd better spend some time choosing the right school. There were only two schools in the Atlanta system that were in affluent Northside neighborhoods, and I picked one of them.

I told Ma that I was interested in their magnet program, international studies. To appeal to her interests, I reminded her that it was in the same district as the middle school Bridgette would be going to next year, so I could meet her school bus and she could ride home with me on MARTA. Ma wouldn't have to worry about picking her up, or as was happening more often, begging the mother of Bridgette's friend to let her spend the night because she couldn't get away. It was happening so often that Bridgette took to keeping extra clothes and a toothbrush at her friend's house. I didn't tell Ma the real story about my selection because it shamed me to think it—that I believed I was safer in places where white people lived in mansions and drove European cars.

When we pulled in front of the school, I realized for the first time that there were varying degrees of rich and white.

The school was ancient, a single, large, red-bricked building that I was certain had been built a few hundred years earlier. Had I arrived at the school straight out of the West End, I'd have thought this place was heaven in comparison. It sat at the end of a quiet residential street in a neighborhood just two blocks off bustling Peachtree Road. Ancient white oaks, a clue on the age of the school, provided shade, and there was a large grass yard out front. But I hadn't come straight from the West End, so I noticed only that the grass wasn't so green and had plenty of brown spots mixed in. There was no great swath of a soccer field. There was a single building from what I could see—no separate library, no tennis courts, no series of buildings connected by breezeways and courtyards, no weeping willow–canopied creek running alongside the property.

We arrived while classes were in session so the halls were empty. I noticed there were only half lockers, not the full lockers I was used to, meaning there was a chance I'd have to negotiate with someone each time I wanted to get into my locker. Paint peeled from walls, and the concrete steps between floors were cracked in places. I was certain the hallways smelled faintly of urine. A passing teacher gave us directions to the guidance counselor's office.

I was in a school office with Ma for the second time in a month, more times than there'd been in the past two years. While Ma made introductions for us both, I realized I was more nervous here, even though there was no one to give me sermons or hand down punishment.

"I've been looking over your transcript," said the guidance counselor, who appeared to be eighty if a day. "I think you'll do well here. Because you were required to take eight classes per semester at your old school and we only require six, you're on track to graduate nearly a year ahead of schedule."

Two things struck me besides wondering why she hadn't yet retired: she spoke as if it was a done deal, referring to my "old school"; and she was a good salesperson, aware that a promise of an early parole would appeal to most any kid.

"Now that sounds promising. A chance to get a head start on college and your future," Ma said with a level of cheer that sounded foreign. She'd turned into June Cleaver between the car and the building. Different school, different agenda, different mother.

"I spoke to your mother on the phone, but I'd like to hear your reasons for transferring to our school."

"I don't have any. My mother has all the reasons." I stole a look at Ma, and her expression told me to drop the smart-ass attitude, so I did. "It isn't final that I'm transferring, but I'm not sure I fit in so well at my current school."

"Yes, your mother told me there was an issue with the homogeneity in the student body over there."

"That's one way to put it."

"Well, I think you'll find a big difference here. The Minority-to-Majority program has ensured that we have students from all over the city, including some from your school district. Our racial makeup between black and white is fairly balanced, and with our International Studies magnet program, we attract students from many different cultures. Our English as a Second Language program is the largest in the school system."

The old woman was a talking brochure, and I wondered why I was getting a sales job. I knew why they did it when I first visited the private school—they had to justify a parent spending half the price of a subcompact car each year. But in public school, I thought the city would just say, attend or don't, your call. I liked the idea of the counselor pitching the school as a place that wanted me, rather than a place I should want to be.

I answered the counselor's questions, surprising myself that my feigned interest had become real by the end of the interview. Ma continued her TV mother impersonation right down to our good-bye, which happened just as the halls began to fill with kids heading for last period. The counselor had been right about the student body. There were faces ranging from Scandinavian light to Nigerian dark and all the hues in between, including mine. Languages other than English were being spoken in front of lockers. There were no uniforms to get just right, no priests patrolling the halls with a ruler in hand to measure the length of plaid skirts. No class stratification made obvious by the quality of shoes, or the authenticity of Lilly Pulitzer Bermuda bags, or the number and type of stones strung on Add-a-Bead necklaces, or the car emblem key chain dangling from Jansport backpacks. For the first time since we'd discussed public school as a real possibility, I thought maybe Ma's suggestion was a good one.

On the ride back home, I was weighing the good and bad of leaving my school, beginning to see more good than bad, when we came to a stop behind a line of cars on a road where I knew there were no stop signs or traffic lights. It was already summertime warm, and with the windows open, I could hear the steady buzz of crickets in the dense growth of grass, weeds, and rabbit tobacco growing alongside the road. I focused on the brush, wondering if I stared hard enough whether I'd spot a body. I'd taken to watching the woods and tall grass alongside the road as Ma's car, or the MARTA bus, sped by an area I thought the killer might drop a victim. I searched the varying shades of green for a color that didn't belong—a red T-shirt, a white tennis shoe, a pair of blue jeans. When we drove a wooded stretch of road and I smelled something bad, I wondered if it was a dead possum, or a dead person. At the time, I hoped I wasn't too sick for having such morbid thoughts. Today, I don't doubt that other folks occasionally thought the same thing while driving past a stand of pine. They might have sung along to the car radio and tried to focus on the road instead of the vegetation along the shoulder, but sometimes they probably couldn't help but wonder.

To push away thoughts of what I might see or smell, I focused on what I actually could sense, the perfume of magnolia blossoms blooming somewhere close, though I couldn't see them. The heavy scent made me see them in my head, though: shiny green leaves cradling delicate white petals, with edges that would already be turning brown by nightfall. I saw a muscadine vine growing wild in an oak tree, and imagined how sweet the fruit would be come August. I noticed how it seemed warm for April, and how the breeze had cooled things off while the car was moving. We'd been idling only a minute and I could feel the sweat beginning to make my forehead damp and wished Ma would turn on the air conditioner.

"What's going on up there, can you tell?" I asked.

"I don't know, some kind of roadblock. It must be for the investigation."

"What investigation?"

"What other investigation is there?"

We crept ahead, and I was able to see officers looking into cars on the other side of the road.

"What are they looking for, drugs?"

"Kids. The Task Force is setting up roadblocks in areas where the kids were abducted."

"I would think the killer would just make a U-turn and avoid the roadblock."

"You're probably right. It's more of a deterrent than anything."

When it was our turn at the checkpoint, I expected Ma to flash her badge and speed on through, but she slowed to a stop, and even after showing her badge, the officer looked into the backseat of our car. I expected him to ask whether I knew this woman, but he didn't, just said a couple of words to Ma and finally waved us on our way.

"Why'd he look into our car when he knew you were a detective?"

"Ever since the mayor said trust no one, not even a cop, everyone's a suspect. Even the good guys."

It was Grandma's day to clean the rich man's house. Once a month she worked a full day doing the heavy-duty cleaning even though the man stayed away for weeks at a time and the only dirt that would accumulate was dust. It didn't matter. He still wanted Grandma to scrub the house down top to bottom. On those days, she'd have to stop in the middle to pick me up, then go back to the house and complete the long list of tasks the man had written out. I could have caught the bus home on those days, but she'd be done more quickly if I helped her finish the list, which I'd do after making myself a snack of the man's gourmet food.

He hadn't been home since Grandma had vacuumed the place two days earlier, so she assigned me the job of running a garden rake over the thick pile carpet to give it some fresh lines to make it look as though it had been vacuumed. She said it wasn't cheating; it was using good common sense. She couldn't see any point in vacuuming a clean carpet or using the energy that would take.

"You been walking around with your lips poked out a mile and wearing an attitude on your shoulders for days, and I'm about tired of it. Now, if you plan on being of some use to me, start dragging that rake across the carpets. I want to get home before rush hour gets too bad. My knees are starting to act up. Must be rain coming."

"It's not like I'm trying to have an attitude."

"Well, what is it you trying to have, 'cause it seems to me that's what you got."

"I just don't know what to do anymore. Ma's saying she's tired of me complaining about going to a school I don't like, and she's tired of paying for it."

"Makes sense."

"It's not like she's paying for all of it. I pay some too."

"I don't think that's the point, and I think you know what the point is."

"I'm just trying to get the best education I can so I get into a good college." I pulled the rake across the carpet, making sure the lines were straight. Grandma watched me while she folded laundry on the man's bed.

"Nothing wrong with that, if that's truly the reason you putting up such a fuss about going to public school."

"That's the only reason. Unless you're trying to accuse me like my friends are. They're saying I've turned, that I'm whitewashed."

"Say what?"

"Trying to act white."

"Oh. Back in my day, we called it playing the house nigger when I was growing up in Georgia. Or trying to be a blue vein when I moved to Cleveland."

"Why a blue vein?"

"That's when you're so fair folks can see your veins through your skin. And I know that ain't you, child—you too dark to play a blue vein. And I raised no house niggers, so I know one didn't raise you."

"I'm not trying to pass for white. That's crazy. Even if I wanted to—and I *don't*—who'd believe it?"

"So what's the problem then?"

"It's true that I hate being at that school, I hate how ignorant some of the kids are." The hair pick incident, and being called the color of shit, was still fresh for me. "But it's safer where I am now. The killer doesn't come out here looking for kids."

"You must be from a different world than me if you believe that." Grandma got quiet then, focused on folding the warm bath towels that looked nearly big enough to be sheets. I thought I saw a look cross her face, and I couldn't decide whether it was anger or disgust. I didn't want to be the cause of either feeling in my grandmother.

"Why?"

"I'm just wondering how in two generations we went from fear of a lynching if we crossed them, to thinking living among them is safer than living among our own."

When Grandma said this, at first I thought she was talking old-fashioned nonsense, and it took a minute to register that she was talking about me. It didn't seem possible. When the kids started dying, my first thought was that it was an outsider, that we had to protect ourselves from the one thing we all knew didn't want us to survive and never had: Southern racists. But sure enough, two years later, I'd done just what Grandma was accusing me of. I'd never known the shame I felt at that moment. I didn't say anything to her because I was afraid of what other shameful things might come out of my mouth. I just took the vacuum cleaner out to give the floor a true cleaning instead of rake lines, and took a bucket and ammonia into the master bathroom without her having to ask me.

On my walk to the bus stop, where I knew I'd be the only student standing on the side of the street for the bus into Atlanta and away from the suburbs, I passed the pickup circle full of fancy cars driven by mothers who didn't work, waiting on kids for whom transportation between school and home was simply transportation and so required no consideration.

At the stop after I boarded the bus for home, we pulled up to a card game in progress on Alabama Street. The men playing the game were so into what they were doing that the bus driver had to ask them if they planned on riding or not. They got on the bus without turning down the volume on their voices to accommodate the fact that they'd just gotten on a crowded bus. I was sitting in my favorite seat, one of the perks of boarding at the hub before everyone else, one row in front of and across from the back door—not too wimpy, not too risky either. Not surprisingly, the card players headed straight for the back of the bus and took the bench seat that spread full across the back.

I shared a seat with either a military man or someone in college ROTC, but it must have been the full-on military because he seemed a good ten years older than I. He was goodlooking, and smelled good too. I was hoping he'd talk to me, tried to get his attention, though I had no idea what I'd do with it even if I were to capture it. He was reading something, I don't recall what. Having next to nothing in my flirtation arsenal, all I could do was open one of the books I'd just checked out of the public library, imagining that, as a reader, he'd look over and ask what I was reading. He did not. I gave up after a few minutes. He was a grown man who'd probably been in other countries. I was a fifteen-year-old girl in a Catholic school uniform who'd been as far north as Cleveland, as far south as Orlando, and maybe a hundred miles east and west.

The card game continued as we left downtown, past the stadium and into Southeast. The card players' voices never quieted, and if anything, grew louder with every mile. I was still able to block most of it out while I stared through the dirty window. It had recently stopped raining as I recall, and I'd been turning over some fifteen-year-old's problem in my mind, probably the school issue. Even though the only thing that was truly Catholic about me was my unwavering sense of guilt and the ease in which I could slip into it, I got religious on this particular bus ride, asking God for a sign that my problems, whatever they were, would get worked out. At the same time, the clouds broke and sunlight filtered through in such a way that any Catholic, even a not-so-fervent one, would take it as a sign.

It was at this moment, while I was enjoying the glow of having gotten some divine attention, that one of the card-playing men shouted, *You cheatin', man, I knew you was cheatin'*, or something like that. I remember exactly the words that followed:

"I'm a kill you, you cheatin' motherfucker."

Then a woman's scream, and another woman's voice saying, "He's got a gun."

I didn't turn around. I was a good five rows in front of whatever was going on back there. If I didn't look the man in his face, he'd have less reason to shoot me. And unless he had an M-16, he couldn't shoot all fifty of us. The man must have started waving the gun around, because more screams erupted, not just from the back of the bus but from the front and middle too. I dove to the floor, crouching down as far as possible, trying to become invisible. Shuffling noises told me others were doing the same thing. The cute soldier next to me dropped too, wrapping his body over mine. The man was at the back door now, yelling, "I'm not gonna hurt nobody, I just need off the bus, now!"

The bus driver didn't stop, and I couldn't understand why. I replayed the last street scenes I remembered seeing before the woman screamed, and realized we were about a half mile from the police substation on Jonesboro Road when the gun came out. The driver was trying to get closer to that substation before stopping the bus. The man with the gun yelled to the driver that if he didn't *stop the goddamned bus, someone was getting hurt*.

The driver stopped the bus and opened the doors, and the man jumped off. The soldier lifted off of me, and I sat up just in time to see the man take off running away from Jonesboro Road and into the residential neighborhood that fed away from it. Sure enough, we were sitting across the street from the police substation, and already a cop was giving chase into the neighborhood. I wondered how he could respond so fast, but I guessed the driver, who'd probably seen some of everything on his job, was more alert than the rest of us to what was building in the back of the bus. He must have read something from the moment the card players got on and phoned it in when he knew it was about to go bad. I realized then that's why he tried to stop in front of the substation.

More cops boarded the bus to take reports from the passengers and the other card players, but those men had jumped off the bus, too, running the opposite direction of the man who threatened to kill them, and away from the cops who came pouring out of the substation. While the police asked questions of the riders sitting closest to the card game, I stared out onto the street, thinking how I could be dead and it wouldn't have mattered a bit to the people who were going about their day. I noticed one of the billboards that had been going up around town, plain white billboards with black lettering that read: *REWARD:* $100,000. THE CHILD YOU SAVE MAY BE YOUR OWN. CALL THE ATLANTA POLICE SPECIAL TASK FORCE. The signs were all over the Southside. I hadn't seen a single one in the North.

Chapter 28

By the time April wrapped itself up, another name was added to the list. Twenty-one-year-old Jimmy Ray Payne went missing on April 22. They found him in the Chattahoochee five days later. That was the same day the Task Force began their surveillance of the bridges over the Chattahoochee and the South rivers. The killer was disposing of his victims' bodies exclusively over bridges now, and watching the bridges was as good a chance as any to catch him. The sad part about that was if the theory was to work, it would mean another victim had been killed. But it was something.

A questionnaire was sent out to boys in Atlanta Public Schools in an effort to get leads. Had the boys been approached by anyone in the last year? Had they noticed something that didn't seem right, anything at all? I wondered what the boys did that night when they went home, sat down with their parents in the place they usually did homework, and told them about the questionnaire. The evening was probably like any other, except for the questions. Dinnertime was likely strained. I'm sure it was difficult for some of them to get to sleep that night because the questions made them remember moments when they came *close,* much closer than they'd ever realized before the cops made them fill out a survey to help find a killer, handed out during a regular old school day.

I wondered about Kevin and the questionnaire since he was the right candidate for it—a black boy going to school in the Atlanta public system. Even though he just lived around the corner, I didn't see him very often. At first I'd see him visiting the girl across the street, but within a few months of his dropping me for her, she'd already been dropped too. He was seventeen by then and driving, so I only saw him once in a blue moon, and then only briefly as he passed by in his parents' car. When I'd see him, I couldn't help but wonder how things would be if we were still together now that he had a car. I imagined us in the backseat, him giving me kisses. Our main impediment had been the fear of getting caught (for him, anyway; my fear was getting pregnant), and a car would have reduced that possibility. So I figured that by now we'd have already done the deed.

Tonight he was filling out the questionnaire, and that made me afraid for him simply because he fit the profile. He'd think it was a waste of time; no killer was going to get him, he was too smart to fall for some offer of easy money. No doubt all the victims thought the same thing because that's the way boys are. But I tried not to worry about him too much when I realized that he probably hadn't given me a single thought in months.

The next morning, Ma still wasn't up when it was near time for me to go catch my bus for work. Even though it was Saturday, we both had to work, so Grandma was on her way over to pick up Bridgette for the day. I was hoping to catch a ride with Ma downtown if she was anywhere close to being ready. When I went into her room, I found her awake but still in bed.

"I had a bad night."

"Finding the kids?"

"Yeah, it knocks me on my behind every time, even when I think I'm ready for it. I guess I won't ever be ready." The curtains were still drawn, making the room dark. She had the television on, turned down low and flickering the morning news. I switched it off, thinking how that was half the problem—she could never let it go.

"You feel sick? Want me to get you some Pepto or something?"

"I don't feel bad that way. This bad goes deeper. I had a dream last night about the kids. They were alive, but they still looked the way we found them in the woods and rivers."

"It's too much trying to work every crime scene," I said, because I was like Ma, always trying to find a solution. "I think you should tell your commander that it's too much."

"It was one of those dreams, the kind when you know you're dreaming and you try to wake up from it but can't. And the kids were begging me to find their killer, crying. And all I could tell them was that I'd try."

"I was thinking I could ride with you into work this morning. We can both make it on time if you get up now. I already made some coffee."

"The craziest thing about it was when I woke up . . . at least, I think I was awake by then, you never know, it was one of those kinds of dreams . . . but when I woke up, those kids were at the foot of the bed, right there where you're sitting now, smiling at me."

I jumped up from the bed, partly because I'd been raised by superstitious women, but mostly because Ma hadn't been one of them and now she was talking about seeing ghosts.

"Let's see, what do you want to wear today? Since it's Saturday, do they let you wear jeans?" My back was turned to her while I went through her closet and so she wouldn't see on my face how much she'd spooked me with her crazy talk.

"Something comfortable. I have to go back out there today to look for evidence."

I threw a pair of jeans and a sweater across the foot of her bed, wondering if I'd disturbed the spirits.

"I've had dreams about the kids too," I said. "Probably a lot of people have, especially the people who loved them."

My words didn't seem to make it any better for her, though she smiled at me like she appreciated the thought. I left her in her bed, yelled at Bridgette to get up and get some breakfast before Grandma arrived, then headed out for the bus stop.

Ma still had questions about the people closest to the girl in her second case. Detectives who'd interviewed the mother's cousin weren't left with the feeling that he could be eliminated from the list. He said he had nothing to do with the girl's death, but seemed nervous and apprehensive throughout his interview. He agreed to a polygraph, but at the time of the test, he fidgeted in his seat, making the testing impossible. He blamed his lack of cooperation on a mistrust of the police and to smoking pot earlier in the day, though the tester didn't believe the pot explanation, saying marijuana alone wouldn't cause such agitation. Mistrust of the police? That part was believable since it seemed most of Atlanta felt the same way.

In the Evans case, she still didn't have enough evidence to make an arrest either. I read another section of an interview she and Sid had with the suspect, hoping to pull a confession from him.

> *Sid:* And did you ever accompany [the victim] to the movies?
>
> *Suspect:* Naw.
>
> *Sid:* Do you go to the movies?
>
> *Suspect:* To the drive-in sometimes.
>
> *Sid:* Did you ever take [the victim]? I guess if you going to the drive-in, you're going to take a lady, right?
>
> *Suspect:* Something like that.
>
> *Sid:* Something like that. You mean sometimes not a lady?
>
> *Suspect:* Young ladies or young players.
>
> *Sid:* Young lady or whatever, or an old lady? Usually a lady?

Suspect: I prefer older women to younger women.

Sid: How old, like Ms. Fuller, for instance?

Ma: I beg your pardon, I'm not an old lady.

Sid: Older.

Ma: [Suspect], do you think I'm older?

Suspect: Well, you're older than I am.

Ma: How do you know that?

Suspect: I guessed it.

Ma: Oh, at least he didn't say I looked like it.

Sid: Do you think I'm older than you?

Suspect: Not that many years, but you are older than I am.

Sid: Not that many years. In my twenties?

Suspect: You might be thirty.

Sid: I appreciate that. You are a good man. Now, if we can get you to tell the truth, I can get your heart beating normally and your hands to be warm. You said earlier that you were a Christian, didn't you? That you believed in a Supreme Being, The Almighty? Did you not?

Suspect: Yeah.

Sid: Let me tell you what we think. Yvonne and I have discussed this case. We discussed you, and I want you to know what we think, and I guess this is the proper time to just tell you what we think . . . We believe that you and [the boy] went someplace. Right now we don't know where, but believe you me, we are digging like hell. We think y'all went somewhere, possibly stayed overnight, somehow, [the boy] was either killed or in effect, died accidentally in your presence, and you disposed of the body. That is what we think. And if that is the case—let me go on—if that is the case, then that would be no murder charge against you. It'll simply mean that you did violate the law by having concealed death. And I'm not sure the DA's office will push to prosecute you for that. They might.

> *Ma:* I would recommend . . . that they not, if you tell me the truth.

The interview ended without the hoped-for confession, and not long after, the man was dropped from the list of suspects.

I could hear a car slowing behind me, and the fear from that spring day a year earlier slapped me, fresh as yesterday. But it was only Kevin, and my body was suddenly full of adrenaline produced by fear, relief, and anticipation. He drove slowly alongside me, my still warm heartbreak and the cause of it separated by a yellow dividing line and one lane of blacktop. We hadn't talked to each other in a long time, but hearing his voice, it seemed to me we had never stopped.

"Don't you want to slow down a minute and talk to me?"

I considered acting nonchalant, but only briefly. I walked over to his idling car and stood on the yellow line, hoping no car came by to run me over just as I was beginning to see a possibility. He looked bigger, like his shoulders had broadened, and there was more hair above his lip. I thought if I looked away for just a second, down the street toward that place where I used to fly on my bike with arms outstretched (was it just two summers ago?), I'd turn back to find he was a full-grown man.

"How've you been?"

"Not bad, just busy, you know, with football and stuff. I'm not around the neighborhood as much."

Was he trying to explain why we hadn't talked in nearly a year, even though we lived an eighth of a mile apart? We were in front of the girl's house he left me for, and I hoped she was looking out of her window watching us. That female predilection kicked in, the one that can turn a single hello into a lifetime commitment. It took only a few seconds for me to understand that he was trying to tell me he'd made a mistake. I thought him shrewd for asking me back and demonstrating to the girl that he'd been wrong, all at the same time. We stared at each other hard, not saying a word, not knowing what else to do.

"Don't you want to give me a kiss?"

I did, and didn't require further prodding. I leaned into his car and gave the most passionate kiss I could muster from such an awkward position, because I thought it held the power to bring him back to me. That kiss had to cover more than a kiss—it had to be me holding him while we watched *Soul Train* in his basement, us swaying together while "Reunited" played, the rush of finding two remote seats in the back of the movie theater for two hours of messing around, including the trailers and closing credits. I was certain I pulled it off when we broke apart and I walked down my driveway, expecting his call later that evening.

"I saw you out there kissing Kevin," Bridgette said when I got into the house, surprising me that there was someone home. "I was watching through the window."

"You like to gave me a heart attack. What're you doing home? Where's Ma?"

"I got sick at school. She had to come and pick me up and bring me home; but then she left for work again. I guess I should be glad she at least came to pick me up, and that it wasn't some black and white pulling up to the school." I noticed for the first time that Bridgette was not wearing her hair in afro puffs or plaits, no ponytail banded with pink acrylic balls, no barrettes. She had made a not-so-effective attempt at using a curling iron that morning, creating a bob that was half flipped up, half curled under.

"You don't look sick." I touched her forehead with the back of my hand. "You aren't feverish. Ma wouldn't have left if she thought you were sick. Maybe she thinks you're faking."

"She knows I'm not faking. The school nurse told her I had a fever, and I puked in the parking lot." Bridgette tried to act like she was unfazed, but the fact we were talking about it made it plain that she was bothered. "She said you'd be home soon to take care of me."

"Well, you seem okay now. Why aren't you in bed if you're so sick, instead of spying on me?"

What was that I smelled on her? How long had she been sneaking into my cologne?

"I wasn't spying. You were right there in the middle of the street kissing on him so the world could see."

The way Bridgette presented it, I imagined hookers in wigs and vinyl leaning down into the cars of their johns.

"What's it like to kiss a boy like that, with your tongue and everything. Sounds nasty to me, but I guess you wouldn't be all the time doing it if it was nasty."

"Now I know you couldn't see all that from the window."

"Not this time, but I've seen you and him once, before y'all broke up. So I guess it isn't as nasty as it looks, then?"

"You don't need to know anything about it. Eleven years old and asking me that." Then I remembered I was only twelve that time between the forsythia bush and the brick wall. "All I know is you'd better not try it."

"You sound just like Ma. Now I got two mothers: one I don't need and one I never see."

Kevin's kiss left me believing we'd be getting back together, but a few days had passed and I'd heard nothing more from him. I consulted on the matter with someone who knew more than I did about boys. Halfway through the second year of school, I'd made almost-friends with a girl outside my usual circle, and regretted that we hadn't gotten to know each other earlier, maybe the school would have been more bearable. But she didn't have many friends at the school, and it seemed to me that she treated the place like a job—come in, do your work, get out.

I always thought her glamorous even though we were in the same grade. She seemed older than the one year in age that separated us, and more worldly. Perfume was already a part of her daily ritual, where for me, on the days that I'd remember to spray some on, it would be an afterthought. I still wore Love's Baby Soft. She wore real perfume, something I imagined Ma might wear but would say to me, "That's too old for you" if I ever tried to use some of it. This girl really knew about boys and sex, or she claimed to know. I guess that's why she shared with me how she and a boy from senior class had done it in the school chapel.

"No, you didn't," I whispered, because we were in the chapel at that moment. We were alone, but it was still instinct to whisper, just like when we first entered and did a halfhearted genuflection in the direction of the altar, while making the sign of the cross. That was instinct too.

"Yes, we did."

"You're gonna burn in hell," I said, not sure I believed her.

"Maybe, but I'll have good memories of how good I felt getting there." We both laughed at that, forgetting to whisper, me acting like I knew what she was talking about. I wondered what Ma would say if I got an extra piercing in my ears. It made Roxy look bohemian, and more like a college girl than a high-school sophomore. I could probably learn all kinds of things about boys from her.

"So what do you think about my story, my boyfriend's kiss?"

"Ex-boyfriend, you mean. I only see two possibilities." She paused, and I waited for whatever she was going to say, certain it would be brilliant. "Either he's a dog and just wanted a free kiss and had no other intentions, or he wanted to see if maybe he made a mistake in breaking up with you, and he realized he hadn't. Either way, it's over."

Her words hit me like a slap, the way the truth usually does when you're not ready to hear it. I pretended that she'd told me something I already knew.

"I figured as much. He was a dog." He was, as well as my first love.

"Most of them are." From her blazer pocket she pulled a

pack of cigarettes, a matchbook stuck between the package and the film wrapper. I waited for lightning to strike us from the altar when she lit up, but the only fire and brimstone in the air was from the meeting of her match and menthol cigarette. To a girl who claimed to have fucked in the Lord's house, smoking was probably nothing.

"Do you do this often?" I asked. "Cut class, I mean."

"It's not cutting class if you have an excuse."

"Yeah, but we're supposed to be in the library helping get ready for the fund-raiser this weekend, and you're sitting here smoking a cigarette and telling me how you got laid in the chapel." When I said that last line, I thought about how much my language had changed in the two years I'd been at the school. Before the school, my friends and I said "did it," or the bolder ones simply said "fucked." We never said "getting laid," and now I said it effortlessly.

"If I'm going to burn in hell, I may as well get my money's worth." She exhaled, creating a bracelet out of smoke, and I was endlessly fascinated.

Chapter 29

Ma and I were in the den watching TV. She was running the videotape of the Dan Rather Special Report about the Task Force Investigation even though we'd watched it before. A fifteen-year-old girl from the Southside was being interviewed, being asked if she was afraid. What a stupid question, I thought, of course she was afraid. She said she always carried a knife in her pocketbook, and when she walked home from school, she put the knife up her sleeve, just in case.

The following day, on my way through downtown, I bought myself a knife with a leather sheath and didn't tell Ma about it. I carried it in my purse, long after the Task Force was disbanded, through college and into grad school. My college friends named the knife Butch. It made me feel better about walking through Washington, DC, after my classes let out at ten at night and taking the Metro home. Years later when I told Ma about it, she yelled at me as if I were still a child instead of twenty-five, and as if the knife were still in my purse: "If you get a chance to use a knife, that means you're too close to him and he can turn it on you. It's a good thing you never got your silly ass killed." Always *too close*. No place ever safe.

Now Ed Bradley was on the screen, talking about how

after nearly two years of killings, kids still weren't so afraid they wouldn't get into a stranger's car. Wanting to see if the student education program was working, the program that was supposed to teach kids how to avoid the killer, some plainclothes cops in unmarked cars went into some of the neighborhoods where the victims had been taken. They drove down the street, yelling to kids "Want to make ten bucks?" It turned out every kid they approached got into the car.

Ma didn't say anything, only shook her head in a way that made me realize she had finally decided it was hopeless. And if she didn't have any hope, how could I?

A day hadn't passed between the time the twenty-seventh victim, a seventeen-year-old boy, was last seen and when he was found dead. His mother last saw him midafternoon on May 11th, and when he didn't come home that night, she reported him missing at two in the morning. There was no way for her to know that by then her son was already gone, that less than an hour before she made her report, her child had been found laying against the curb on a street in DeKalb County by a passing motorist. The boy had been both strangled and stabbed, as if the killer wanted to make some kind of point.

"Or as if he was angry," Ma said.

"But how can you be angry at someone you'd known for hours?"

"The boy may have known his killer. Either way, the killer probably wasn't angry at the boy. He's either angry at what he thought the boy represented, or he's mad at everything that isn't the way he thinks it ought to be."

I was old enough to know things rarely went the way you expected them to, nothing worked out perfectly. What I wasn't old enough to understand, and still don't, was how the same disappointment most of us just deal with can drive some peo-e to an anger so hard that they can kill a child. I didn't under-nd why after nearly two years of killing, the murderer still couldn't see that it wouldn't make the anger or the disappointment go away. It was scary to think the killer would never be satisfied, would never stop killing, until something stopped him first.

On Friday morning in the third week of May, Ma woke me early to say she had to get into work right away. One of the bridge stakeouts might have finally turned up a suspect.

All through school I couldn't wait to get home and find out if the killer had been caught. Ma didn't have any details before she left for work, but I could hear the relief in her voice at just the possibility. I wanted to tell the kids at school that maybe it was over, though it probably wouldn't have generated much excitement. Nearly two years after the murders began, my classmates still expressed little interest in the killer or the dead kids.

When Ma got home late that night, I had everything done so she wouldn't have to do anything but tell me the news: dinner eaten, dishes cleaned, homework done, baths taken.

"So, did you catch him?"

"Can you let me get in the door first?" Ma said, but there was a lightness behind the question that told me right away they'd at least caught a good break, if not the killer. After she put away her purse and gun, dropped her briefcase on a chair in the dining room, and took a Miller High Life from the refrigerator, she was finally ready to talk.

"So, there's some good and some bad."

"Good first," I said, tired of so much bad.

"Early this morning, a recruit on stakeout under a bridge heard a loud splash in the Chattahoochee, like something big had been dropped in the river from the bridge. He saw the headlights of a car slowly passing overhead. He radioed uniforms on either end of the bridge, they followed the car that was crossing the bridge just after the splash was heard, and a mile down the road, they stopped the driver." Ma spoke in a flat news reporter voice that told me she'd recounted the story many times since this morning.

"So you caught him?"

"We have someone we're questioning."

"Who?"

"I'm not going to say. The media hasn't caught on yet, and we need to take advantage of that as long as possible."

Did she think I'd tell? My feelings were slightly hurt, but for Ma to be so tight-lipped, I knew it was a good lead.

"So, what's the bad part?" I asked.

She finished off the pony-sized bottle of beer and asked me to get her another. I always wondered why she bought the little bottles when she'd always drink two of them, which equaled more than one regular bottle. I went and got the beer, uncapped it, and brought it into the den where she picked up as though I'd never left.

"For one thing, I know the suspect from my patrol days, and my first instinct is that he couldn't have done these murders. But that was a long time ago, people change. The biggest problem is that no one actually saw the man, or anyone, on the bridge. His was the last car to go over the bridge immediately following the splash. No one saw anything dropped into the river. And we couldn't find anything that had been dropped in the river."

"But I thought there was a stakeout? Seems like somebody should have seen something."

"Seems like. That's why we shouldn't have had recruits on the stakeout. There was a uniform and an FBI agent at the end of the bridge, but they sent a recruit underneath. The position nobody else wanted, so they gave it to a recruit who had about three minutes' worth of experience doing surveillance."

"He's in jail now, right?" That was all I really wanted to know. Could I go to sleep tonight without worry, stand at the bus stop in the morning without fear?

"No, officers and FBI agents tailed him for a while, pulled

him over, questioned him, searched his car. Then they let him go."

"Let him go?"

"The FBI took the lead and said there wasn't enough to hold him. I wasn't there, so I have to believe that. Right now, all we have is a man driving across the Chattahoochee on the Jackson Parkway bridge and the sound of a splash."

Two days later, the Task Force had more than the sound of a splash. They had the body of the twenty-eighth victim, found in the Chattahoochee just a half mile downstream from where the splash had been heard.

The Monday following the Splash was the first time I could recall making the early-morning walk through downtown and not being afraid. The first time I'd walked through Central City Park in the dawn, promising God I'd never do it again if he let me make it to the other side, was a month after the first two bodies had been found and my first day of school in the suburbs. Now I was starting the final week of my sophomore year, and it was the first time I didn't imagine a child killer lurking somewhere, watching me. Instead of walking around the park, I walked straight through it. Instead of going directly to the bus stop, I used the ten minutes between buses to buy a fresh-from-the-oil doughnut from the Federal Bakery. I'd planned on waiting to eat it on the bus, hidden behind my science notebook, but couldn't hold out and feasted as I walked down Forsyth toward my bus and Luckie Street, which I called Rat Street. In the morning hours before the sun came up, the rats that roamed around Luckie and Poplar were fearless and thought nothing of running right past the feet of people scurrying to make the bus. That morning, I barely paid the rats any mind.

Ma said they weren't sure the man from the bridge was the killer, but they were questioning him, and the FBI was getting warrants to put surveillance on him. I was satisfied. They had someone, and the cops were watching his every move. He wasn't waiting for me around the next corner. Once I was past the initial relief that there was a suspect, I wondered who he was. Ma said it was someone she knew from her patrol days. I tried to remember those days, but I was too young to have retained much memory of them. She worked in Zone Four, that much I remembered, somewhere off Campbellton Road. Angel Lenair was found off Campbellton Road. Greenbriar skating rink was there too. It was the street I'd had a hard time imagining a Klansman cruising for prey. But maybe it wasn't a Klansman, just an angry white man who felt we'd wronged him, all of us, and he wanted to set things straight. There weren't many white people living around there that I knew of, even six years ago, so I wondered how Ma knew the man. It didn't matter that recent leads had pointed to a possible black suspect, I didn't believe them. There was no way a black person could do this to his own. Even an FBI profiler said as much.

It had been hard for me to keep quiet about what I knew when I played basketball down the street on Saturday, or worked the Sunday morning shift at the restaurant, but I did. On the same day of the Splash, the paper ran an article about an out-of-state suspect in the death of the twenty-fourth victim, but the media didn't have information on the Splash yet. On Monday, everyone was talking about a suspect, but not the one the police caught on the bridge. I even heard some kids talking about it in chemistry class in the minutes before the bell rang to start class.

"I heard they might know who that killer is."

"What killer?"

"You know, the one that's been killing those kids in Atlanta."

"Thank *God.* Maybe they can talk about something else on TV for a change."

"I know. It's on the news all the time. I'm so tired of it already."

"Totally."

I wondered how many demerits I'd get if I slammed my chemistry book down on their heads. Between the assault and the class disruption charges, and the fact that I'd already used up ten demerits, I was certain I'd be expelled. Luckily for all of us, they moved on to another topic.

"I love your hair. Those braids are so tiny. How'd they get the beads on?"

"I did it myself over the weekend. I thought it was too much to do all of it, but I thought a few placed here and there would look bitchin.'"

"It *is* bitchin'. It's so Bo Derek in *10*."

I wanted to yank the girl's beaded braids from her scalp and beat her with them while I educated her on the fact that Bo Derek had not invented the style, African people had about a million years ago. And they'd see black folks wearing braids all over Atlanta if they ever ventured beyond the five-mile radius that encompassed school and home. And besides, *10* was in the theaters two years ago. It seemed to me they were always the last to know, but always the first to lay claim.

Chapter 30

For the first time since Ma joined the Task Force, she became secretive about the case, taking all work phone calls behind her closed bedroom door. If someone called about the case while we were having dinner, she'd leave the table, asking me to hang up when she got on the line. If a call came while we were watching television on her bed, she sent us away. The media still didn't know who the suspect was, and it was easier for the Task Force to start building evidence for his arrest without media scrutiny. Even the identity of the body found downstream from the Splash was kept a mystery for a few days, although I overheard his name—Nathaniel Cater—when I walked into Ma's bedroom while she was on the phone, and before she abruptly stopped her conversation and shooed me away.

So I had to find out from the evening news that the suspect stopped on the bridge that night was a black man. Not a Klansman, not an angry white man, but someone with brown skin like mine. As much as I respected the police, knew that there were some good detectives on the Task Force despite what the rest of Atlanta thought, I refused to believe it. So did some of those detectives, including Ma.

Like many patrol officers who worked in her patrol zone in the mid-seventies, Ma knew Wayne Williams long before the kids started dying. He and his father had a small-time radio station in the same building that housed her precinct when she was a street cop. Ma remembers the father being a friendly man, and she and the other cops would chat when they passed him in the hall, the way tenants do who share a building. His son always wanted more than pleasantries from Ma and the other cops, asking about the cases they were working on or whether anything big had gone down that day. Ma pegged him as a cop wannabe the first time she met him. He was always asking about police procedure, listened to calls on the police scanner, sometimes arriving at the scene at the same time as the responding officers. She said one time she pulled up to the scene of a call and Williams was already there, directing traffic to make way for the real police. Her acquaintance with him was nearly forgotten by the time he crossed the Jackson Parkway bridge in 1981, and she was caught off guard by the FBI's insistence that Williams was a viable suspect.

Ma just couldn't see Williams as the killer. She questioned his size, only 5'6" and 160 pounds, and whether he could easily overpower streetwise teenage boys and discard their bodies so easily, hauling dead weight over bridges. From what she knew of Williams back in her uniform days, she couldn't match his personality to that of a serial killer's profile, though she was the first to admit he was a little strange. Specifically, he didn't fit the original FBI profile—a white man or group of white men who belong to a racist organization like the Klan. Ma had always believed that the majority of the murders were committed by a person who matched the profile, but she also admitted she'd been in police work long enough to know that you just never know.

She was willing to concede that some of the evidence did point to the strong possibility that Williams was involved in at least some of the latest murders. His interest in all things police related got him arrested in 1976 for impersonating an officer, driving around with a blue light affixed to the top of his car, though the charges were later dropped. This jibed well with one Task Force theory that the killer was pretending to be a cop, something that would explain why street-smart kids would get into a stranger's car. He matched the physical description witnesses had given months ago on the driver of the car some of the kids were last seen getting into—a short, slightly heavy, young black man.

Williams had contact with some of the victims before their deaths through his business as a talent scout. He'd handed out flyers at several Atlanta public schools soliciting his services, calling for young people aged eleven to twenty-one to work with "professional recording acts, no experience necessary, training is provided." He'd also handed out the flyers in the neighborhood of some of the victims, and through witness interviews, the Task Force had been able to conclude Williams had crossed paths with some of the victims. But so had I. So had half the population of those neighborhoods. Until the Splash, Wayne Williams was no more and no less a suspect than anyone else in Atlanta, whose mayor had said that everyone was a suspect until the killer was caught.

It didn't matter what Ma thought, or how surprised most black folks in Atlanta were when Wayne Williams was named as a person of interest. The FBI, with the full support of the mayor, named Williams the prime suspect, so Ma and Sid and the rest of the Task Force had to get to work finding enough evidence for an arrest. The district attorney had grown increasingly worried about having a prosecutable serial murder case, and he and his staff weren't that confident in the FBI's ability to provide the evidence needed to try it. All the fibers in the world still amounted to circumstantial evidence, even if excellent circumstantial evidence, and they wanted more to build the case on. Fibers were collected, personal items searched, but no one would ever know what Williams had gotten rid of the night of the Splash when he was allowed to go home. Neighbors said they saw him burning something in his backyard.

Even if Wayne Williams hadn't committed the crimes,

there was no overwhelming evidence that would help clear him. There was his weak explanation for being on the bridge that night that didn't check out—that at three in the morning he'd been scouting out the location of a potential client's house in preparation for a seven-o'clock meeting that morning. Williams told police his client's name was Cheryl Johnson and that she lived in the Spanish Trace Apartments, though he couldn't remember the apartment number. He even provided a phone number, which he said he'd tried to call the morning of the Splash, sometime around two o'clock. The first time he got a busy signal; the second time someone answered but said there was no Cheryl Johnson living there. He'd only stopped at the bridge to verify that he'd dialed the right phone number. The police could never locate a Cheryl Johnson and surmised he'd made up the client.

There was Williams's story that a few hours before the Splash he'd visited the Sans Souci Lounge downtown to get back a tape recorder he'd loaned the club manager. The club manager said that visit took place on a different night. There were bloodstains found in Williams's car that matched the blood type of two of the victims who'd died from stab wounds. And most damning were carpet fibers and dog hairs found on Williams's personal belongings that could be matched with fibers found on multiple victims.

While investigating Williams, Ma and Sid worked to eliminate other possibilities, following hunches and facts. The body found downstream from the Splash was Nathaniel Cater, who coincidentally lived in the apartment above Latonya Wilson's family at the time she was abducted from her bed. Ma had already concluded that her parents had not harmed the girl, but still wondered if they knew anything about the disappearance, if perhaps they or their children had been threatened by the killer into silence. The discovery that Cater lived just upstairs seemed too coincidental now that he was found in the Chattahoochee, leading Ma to speculate on a few theories.

The first was whether Cater had killed Latonya, especially since his build matched the physical description given of the man, or the silhouette of a man, a neighbor had seen carry the girl through the bedroom window. Perhaps someone in Latonya's family had the same theory and sought revenge against Cater by making it appear he was the victim of the killer who was dumping bodies into the Chattahoochee. The theory was weak, but she couldn't shake the coincidence of proximity between the two victims, nor could she build a stronger theory. Her other theory was Cater had an accomplice in the murder, the second man the neighbor had seen at the window, who had killed Cater to eliminate him as a witness.

During a canvas of the Verbena Street neighborhood Latonya and Nathaniel had lived in, Ma and Sid found a young girl who said she'd seen a man in a neighborhood park with his dog a few times. Her description of the man and his dog matched that of Williams and his dog so closely that they had the girl polygraphed and got a positive reading. But this lead was as circumstantial as the fiber evidence.

The FBI said as early as the second week of June that they had enough evidence to arrest Wayne Williams, basing their claim on the fiber evidence, but local authorities—the Atlanta police chief and the district attorney—didn't agree, and they were the people who needed to make the decision. They were close but weren't ready to say they had enough to build a case. Ma, who'd be on the team responsible for the criminal investigation of any case the district attorney would finally elect to prosecute, still wasn't convinced Wayne Williams was the killer, at least not in all of the murders. A political tussle ensued about whether to arrest Williams: the FBI and the mayor on one side, the district attorney and police chief on the other. Ma thought the FBI, which had been claiming victories throughout the investigation that didn't pan out, wanted to finally have a real success, and then extricate itself. The mayor wanted to get back to running the City too Busy to Hate. The district attorney and the police chief knew that when it all hit the fan, they'd be the agencies blamed, so they were reluctant to move forward with anything less than a tight case.

Eventually, a compromise was made. To try a homicide case, a suspect need only be arrested for a single murder. On June 21, 1981, Wayne Williams was arrested in the Missing and Murdered Children case, charged with murdering Nathaniel Cater, who had been a grown man and not a child at all.

Chapter 31

My mother didn't need me as much after the arrest. There were no more Missing and Murdered Children crime scenes, no nights where she came home and asked me to help her pull off mud-caked boots or fix her a little something to eat that she'd pick over while she talked to me, trying to let go of the day's bad. Before the arrest, I'd give her the plate I'd kept warming in the oven, and watch the tines of her fork tap at the drying edges of meat loaf, stab at shriveled green peas while I tried to think up something to say. I'd struggle for the soothing and supportive words a grown-up would say, but most times all I could come up with was a question, something innocuous that didn't demand anything of her. She didn't seem to mind. But we didn't have many of those nights anymore.

Ma no longer needed me to be her surrogate to Bridgette, because most nights she was home to cook dinner or help with school projects. This took some getting used to because I'd grown accustomed to running the house, and though we both missed her, Bridgette had grown used to it too. She was happy to have more of Ma, but missed dinner in front of the TV (because Ma said she didn't raise any savages and we had to eat dinner at the table) and staying up late watching old scary movies like *Attack of the 50 Foot Woman* and *The*

Blob. When the kids began dying, I was a girl, more responsible than most thirteen-year-olds, but still a girl. After the arrest, there were two women in the house, but I was a lightweight trying to hold steady against a heavyweight. There is room for only one woman in any house, so I deferred, waiting for the moment she would need me again.

On the last Friday of February 1982, I thought she might need me. Jury deliberations in the Wayne Williams trial were expected to begin, and though the odds were against it, people hoped that a verdict might come quickly. Whatever the verdict would be, I thought it would leave Ma spent and that she might need me close by like she did those nights I waited for her to come home from a crime scene.

That's why I decided not to take the second bus once I reached downtown from school. Bridgette, who had started middle school earlier that fall, now made the bus ride from the Northside with me. Her school bus dropped her off a block from my new school, and from there we caught MARTA home. When we got off the train at Five Points and rode the escalator up into the street, our eyes adjusting to natural light, I said, "Let's see if Ma's car is there."

The courthouse lot sat between Pryor and Peachtree, taking up nearly the whole block. It looked as though someone had razed a building to expose the underground parking lot, a pit filled with cars. It was protected by a chain-link fence, put there to keep pedestrians on Peachtree Street from stumbling and falling twenty feet down onto the roofs of Fords and Chryslers. Ma always parked in the same section, and when I'd ride past on my bus in the afternoons, I'd look for her car. When I saw it, I'd be relieved that she'd made it to the end of another workday, no bad guy had wrestled her gun away, no visit to a witness's house had gone bad.

"I don't see her car," Bridgette said. "Maybe she isn't there."

"Where else would she be on the last day of the trial? Maybe she had to park someplace else because of all these people coming down here to gawk."

Pryor Street in front of the courthouse was clogged with

traffic, the far right lane of the one-way street turned into extra parking for media trucks. Across the street in the vacant lot that had been the old entrance to Underground Atlanta were groups with signs that let the world know on which side of the verdict they stood. Officers were stationed at every corner, making sure almost three years' worth of anger and fear didn't erupt in front of the building.

I doubted whether we'd make it inside the courthouse. I knew most of the sheriff's deputies who worked the front entrance, who had not long ago been reinforced by metal detectors and the right to search through purses and briefcases. This meant on the days I carried my knife, I'd have to call Ma from a pay phone to ask if she was going home anytime soon and if I could get a ride. Had I ever forgotten, Ma would not only have learned about the knife, but might also end her day bailing me out of jail for carrying a concealed weapon. On that day, I'd left the knife at home and the deputies, who called me Little Yvonne because they said I looked so much like her, let us in.

"Go straight to the fifth floor, you hear?" the deputy said, referring to the floor where the crime investigators' office was, and not the floor where the trial was taking place. We did as we were told.

"Your mother isn't in her office right now, but you can go on back," the secretary told us when we reached the fifth floor.

Her office smelled of Chanel N° 5 and mildewed paper. It was tiny, with just enough room for her desk and two chairs, hers and the chair where people sat and gave her the information they hoped would clear someone they loved, or sometimes if the person they loved had done them wrong, the words that might send them away forever. But it was private, not like the car-dealership-turned-Task Force building where I sometimes felt in the way. Since it was just before five o'clock, I thought we might be waiting a while, but Ma surprised me when she stepped into the closet-sized room.

"What are you two doing here?"

I wanted to say that I thought she might need me today, but instead I said, "We thought maybe we could get a ride home."

"Today of all days? It's crazy around here, I'm not sure when I'm going home."

It didn't look crazy to me, at least not in the crime investigators' office. The head investigator, the one I couldn't stand because Ma couldn't stand him, the one who liked to imply Ma might not be a clean cop because she managed to buy a house and send her kids to private schools without benefit of a husband, appeared at the doorway. He asked if he could have a word with her. She left with him, and Bridgette voiced my own worry.

"You think she's in trouble because we're here?"

"Grown people don't get in trouble. This isn't school."

"Grown people can get fired, though."

"She won't be fired because we're here," I said, my tone relaying how little Bridgette knew about grown folks' business, though I was thinking the same thing.

Ma returned in a minute. "Come on, it looks like my day is done after all."

On the walk to her car, which turned out to be in the parking lot but far from her usual space, I tried to understand what had happened. Surely Bridgette hadn't been right, but neither of us said anything because Ma hadn't said anything. During the drive home she was quiet, so I stared out the window as if the scenery were new to me, as if the Fulton County stadium had appeared overnight and the people pushing all they owned in rusted grocery carts down Capitol Avenue was something I'd never seen. Bridgette sat in the backseat and pulled out the leftovers of her lunch, a banana and half a peanut butter sandwich.

"Put that away, the smell is making me sick." Those were the only words Ma said the whole ride home. I wanted to look back at Bridgette to sympathize, but anything could set Ma off when she was angry. I knew whatever she was thinking about, maybe what her supervisor had said, was making her angrier by the minute. So when we got home, Bridgette offered to make the salad, and I told her I'd start cutting up a chicken. Ma just went straight to her room and turned on the evening news. When the chicken had been browned and the onions caramelized, all of it poured into a casserole, smothered with a can of cream of mushroom soup and put into the oven, when Bridgette had sliced the last tomato into the salad, we went into her room and sat on the bed.

"Ma, did we get you fired today?" Bridgette asked, and I thought she was braver than I.

"Why do you think you got me fired?"

"Because we came to your office when all the Wayne Williams stuff was happening; then that man came to talk to you, and you've been mad ever since."

"I'm not mad at you. And he didn't fire me. He can't fire me, only Slaton can do that. But he did let me know that Slaton wouldn't be needing me in the courtroom, and that there was no sense in me hanging around waiting to be asked. And he was right, there was no sense in that at all."

On the TV screen, the cameras panned the Fulton County Courthouse, the prosecution team walking down the steps while reporters stuck microphones in their faces. My mother's face was not among them because she had been dismissed and was sitting on her bed with us. That's when it occurred to me that hers had never been among the faces during any of the news film during the eighteen days the trial had dragged on.

"Ma, why aren't you ever on the news walking down the courthouse steps?" I asked.

"Because I wasn't part of the courtroom team."

"But I mean before today."

"I've never been part of it. I was good enough to represent the DA on the Task Force, good enough to help build the trial investigation. But I didn't make the cut when it came to the courtroom team for the biggest trial we've ever had."

When she said that, Ma looked the way she did on too

many days before the arrest—broken down and defeated, her hope drained into the soft riverbank soil of a crime scene. All my anger of the last two years was fresh again in that moment. I remembered being called the color of shit. I remembered the nights and weekends without my mother, the childhood I gave up so Bridgette wouldn't have to give up as much of hers. The phone calls from Ma when she couldn't hide the panic in her voice because she'd already called ten times and I hadn't answered because I'd missed my regular bus and had gotten home late. My fear for all of us when my strong-as-blue-steel mother told me she saw the ghosts of children.

The newscaster came on and said that the jury had not reached a verdict, so there would be another day of deliberations. Another day of waiting.

The next day was Saturday, and Bridgette and I stepped delicately around Ma because even though she wasn't angry with us, she was still angry. I wanted to stay close by because I still thought she might need me, so I called work and said I was sick. By evening, her anger had softened into a kind of sadness, so we sprawled on her bed again as though it were any other night, bits of pecan shell lost in the stitching of her thick comforter, camouflaged by its brown and tan print. Copper snored loudly at the foot of the bed, and I could feel the vibration of it.

"I wish *The Carol Burnett Show* was still on," Bridgette said, sounding the way old people do when they wish for things they can't bring back, and would surely find lacking even if they could.

"Quiet, the news is coming on."

"But you already know the verdict," I said. She had received a phone call, and I knew from the way she wore her relief that a verdict had been reached, but she didn't tell me what it was. As she'd done since the arrest, Ma was still holding back because it was part of her job as a cop or as a mother, I wasn't sure which. I thought maybe she didn't need me at all.

There was more film on the courthouse steps that didn't include Ma, more pictures of crying mothers, pulled from two-year-old footage in case we'd forgotten how painful it had been. The news anchor announced that a jury had convicted Wayne Williams on two counts of murder in the cases of Nathaniel Cater and Jimmy Ray Payne. Then Ma began to cry right in front of us, not saving it for when she was behind her bedroom door, and I didn't know if it was from anger, frustration, sadness, or relief. I figured it was all those things and more, because soon enough Bridgette and I were crying too. When we got it all out, we acted as though it had never happened, because that's the way we were, that was how we needed each other to be. And that was fine.

Bridgette fought with me over who would go get more pecans from the big burlap sack, brought home from the farmer's market on a late autumn day when they were at peak season.

"Don't tell me what to do, you aren't my mother."

"Yeah, but I'm the oldest."

Ma said, "Hush the both of you," and went to fill the bowl herself.

Epilogue

After the conviction, my mother continued to work as an investigator for District Attorney Slaton until the last day of 1987, when a construction crane working on the new Underground Atlanta complex dropped a beam on the car she and her partner were in. The difference between them living and dying was a few inches. Ma's back was injured and she had to take a desk job in the solicitor's office to earn enough years to receive part of her pension. She figured it was a sign anyway, an omen that she'd better get out of police work before some crackhead shot her first.

During those years she dreamt of leaving, she met a public defender who was her nemesis in the courtroom but whom she chose as a life partner outside of it. Three years before she gave up her badge and government-issued gun, she married and brought home a white boy, proving anything is possible. They still work together in Atlanta, but on the same side—he's in private practice as a criminal defense attorney, and she does the investigative work for his office. They gave Bridgette and me the gift of another sister, and a brother.

For a long time, I followed the plan I laid out for myself when I first started at the private school. I earned degrees from a mostly white undergraduate school, then a mostly white graduate school, because I bought into the belief that it was required to succeed. I learned to play the game, too, steadily reaching my goals of making it in white America—a six-figure corporate job with a nice title. Eventually, I understood that the middle management position would never lead to upper management no matter how well I played the game or how many superlatives were added to the nice title. When I realized things hadn't changed as much as they should have since the day my mother wasn't made part of that courtroom team, and that playing the game had worn me down, I decided to write again, calling up a forgotten childhood desire to become an author. As for my mother's admonishment to never bring home a white boy, and my certainty that I would only come home with someone who looked liked me, I did neither. I married a Korean man, which brought with it another set of lessons, along with enough joy to make the effort seem inconsequential.

Bridgette grew up, got married, and has kids of her own. She always had plans of opening a hair salon, but in her thirties, she went back to college to complete the degree she left unfinished when she married. She's working on a master's degree in sociology, and is now a social worker for inner-city kids, children who matched the victim profile of the cases the Task Force cops worked. She specializes in coaching parent–child relationships. Even though I'm sure it influenced her career decision, I'm glad Bridgette was young enough to avoid being as affected by the investigation as I was, because today it no longer has the immediacy for her that it still holds for Ma and me. She's managed to hold on to a few of those childish things, a gift to her children whether they realize it or not. And even now, we wonder if there will ever be a time when we see each other more as sisters, and less as mother and daughter.

Questions still remain about who killed Atlanta's children, within our family and among Atlantans. In May 2005, the police chief of DeKalb County reopened five of the closed cases. He was an investigator on the Task Force and never believed Williams killed anyone, even the two adults he was convicted of murdering. A year later when the police chief left office, the case was closed again, but in early 2007, the district attorney granted Williams's defense team permission to perform DNA testing not available during his trial. Perhaps now police can look at the case with the benefit of what twenty-five years can bring: better methodology, stronger science, and more perspective. I still hold out hope that the case will be reexamined, even though it might mean that my mother's involvement in the investigation didn't end in 1982 after all.

Author's Note

Writing one's own story naturally goes the way the writer remembers it, and while I tried to be as true to the facts and to my experience as possible, surely someone will interpret the same event a different way. I don't mean to contradict them, but I can tell the story only as I know it.

The changes it caused my family, not the investigation itself, is the story I tell here. But the investigation gives the story its backdrop, so I didn't rely only on memory for the details of the case. I was supported by case documents, my mother's notes and accounts, and the occasional news article.

With the exception of using real names of my family members and any names made public during the investigation, all character names have been changed, but each "character" is a real individual, and not a composite of people I knew. The locations I describe around Atlanta are real and distinct places, as best I can recall them—or they used to be at one time. A lot changes in twenty-five years, but I hope folks who were there still remember some of those places.

While I believe I have a great memory, there is no way to remember people's words just as they said them—no one expects they'd ever have to—so the dialogue here is not an exact retelling, but it is true to the story.

A READING GROUP GUIDE

NO PLACE SAFE

Kim Reid

The following questions are intended to enhance your group's discussion of this book.

DISCUSSION QUESTIONS

1. The subtitle of this book reads "A Family Memoir." What do you think this means? How does a family memoir differ from other types of memoirs? How might the story have been told differently?
2. How does the author present the theme of race, both in her personal life and in the murder investigation? Do you think her personal experiences with racial issues paralleled those of other Atlantans during the investigation?
3. Have you experienced occasions when you were in the minority, whether because of your race or color, your political or religious beliefs, your gender, or other attribute? Did reading *No Place Safe* make you think differently about a time when you were in the minority?
4. Did you feel sympathy for the author's mother, both as a cop and as a single mother? Do you think she faced difficult choices as she balanced her commitment to the murder investigation against her love for her family? Did the story change any of your ideas about police officers?
5. How would you compare the scant early coverage of the missing and murdered children's investigation with the extensive media coverage of the JonBenet Ramsey case? Do you think the media continues to give more attention to missing white college girls or lost white Boy Scouts than they would to people of color in the same predicament? If so, why do you think that is?
6. Do you see *No Place Safe* as a coming-of-age story? What other books have portrayed this theme? How does *No Place Safe* compare to them? How does it compare with your own experiences in growing up?
7. Thirteen-year-old Kim questions why her mother has to pretend to be strong in front of her, and in other in-

stances, she fears the moment her mother will finally let go. How do you interpret this conflict? What do you think it says of Kim's relationship with her mother? Do you think their relationship was similar to or different from other mother–daughter relationships?

8. How would you characterize Kim's relationship with her sister, Bridgette? How does it change as the investigation continues and as their mother's role in it escalates?
9. Kim says she didn't miss having her father around because she had a strong mother and was surrounded by good men. But she also writes, "Even at twelve, I loved men, or men-in-the-making." How do you think she really felt toward her father?
10. What other conflicts do you see in Kim's life? What other opposing or contradictory forces did she have to deal with?
11. Do you think *No Place Safe* is only about a certain time and place, or do you think it expresses themes that transcend its specific setting?
12. When you finished reading *No Place Safe*, did you want to know what happened to the people in the story? Did the epilogue satisfy your curiosity about them?